Joy in the the Mourning

VIEWING THE RAINBOW FROM THE VALE OF TEARS

LESLIE I

D1502782

LCCN 2018910136

ISBN 9780692091043

Leslie L. Harder
Roanoke Rapids, NC 27870

FIRST EDITION

Publishing services by Word Pearls Press, LLC

• •

Suggested list of subject matter:

1. *Child loss—Biography.*   2. *Bereavement—Religious aspects—Christianity.*
3. *Grief—Religious aspects--Christianity.*   4. *Hope — Religious aspects—Christianity.*   5. *Death—Religious aspects—Christianity.*   6. *Christian—Biography.*   7. *Mother—Biography.*

prologue

There are a lot of ways this book never happens, and probably only one that it does. That one is Donna Clements. God has written this story, and when I began it, it was for my own benefit. Writing is how I process. But God, in His infinite wisdom, was at work on this long before I ever knew it was coming. Many years ago, Donna and I worked together, and we became friends. Though God called us to different paths, we kept in touch. Through her asking about my loss and me sharing some of what I'd written, Donna was given a vision by our Father. Through her coaxing and cajoling and, yes, sometimes admonishing and prodding, this collection of vignettes of how God has walked me through the hardest season of my life has been born.

While Donna was given the vision for this book, her daughter Gesine Lynch and Gesine's husband Levi were blessed with the talent and skills necessary to make it a reality. Their dedication and sacrifice are what transformed this book from a lengthy word processing document into the work of art you now hold in your hands. I am immensely grateful to them for their desire to be a part of telling this story, and I can't thank them enough for their patience with my inexperience and their commitment to spreading this message of hope.

If I took the time to list everyone that God has used along this path I've trodden, this would be a very unwieldy tome. I hope it will suffice to say that if you have spoken to, prayed for, or encouraged me at any point in this journey, this story is yours as much as it is mine. This is the story of my journey, yes, but it is also the story of the body of Christ being the hands and feet of Jesus at every turn. It is also the story of our loving God revealing Himself to His children so that they can be encouraged

When you ask Jesus to be your Lord and your Savior, there is never a moment afterward where you are alone. Did you hear me? You. Are. Never. Alone. Don't let your feelings overrule your faith. Whatever circumstance you face, whatever hardship or tragedy or loss, as a child of God you do not have to face it alone.

If you don't have that assurance yet, I challenge you to read on. Finish the book, and decide for yourself. Do you want the assurance that I have? It's yours for the asking, and the details on how to get it are within these pages.

introduction

Donna originally asked me to share my journey so that she could, in turn, share it with others who might find strength and encouragement for the challenges they face. Let me preface by saying that any strength or encouragement you find in here comes directly from God, my Father. I have no strength or encouragement, except what He has graciously bestowed on me - sometimes through His Word and His Presence, and sometimes through His children, but always by Him. I am so blessed.

First, a little background. My mother had a heart condition. It often caused small illnesses to be aggravated. One such instance occurred in early August of 2016. What started out as a visit to the emergency room for antibiotics quickly became a stay in ICU and frantic calls to immediate family to come and visit while she could still enjoy company.

But God was merciful. And miraculous. My mother recovered, much to the surprise of the medical community. After several days in ICU and couple more in a regular hospital room, she was off to a rehab facility. Her first two days there were good. She made progress. She groused about her roommate. Life was back to normal.

Then the phone call. Sometime in the evening on August 18, after a day spent with my sister and her family, Mom passed. Just like that.

We were not so much shocked as just surprised. After all, she'd had heart health issues for a long time. We all expect to bury our parents. That's the normal way of things.

Normal stopped for me five days later, on August 23, 2016. After another phone call.

What follows below are narratives written at those critical points that have come in my journey so far. I thought about rewriting them, but I think they'll feel more honest if I leave them as is, other than some necessary editing. Some of what you'll read is social media posts, because our family and friends are scattered across the whole world. The fastest way for us to keep in touch is through technology. Some is just the workings of my heart as I try to follow God's example of trying to use what the enemy meant for evil in my life to bring good to others. It skips about. It rambles. I probably double back and repeat myself, and I'm sure, despite my best efforts, it is riddled with typos. However, it is real. It is the living, breathing testimony of what it has been like to try and cope with the loss that no one ever expects. For the sake of privacy, I have sometimes removed the names.

If there's a message to be gleaned from this path I'm on, let it be one of hope and encouragement. God is in control. I don't have to know why. I don't have to like what has happened. But I DO have to trust Him. If I am His child - and I am - then I need to walk what I've been talking all these years. I refuse to allow the enemy to gain a toehold in this situation. I know - not believe or think - I KNOW that God can use even this for His glory, and I will trust in Him.

step 1

Finding My Feet

If one person falls, the other can reach out and help. But someone who falls alone is in real trouble.

- Ecclesiastes 4:10 NLT

August 24

I have waited to post this because I am still cracked and bleeding from my heart splintering in pieces. My older son passed away sometime yesterday morning. We don't know how. We may never know why on this side of heaven. BUT my God is faithful and true. There is no circumstance that He can't get me through. I will cry. I will grieve. And when I run out of tears, I will cry some more. BUT I WILL TRUST IN GOD. There is no one else that can get me through this.

I would appreciate your prayers for me and his family as we try to hang on through this storm.

Thank you for lifting me up.

August 25

Thank you so much, my friends, for upholding my family throughout this difficult journey. I wanted to just update you and ask you to pray for the next tasks ahead of us.

First and foremost, I want to assure you all that I am at peace about where my son is. He asked Jesus to be his Savior at a very young age. But I am still reeling from the shock. However, God is faithful. He will find a way to use this in my life. I certainly have a new perspective on the sacrifice God made when He sent His Son to die for us.

There are people all across the nation praying for us, and it has made all the difference. Relationships are being mended. Decisions are being made. Plans are slowly falling into place. Every time I think I cannot find the strength to take one more step, God sends someone to help. I am so very blessed.

I will appreciate your prayers, especially for the next three days. My son's ex-wife is bringing my grandson to Mom's services at his request. Many of my friends and family that will come to these will have already heard about my son, so it will be even more difficult for us all.

But that's not the hardest part of my weekend.

Saturday I have to go to my son's apartment and pick up some stuff for my grandson, because he doesn't have much in the way of anything right now, and he needs the security of his own things. I. Can. Not. Do. This.

But I can do all things through Christ Jesus, Who strengthens me. Church family has already agreed to meet us there if we ask them to and walk this road with us, and there are many, MANY prayer warriors who are storming the gates of heaven for us. Like I said before, I am so very blessed.

Many of you know I've been praying for my son to mend his relationship with God and return to serving Him. God has answered that prayer--not in my way--in His way. However much that hurts, I will thank Him for that. He sees all and knows all. I will put my trust in Him.

Thank you so much for your love and prayers, my friends. God is still on His throne, and we can trust Him because He loves us.

Blessings through the tears,

Me

August 26

Dear friends,

Your love and support and prayers have been such a blessing to me. These past two days have been hard, but God is faithful. Burying my mother, knowing that my son will soon follow--there are just no words. At each point where my steps have faltered, God has used your prayers to bolster me. In some cases, He saw me through a moment of unfathomable grief. At other times, He removed what I perceived to be an obstacle I would have to overcome. He has blessed me so much with a family that's grown far beyond my blood kin. God blessed me with my sister, who has stepped in countless times in the last two days to take care of tasks I never imagined I would have to do for my own child, who has repeatedly answered my questions when my brain can't seem to retain the answers, and who has let me cry and cry and CRY on her loving shoulder. God has strengthened William's father (my ex-husband) to take on the herculean task of notifying all the authorities and gathering all the documentation to get us through this next week, in spite of the fact that he lost his younger son in 2007 at the tender age of 15. God blessed me with an extended family that includes people that were important to my son, like his best friend, who are stepping up to make sure that things are being done the way my son would have liked. They are selflessly shouldering burdens that God knows I shouldn't tackle alone. Brothers and sisters in Christ are coming alongside us, bearing us up with prayers, support, help, encouragement, compassion, and yes, even tears. Your words are a balm to my shattered, broken heart, and there aren't enough words to express my thankfulness to God for you all.

I can almost literally feel you all storming the gates of heaven on our behalf. Moments when I'm almost incoherent with grief become drenched in a peace beyond comprehension, peace that you, my friends have petitioned God to give me. I thank you and I thank God.

Blessings continue through the tears,

Me

August 27

(This announcement was posted with the link to my son's obituary.)

As a parent, you never imagine you will have to announce this. If I didn't know my Savior, and I didn't know my son knew my Savior, I can't begin to fathom how I would survive this journey. Those of you young ones who are friends with him, please learn from this that you have no guarantee of your next breath. Each one is a gift from God. If you only think you might go to heaven or that you've been a basically good person or you go to church so you're good with

God, the bald truth is that that won't cut it. This is a decision, dear ones, that you have to make. God offers you eternity with Him when you admit you can't get to heaven on your own, and ask Jesus to be your Savior. If you want help, or you have questions, please don't hesitate to ask. Let what happened here bring you to a better place. Don't let your preconceived notions of "Christians" hold you back from heaven. We're as imperfect as everyone else. We've just admitted it to God and asked Him to save us in spite of it. My son lived a full life. Let his legacy be that he will get to see you all when you join him. But unless you make the decision that he did, that's not going to happen.

God bless you all for your thoughts and prayers for me and all of his family.

August 28

Thank you to all my brothers and sisters in Christ at our home church who prayed, wept with, encouraged, hugged, and loved on me today. The body of Christ is truly obeying God's call to love one another. I really appreciate everyone's continued prayers as we put our life on hold here while we deal with saying goodbye to my son. God continues to use what the enemy meant for evil to bring good to His children. Relationships are being mended, hearts are being prepared to hear the gospel, and God has even blessed me with my son's best friend - now my new son. :) Also, many of my sisters in Christ who have had a similar experience have come alongside to share with me the comfort God gave them through their journey. I am so blessed. There are many people who will be traveling in the next few days and many details that we are still working out, and I appreciate you lifting us all up to our Father, that we might find grace and help in our time of need.

August 29

This is my son's childhood friend, Daniel. They were practically inseparable until Daniel's family moved, when they were both in their teens.

I wrote the post below after spending the day with my son's childhood friend and his wife. They sacrificed their time, left their three children with Daniel's parents (longtime friends of ours), drove down from Michigan and spent the day with us. Daniel has military commitments that will make it impossible for him to attend my son's services, but he came to be with us today.

God knew we needed his presence, and perhaps he needed ours.

Daniel and William were lifelong friends. They lost touch as adults, but they had reconnected about a year or so ago. Daniel had even managed to get down to see William, which, looking back, was truly a blessing. We spent the day just talking. Reminiscing. Laughing. Crying. Another friend had given us a gift card to a local restaurant, so we went out to eat. We learned all about Daniel, how he and his family were faring. How he and his wife are looking forward to the end of the year, when their 8-year-old daughter will finish treatments for leukemia. As they were leaving, Daniel made me do something I didn't think possible, at least not at this point in my life.

He made me laugh.

We were actually discussing something that weighs heavily on the heart of Christian parents whose children are believers that are struggling in their relationship with God. Did they really accept Jesus as their Savior? Or did they just parrot what they heard? As my husband and I expressed these concerns,

Daniel interrupted. "Oh, I KNOW William is in heaven. I don't have a doubt," he said. "And it really sucks, too, because he got there first."

Thank You, God, for friends like Daniel and his wife, Sarah. Thank You for their heart for us in our grief and for their sacrifice to bring us comfort.

"Many thanks to my son's closest childhood friend and his wife for coming down from Michigan and spending today with us sharing memories. Hats off to you on your 'memorial' rental car, a 2016 Mustang in honor of my son."

September 3

I laid my firstborn to rest yesterday. Those are hard words to say, even harder to comprehend. I wish I had had the strength to say these words yesterday, but perhaps God knew that more of you would be able to hear them, now that the initial shock of grief is beginning to ebb.

My son's life had purpose and meaning, and I don't think any of you would disagree that he lived it to its fullest. His greatest joy was raising his son, and they were truly a dynamic duo. I would appreciate your prayers for him as he continues on his life's journey. Share your memories with him. Ask him to share his with you. He is a wonderful young man with an incredible future ahead of him.

As fully as my son lived his life, I don't want his death to be in vain. Please, dear ones, PLEASE learn from this that you have no guarantee of your next breath. Each one is a gift from God. My son lived a full life. Don't let yesterday be the last time you see him. Let his legacy be that he will get to see you all when you join him.

Unless you make the decision that he did, that's not going to happen. If you only think you might go to heaven, or that you've been a basically good person, or you go to church so you're good with God, the bald truth is, that won't cut it. This is a decision, dear ones, that you have to make. God offers you eternity with Him when you admit you can't get to heaven on your own, and you ask Jesus to be your Savior. If you want help, or you have questions, please don't hesitate to ask.

Let this difficult, heart-wrenching experience lead you to a better place. Don't let your preconceived notions of "Christians" hold you back from heaven. We're as imperfect as everyone else. We've just admitted it to God and asked Him to save us in spite of it.

On behalf of my son's family and friends, I thank you again for walking this excruciatingly painful journey with us.

God bless you all for your thoughts and prayers.

September 6

The cemetery called today to confirm all the information for my son's marker. In addition to the facts, it will also have the Christian and Missionary Alliance symbol, because that's the denomination of church we were attending when he asked Jesus to be his Savior. There were two short lines for terms of endearment. They will read:

BELOVED SON
DEVOTED FATHER

Such small words to describe such a big heart...

September 9

Today I went to a local business to print some copies of the memorial bulletin from my son's service. The gentleman was very nice, and he did a fine job. When the print job was done, I asked, "How much?" He replied, "No charge."

God bless you, sir. In a world where many are looking out for themselves, you are showing love and compassion for your neighbor. You really touched my heart. (And I apologize for the tears. They sit very close to the surface these days.)

September 10

All along this incredibly hard journey, God has given me moments where I could clearly see His hand at work. Once while I was being hammered by my grief and shock, as well as the grief and shock of others, I got a text from one of my dearest prayer warrior friends saying that she was thinking of me and praying for me. When I posted times and dates of some of the hardest tasks it became my duty to perform, I would receive texts and messages from many of you telling me that you were storming the gates of heaven on my and my family's behalf. The instances are so numerous, and I freely admit some of those days have yet to come fully into focus, that I couldn't possibly list them all here. Please trust me when I say God used and is still using all of you to help me through this valley.

There is one instance, however, that I did want to share with you today. About three days after my mother's funeral, I went to my sister's home. While there, she pulled out three palm-sized magnetic medallions that were part of my mom's funeral package. They had different designs, and my sister told me to pick one. So I did. You can see it in the picture below.

Just a few days later, I was at the same funeral home, preparing to escort my son to his final resting place. Even as I write this, my eyes fill and my heart cracks a little. The pain of knowing what had to be done, combined with the stress and grief of others...it's almost impossible to put it into words. Your heart is saying, "I don't want to be here. I don't want to do this." Your head is saying, "This has to be done, and it has to be done now." People are asking questions. You're trying to answer in what you hope are words that make sense. Like I said, it's impossible to describe.

In the midst of all of this, the funeral director, the kind soul that walked us through this most crushing experience, walked up to me with a small, black velvet pouch in his hand. Apparently, my son's funeral package came with three coin-sized medallions. The funeral director handed me the pouch and explained what it was. I opened the pouch and looked inside. The second picture is the coin he handed me.

Remember, the funeral director had no idea which of my mother's medallions that I had chosen.

I. Do. Not. Believe. In. Coincidences.

Jesus loves me, this I know,
for the Bible tells me so.
Little ones to Him belong. [1]
I am weak...
but He is strong.

Yes, oh yes, my friends, Jesus loves me.

September 18

When I woke up a month ago today, my little world was a vastly different place than it is now. My mother was in her second day of what we'd been told would be a short stay in rehab, and, because of her recent illness, I'd had my whole little family under the same roof for a couple of days. It was nice, because it so very rarely happened.

Then my mother, on August 18, in the evening, after a day of rehab and visits with my sister and her family, fell asleep here and awoke in the arms of her Savior. She was 84. She had some health issues. We did not anticipate losing her at that moment, but we knew the reality of a parent in fragile health. And, most of us expect to outlive our parents.

I did not expect to outlive my son, but, five days later, I did. God, have mercy on me. To this day I still can't seem to completely embrace that concept in my head. You know all the cliches from the movies, where you rolled your eyes when the overdramatic actors exclaimed, "I just can't believe it! I keep hoping I'm just dreaming, that I'll wake up soon and find out it was all a nightmare!"?

They are not cliches, my friends.

Momma, I know you won't see this, but I need to say it. I love you. I miss you. I'm sorry you had to go when you did, but I understand now that your being here would have been much harder for you than meeting your grandson in heaven. Give him a kiss for me.

Heavenly Father, thank You that we can't see the future. Thank You, that no matter what the enemy throws at us, You are with us. You comfort us. You strengthen us. Thank You for Your saints that continue to hold me and my family up in prayer. Thank You for my mom. Thank You for my son. Thank You that they both had accepted You as their Savior, and because I have, too, thank You for the knowledge that I will see them both again. In the mighty name of Jesus, I pray. AMEN

I woke up this morning a little heavy in my heart. After I wrote the above, I pulled out my Bible for my daily devotional (http://odb.org/2016/09/18/making-preparations/). In the devotional, the writer mentions:

"when my mother-in-law died, one of the children slipped a set of knitting needles under her fingers." [2]

My mother was an avid knitter. She made many hats to distribute through a local homeless ministry. She also made scarves, hats and afghans for family members.

The Bible reading for today was John 14:1-6, the one I typed in the memorial bulletin that was distributed at my son's funeral service.

God is aware of your anguish, your pain. The God who cares enough to count the very hairs on your head is not going to abandon you to your grief. It is hard. I know it is hard, but, at your lowest point, when you don't think you can continue for one second longer, look up. Listen. He's there. He's listening. And He's reaching out to you, speaking through the music you listen to, the books you read, the things you see.

Can you hear Him?

step 2

Claiming His Strength

The Lord is my strength and shield. I
trust in Him with all my heart.

Psalm 28:7a NLT

September 23

One month ago tonight, I received a call that rocked my world and forever changed my life and the life of my loved ones. And while I waited for two hours for officials to confirm what I knew in my heart, I prayed I was wrong. But I knew. Oh yes, I knew. Nothing short of death would have kept my son from making sure his child was picked up from day care.

A lot of things run through your head in a two-hour wait like that. I shot prayer requests by post and email and text, and I thanked God for the means to alert so many people to my need so quickly. Surely it was on the strength of those prayers that I was able to hear by phone what no mother ever wants to hear, and then pray with the person who had to give me such shocking news. I certainly couldn't do it in my own strength. No mother could.

I've been humbled through this experience, because I've learned that a lot of the cliches about this type of tragedy are based in truth. At times, the only thing I can do is cry and say, "My baby...my baby." At times, I wake up and I really do try to convince myself that it's some horrible dream, and that perhaps today is the day I truly wake up. I've also learned that well-meaning friends and family repeat some of the cliches as well, because there just really isn't anything else you can say.

Except one thing.

"I love you."

I can't begin to tell you how many of you have simply walked up to me, wrapped me in your arms, and whispered "I love you" in my ear. And you can't even begin to fathom how immeasurably comforting that has been, because love really does say it all.

"Love bears all things [regardless of what comes], believes all things [looking for the best in each one], hopes all things [remaining steadfast during difficult times], endures all things [without weakening]. Love never fails [it never fades nor ends]."
1 Corinthians 13:7-8a AMP

I am so blessed.

As I go through this day, it will be your prayers and love that God uses to carry me through the tough places. It will be your cards and texts and posts that will encourage me to keep on keeping on. I've tried to respond where I could, but I have to tell you again that many times just before or after a particularly rough spot in this journey, I'll receive a call, text, or post from one of you that reminds me that God is still at work, I am not alone, and He knows how difficult this is. Whether you believe in Him or not, you can't change the truth of who He is and how He has used you.

My son was a lot of things to a lot of people, but God is more. I know where my son is. I KNOW. Do you? I know I'll see him again. Will you? I can tell you how to make that happen. Even if you never step foot in a church in your life, you can still make the choice to see my son again. My son knew he wasn't perfect. He knew nothing he did would earn him a spot in heaven. Long ago, he admitted that to God and asked Jesus to be his Savior. Did he live a perfect life after that? No. None of us have. But because he made that choice, he met perfection when he stepped into the arms of Jesus one month ago. He would want you to have that chance, too.

Please, consider your life beyond this earth today. I'll be praying for you.

Blessings and prayers through my tears,

Me

September 27

(This was posted with a link to a memorial video of my mother.)

All day long yesterday I fought tears. I couldn't pinpoint any obvious reason why, other than this is a season of mourning for me. Then it came to me this morning.

We buried my mother a month ago yesterday. It's to my shame that her passing has been overshadowed by the events that followed. And while I truly miss her, I understand her passing now.

So, let me introduce you to my mother. I love her. I miss her. I'm glad she asked Jesus to be her Savior. I won't see her again in this world, but I'll see her in the next. If you've asked Jesus to be your Savior, too, then perhaps I'll get a chance to truly introduce you in heaven.

October 1

Woke up in tears this morning.

Again.

I always try to make my first conversation of the day be with God. I didn't voice them, but I was having whiny, pity-party thoughts. Got up to start the day with quiet time with God and my devotional was titled, "Hold On" (http:// odb.org/2016/10/01/hold-on-2/). This was His message to me:

"We have no resources of our own. We depend fully on Christ to keep us moving forward. He will take us through the greatest challenges..." [3]

If you've read my previous post, you know I woke up in tears - again - this morning. I was working on something and scrolling back through my posts, and among the many responses I had, there was one from a stranger. I didn't recognize her name, and I honestly never noticed the post, because I made a point of clicking "Like" when I read them, and this one was unchecked. A little investigation revealed that she is a friend of my sister. This special woman sent me a beautiful note and a link to a song. So I clicked on the link and listened and read the words and allowed God to work in my heart.

And He did it again.

Very few people are aware that I've been working on thank-you notes for a couple of weeks now. It's hard, and it's not a task I ever thought I'd be facing. It is my hope to finish the majority of them today. (I've done 30+ so far. My son was well loved.) At the bottom of each one, I've been writing out Psalm 34:18.

At the very end of that music video was that very same verse.

God is watching out for me. He's watching out for you, too.

Blessings through still more tears,

Me

October 2

When my mother passed away on August 18, I began a journey down into a valley. Five days later, the enemy crept up behind me and pushed me headlong into that abyss with the sudden death of my son. That's exactly what it felt like. I landed HARD. I was stunned, numb with shock from the impact. And then, all my nerve endings roared to life. Physical pain is bad, I admit. Spiritual pain, however, has no equal. If what I felt is even an iota of what God felt at the death of His Son at our hands, then His love is all the more precious to me.

I have been wandering around in this valley for over a month. It's long. It's deep. It's dark. It's full of pits and stumbling blocks. And I'll be frank--I don't like it one bit. Yet...there is a path through it; but, it's difficult to see it in the dark.

Thank you, Lord, that Your Word is a lamp for my feet and a light for my path.

Oh, the pits and stumbling blocks are still there, but with God's help I can see them, and I can choose to avoid them. The path is difficult and narrow, but I've also learned the absolute truth of "I can do all things through Christ Jesus, who strengthens me."

In Christ's strength, I can excuse myself in the midst of my mother's visitation service, and go sign the papers to authorize my son's autopsy.

In Christ's strength, I can bury my mother at 9:30, knowing my son's autopsy starts at 10:00 and will, in all likelihood, be ongoing while I attend her memorial service at 11:00.

In Christ's strength, I can bury my mom on a Friday, and select my son's casket on Saturday.

In Christ's strength, I can walk into the home where my son died, and select the clothes in which he'll be buried.

In Christ's strength, I can type the memorial bulletin for my son's funeral service.

In Christ's strength, I can look into the face of the first child to call me mother, touch him one final time, and bid him goodbye.

In Christ's strength, I can stand and speak at my son's funeral. I can sign "Tell Your Heart to Beat Again" [4] by Danny Gokey, when the wound in mine is still bleeding.

In Christ's strength, I can choose the terms of endearment for my son's grave marker.

In Christ's strength, I can read my son's autopsy report. "Diffuse pulmonary thromboembolization." Three awful words to sum up what might have been treated, had it been correctly diagnosed. At present, I'm not at liberty to say more than that.

Today, it's been one month since we buried my son. I still don't see the end of this valley, but I know it's there. And I know at some point I'll have to begin climbing out. It's going to take determination. It's going to take strength and stamina. And it's going to take prayer. A lot of prayer; because, in addition to being narrow and strewn with pitfalls, that path will be steep. And the enemy would really like to keep me wallowing around down here.

But I CAN do all things through Christ Jesus who strengthens me. The devil IS defeated. God IS exalted. And Jesus Christ IS Lord to the glory of God the Father.

Christ can strengthen you for the struggles you face, too. If you've already admitted you aren't perfect and asked Him to be your Savior, then you've experienced His strength firsthand. If you haven't made that choice yet, please consider it. Learn from what happened to my son. Your next breath could be your last--it literally could be. The time to make a choice is now. I can't stress that enough.

A final note: I never understood taking pictures at funerals. Before God and you, my friends, I'm asking forgiveness for my ignorance in this. At a time when all you want to do is not be where you are, your brain is not making many good memories. My deepest thanks to those who memorialized my son's service in picture for me. They're still hard to look at, but I know that, in time, those moments captured on film will be precious to those of us who feel his loss so deeply.

Thank you, friends, for your prayers, support, and encouragement. A special thanks to my sisters in Christ who've walked this path before me, and who've shared their pain in order to ease mine. It means more than I can ever say. You are all truly blessings from God.

More proof of God's timing. These are excerpts I read today in a book I started about a week ago. I should add that this is a fiction book, and this is a journal entry from a secondary character in the story. I didn't select it because this subject resonated with me. I picked it as an amusing, light read. Lesson learned: God can use ANYTHING and ANYONE to get His message to you.

"How could God take my son? Yes, I understood the parallel. God had sacrificed His Son for all humanity. But where was the good in Peter's death? I still don't see it, but I can accept that God's ways are higher than mine. When I get to heaven, I'll understand the reason why, or I simply won't need to ask."

"So what is the point? Simply this. The Bible says, 'For now we see through a glass darkly...' We don't always understand what happens to us or why, but if we could see through the lens of eternity, we'd weep with joy. Faith is what allows us to believe in the beauty behind that dark glass."

"It's a gift from God, not something we can conjure or create. It's a gift we choose to accept, much like a child opening a box on Christmas morning. I pray you will receive that gift and live your life to the fullest as God intended – with hope, faith, and the courage to love." ---from *Until I Found You* [5] by Victoria Bylin

October 13

I need to preface this post with an explanation of a couple of terms. A friend shared with my ex-daughter-in-law about an article she read on grief that explained it in terms of "hammer moments" and "feather moments". In her words, "Hammer moments are the big ones that you know are coming and are going to suck - birthdays, holidays, etc. Feather moments are the ones that sneak up on you and you don't see coming. Hearing a favorite song on the radio, smelling his cologne on a stranger…"

That being said…

I would really appreciate your prayers throughout this month. I expect my son's birthday to be hard. That's a given. What I did not expect, was this whole month to be a series of "feather moments" that would sneak up on me and choke me (metaphorically). I think I finally figured out why.

Thirty-three years ago, I spent this whole month anticipating the birth of my first child. This year I am spending this whole month anticipating how I'm going to get through that child's birthday without him. I think I would call this one a "sledgehammer moment".

But God is so faithful. When I got up this morning, I had a message waiting from a friend who's having struggles as well, but who's holding on to God with both hands and using her recovery time to reach out to others. I would appreciate your prayers for her.

Please pray for me to keep my eyes on today, not the future. God will give me His strength when I need it, and not a moment sooner. I will trust in Him.

October 17

TISSUE ALERT! I was sitting last night thinking about my son, and I all of a sudden remembered his first birthday, which is on Halloween, and I remembered his first (theologically incorrect, but still cute) costume. Oddly enough, it hasn't made me cry. Instead, I got tickled because part of his halo is sagging.

When my son's things were packed up and moved here, most went straight into a storage unit. I haven't yet been given the strength to go there. However, in the way of God's perfect planning, a few arbitrary boxes ended up at our house. When I say arbitrary, I mean just that: stuffed animals, dirty socks, old bills (years old)... But, among these items I found some t-shirts. Now, you have to understand that my son was somewhat of a t-shirt tourist, so to speak. If he went somewhere, he usually got a t-shirt. As I was going through the shirts, I found one from his Navy recruiter days. I also found one from his sky diving trip. It was the sky diving one that caught my attention, because his best friend had recently posted a picture of them together on that day and was telling about how much fun they had and how fondly he remembered that day.

I decided that God must have had those t-shirts land here so that I could send them to my son's best friend, but at the time I considered that, I didn't have his physical address. I figured that was the end of it. Well, God worked that out, because after the dust settled from the trauma of what had happened, he and I exchanged contact information, and even though I didn't ask him for it, he included his physical address. Another nudge from God.

Writing the letter that went with the t-shirts was hard. Of course, all of this journey has been hard, but God has never failed me before, and He wasn't about to fail me now. So I got out my hanky, picked up my pen, and put it to paper. I packed up the shirts, put them in the post, and sat back for a week, second-guessing myself on whether or not I had done the right thing.

I checked the tracking number throughout the week, waiting to make sure the package arrived. I had learned enough about my son's best friend (who has adopted me, by the way) to know that he would acknowledge the package when he got it.

He got it Friday. By Saturday afternoon, I was a little concerned, so I sent him a message and asked if he got the package. He sent back a message asking me if I got his text.

Oh snap. I never remember to look at that cell phone.

I retrieved the phone, pulled up my messages, and there sat one from my "adopted" son that had come early Saturday morning, and here is what it said:

"Good morning Mom, hope your weekend is going good. I received your letter and package last night and can't be more grateful for your love and acceptance during this part of our earthly journey. I have struggled in my faith as a young adult and honestly would have found it even harder to have faith in Christ through this living hell. But by example you have renewed my faith and given me a way to see the light in a way I could have never understood without YOU! Those two t-shirts are a great reminder of my connection to Wil and can't thank you enough for sending them. You have discussed how there are hammer moments and feather moments that remind us of him, but the strangest thing I have discovered is the same is true in Christ. There have been so many feather moments that make me look up and let God know I see Him working!"

I bawled like a baby, and for once in what seems like a very long time, there were some happy tears mixed in with the sad.

I say all this to encourage you all and thank you all for your prayers for me and my family throughout this whole ordeal. I wanted you to see that God is using your prayers to bring glory to His name, to change hearts, to heal wounds.

Thank you again for your support on this journey. I am so blessed by all of you.

Blessings with less tears and more joy,

Me

October 20

Today's devotion in Our Daily Bread was entitled "Your Journey" [6] (http://odb.org/2016/10/20/your-journey/). It resonated with me, because "journey" is the term I've used to describe the last two months in many of the posts on social media. I've occasionally referred to it as a tragedy or a trauma, but that's really just a human viewpoint. From God's point of view, it's the journey that will take me from where I am to where I AM resides.

Certainly "journey" describes life in this broken world. On the way we encounter mountains and valleys, rivers and plains, crowded highways and lonely roads—highs and lows, joys and sorrows, conflict and loss, heartache and solitude. Often the twists and turns make it hard to see the road ahead, so we must take it as it comes, not as we wish it would be.

October 22

(Chapter 1 – A story in three parts.)

Tomorrow it will have been two months since my son died, and I think I've begun the ascent out of the valley. I don't know if I can honestly say the pain has lessened, but it's certainly not as sharp. I can look at a few photos without tears coursing down my face. I can talk about him without my heart feeling torn in two........And, I can sense an almost imperceptible turning away from the pain of the loss and toward the joy of watching God at work. Loved ones are turning toward Him. Seeds of hope are being sown in sorrow-filled hearts. Prayers - YOUR prayers - are being answered.

A friend has shared with me that science has discovered grief to be an actual physical process of reconciling memories of the past with the reality of the present. As I write this, I'm envisioning a process reminiscent of labor: pain, hard work, stress, exhaustion, moments of helplessness - and at its completion, a life forever changed. But, where the pain of labor fades in the joy of motherhood, the pain of grief can only fade in the joy of my Father's arms. Yes, there can be joy in the mourning.

I don't know exactly where I am in this process, but I can tell that I am moving forward. Like labor, grief seems to come in stages. I think I've passed through the most painful part. There are still feather and hammer moments filled with tears and sorrow, but God is helping me come to terms with my loss. He's given me memories to cherish - some older, some newer, and some a blend of both...

like the one I'm about to share.

The routine began in our home when my firstborn was small. Every night when we went to bed, we exchanged goodnights. It varied little, and seemed to finally settle on three short sentences that we would echo back and forth:

"Good night. I love you. See you in the morning."

Over the years, routine became tradition. Then my boys grew up. My oldest son moved, married, and began his own family and his own traditions.

But a mother's heart can't be denied. Your children become adults, but *they're still your children*. And, surprisingly, technology came to my aid.

Me, one of the worst dissers of cell phones.

I bit the bullet, learned to text, and resurrected the tradition of telling my boys good night. At first it was just my younger son (who still lives at home), because he was often out when I turned in. At some point, I added my oldest back into the mix; I even learned a little "text speak", which I believe both tickled and astounded him. Oh, I admit I forgot to send it out at times, and if I happened to be up late, he wouldn't see it until the next morning. It would be waiting for him when he got up.

That's one good thing I can say about cell phones.

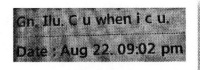

This is a photo of my last text to my oldest, sent to him the night before he died. I don't share it lightly, and I don't share it to distress, but to show you God's mercy in the midst of my mess.

How many people, faced with the sudden, unexpected loss of their child, can say that their last words to them were ones of love and hope?

My Father loves me so very much.

And, if the story ended here, it would be amazing just as it is.

But God wrote a second chapter.

I'll share it tomorrow.

Thank you again for continuing to pray for those who love my son. I appreciate it more than I can ever say.

Blessings with less tears and more joy,

Me

step 3

Walking His Way

Seek His will in all you do, and He will show you which path to take.

Proverbs 3:6 NLT

October 23

(Chapter 2 – continued from yesterday.)

There's a new tradition at funeral services, especially for those who die young. Our funeral director shared it with us before my son's service, and we decided to allow it. God was in that decision for sure, because on that day all I could do was show up. The Lord did the rest. That's the only way I can explain it.

At the conclusion of the service, the funeral director spoke about how my son had made a mark on the lives of those present. Then he produced a large Sharpie and invited those present to leave a mark, or message, on my son's casket. Even though I knew it was coming, I didn't realize that my grandson would be the first to take up the pen.

Or that I would be the second.

At my ex-husband's encouragement, I followed my grandson up to the casket that cradled my firstborn, and I watched as he lovingly and sorrowfully penned his words. I know God stood there holding me up, because that child's message pierced my heart.

Then he handed me the pen.

I honestly can't remember having a single coherent thought in my head at that moment - not one. But I uncapped that pen, and in that moment, I learned firsthand the truth of Romans 8:26.

"In the same way the Spirit [comes to us and] helps us in our weakness. We do not know what prayer to offer or how to offer it as we should, but the Spirit Himself [knows our

need and at the right time] intercedes on our behalf with sighs and groanings too deep for words." AMP

The message, written in an unsteady hand by a mother bowed down in grief, seemed to just flow out of me:

"Gn. Ilu. C u in heaven. Mom XO"

Lord, throughout this journey I have never doubted Your love for me, and I have repeatedly reaffirmed my trust in You. Over and over, You have shown Your faithfulness and Your love to me through Your Word and Your children. However, we both know I've been less than forthcoming with what I'm about to say - not because I didn't feel it, but because my wound went so deep... Just excuses, I know. Please forgive me for holding back. The wound isn't any less deep, but You in Your mercy have continued to reach out to me. And I want to be My Father's daughter.

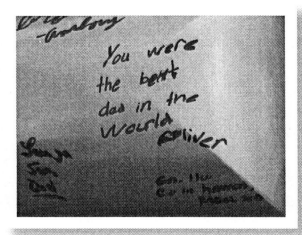

I love You, Lord. I love You.

My heartfelt gratitude to all of you for continuing to pray for those of us who love my son. God continues to answer, and I continue to trust Him.

Blessings and peace,

Me

(Chapter 3 – Continued from yesterday and earlier today.)

I didn't intend to post again today. I really didn't, but God is nudging me to get this out there.

I wrote the rough draft of today's previous post beforehand. It started out as part of yesterday's post, but it was so long I decided to split it in two. But, my Father apparently prefers to do things in threes.

Because, before I could get my earlier entry posted, he wrote Chapter 3.

This requires a little background. If you've followed my journey, you know that, right after my son died, I was contacted by his best friend. My first text from him arrived less than 24 hours after I got the news, and he explained who he was and offered his help. I knew him only by what my son had said - I'd never met him. His second text came just a couple of days later, at a very low point for me. I had buried my mother that morning. I was set to plan my son's funeral and go to his home to pick up some things the next day.

Like I said, low point. Then, that evening, I got a text.

Now, if you've ever gone through a loss like this, you'll understand how this touched me. There's a place in me that's broken forever. Nothing can change that. But the fact that a young man that I never met and only knew by association would reach out to me and try to heal that breach? That is truly a God moment. That he would adopt me sight unseen is evidence of God's love for me.

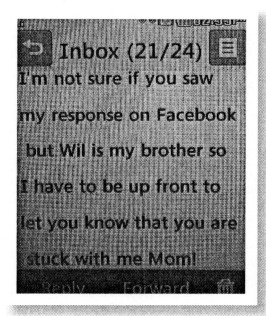

If the association stopped here, it would be a wonderful testimony, but it continues to this day. I recall receiving a text, I think as we left the funeral home after planning my son's service, telling me he was thinking of me. I can't remember the exact words, and I'm afraid I lost it in the shuffle, but it came at just the right time, and at that very moment I gained a new son. I remember responding to the text and asking if he thought it would be creepy if I told him I loved him, but he was gracious about it. My heavenly Father knew what we both needed, and He provided.

I did get to meet my new "son" and his lovely wife, to speak with them, cry with them, mourn with them. They've been such a blessing. They prepared a beautiful video photo montage of my son that I hope one day to be able to view entirely (I'm not there yet, and because I'm not, I realize how great a sacrifice they made by sifting through those pictures to produce that love offering). They don't live locally, but we keep in touch.

God bless technology!

Fast forward to last night. I had posted Chapter 1 yesterday morning, then worked most of the day. Late yesterday afternoon while surfing social media, I read a post saying that a dear friend of mine had just suffered a shocking loss. In my concern for her, I pulled out my cell phone to check with a mutual friend to make sure I had read the post correctly. I sent a text, laid the phone on the end table, and forgot about it.

I never keep my phone out unless my youngest is away from home. Really. Ask anyone. I used to get texts from my best friend that said, "Go plug in your cell phone" on THE cell phone to which she was referring. It spends most of its life in a pocket on the outside of my purse (and really is usually dead when I need to use it).

But, last night, it lay on the end table, initially because I was waiting for my friend to respond, and later because I forgot about it...until it buzzed, a little after 9:00.

I picked it up, remembering that I was awaiting a response from my friend. When I did, I noticed it said I had two messages. Two? I only contacted one friend, and I knew she wasn't likely to send back-to-back messages.

I scrolled up, and, I admit, checked the unknown message before I checked my friend's. It was my new "son":

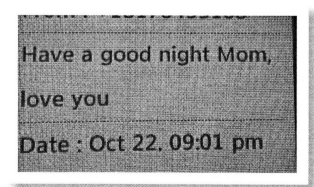

God, in His infinite mercy, didn't want this part of my story to end at my firstborn's grave. He wanted to show me - and my new son, too, and maybe all of you as well - that our life does not end at death, whether it's ours or our loved one's. It just begins a new chapter.

Writing this has brought to mind part of the words to the song "Tell Your Heart to Beat Again"[7] sung by Danny Gokey that I signed at my son's funeral - actually not a song that I picked, but was chosen by my niece. The song urges us to look at even our lowest of lows through the eyes of God, who can and will redeem each pain and each sorrow that we experience.

Blessings through tears of joy,

Me

October 26

Most of you know that earlier this month I was fretting about my son's upcoming birthday, so much so that I had crossed into enemy territory, and, as a pastor friend would say, I let the enemy eat my lunch. But, I repented, sought help and encouragement from brothers and sisters in Christ, and God has forgiven me. He also used a dear friend to share with me how to live in this moment, not reaching into the future to grasp things for which I won't be equipped until their time comes.

October 31 still looms. It is still a day filled with uncertainty for me. But God has certainly not abandoned me throughout this journey. There is absolutely no reason to believe He'd start now. I couldn't figure out how He'd work this one out, but, after the encouragement from my friend, I let go and just focused on the day at hand. And Thursday, I began to see God at work.

At a church meeting, we were discussing October birthdays. Just before the conversation came to a close, the group leader reminded everyone that one of the young men in the group had a birthday coming up.

On October 31.

And it wasn't just any young man. It's one of the men for whom my younger son has worked the last couple of years. And just so God was sure He had my attention, He sent a second person into the mix last night, when I discovered a friend's daughter is dating a young man who also shares my older son's birthday.

In all of my son's 32 years, I never met a single person that shared his birthday. In the last seven days, God sends two.

Young men. In my church. One a close friend.

I may not be celebrating on Monday, but God has given me two young men (and their families) for whom I can pray. When the enemy drops sadness on me like a lead apron, I will not be flattened by the grief. I will instead turn my mourning into praising God for these two young men and asking His blessing on their families.

Our God is so awesome. If you've never met Him, I'd love to introduce you.

Blessings,

Me

My husband must have found this among my son's things (along with the policy renewal notice, I might add), and he left it on my desk. I saw it, got curious, and picked it up.

11/30/09

William,

From the time you were a baby, I kept a small life insurance policy on you, in case, God forbid, the unexpected happened. I kept it up and increased it a little as you got older. Now that you're married and settled, I'm going to leave it up to you on whether to continue this policy. I'm enclosing the paperwork, but not the actual policy, because I believe it's buried deep in the letters we still haven't gone through from our old file cabinets. If you decide to keep it, you can change the info to your address, etc. If you have any questions, you've got my number.

Love, Mom

It seems it's possible to have a feather AND hammer moment. I expect the enemy hoped to strike my heart with this reminder that the unexpected has, indeed, happened, and to pour salt in the wound by pointing out that God didn't forbid it.

Perhaps the enemy should have started reading at the very TOP of the letter, above the date:

Arise and shine, for your Light has come, and the glory of the Lord rises upon you.
Isaiah 60:1 NIV

Either I'm in denial or I'm moving forward. The one thing I'm NOT doing is crying, which makes me curious...and thankful. Sounds crazy, doesn't it?

October 28

The following entries show how much God loves me. It started with a picture I was posting to my son's memorial page. By the time I finished the caption, tears were flowing...

"I don't know that William would have called himself a hero, but he would defend the defenseless. I've seen him call a cousin to account for snarking off at another relative. I've known him to blow up the phone of a scam caller that harassed his grandmother. And I've heard him speak with respect about his son defending someone at daycare that was being harassed, because that's what his daddy taught him to do. He would assist anyone that he saw in need, and if you asked him, you knew he'd do everything

he could to help you. Was he perfect? No. But he was - is still - loved.

Oh, baby, I miss you."

A few minutes after I posted this, while I was still fighting tears. I saw the following post.

 Tequila Sunrise Music
12 hrs · 🌐

Hey guys we are 10 likes shy of 600 Likes. I know we have several friends that have not liked our page yet. So I am asking everyone who has not liked our Tequila Sunrise Music Facebook page to please do so. Thanks

1 Share

Now, the God thing is that the post was obviously hours old, but it didn't show up in my news feed until AFTER I had posted about William always helping others. And, remember the two young men that I mentioned that share William's birthday? This company is co-owned by one of them. He's the young man that my younger son has worked with for two years.

You can clearly see why I don't believe in coincidences.

My Father loves me so much...

October 29

It's two days before my son's birthday. Since I knew the weekend was going to be challenging anyway, I made my first trip to the storage unit we opened when we had to hastily empty my son's apartment. I had put it off for two months.

I wish I could have put it off for two years.

I didn't make a promising start to the day. I had a meltdown all over my husband before we ever got out of the house. My husband said we would be there about two hours. I wasn't sure I could get through one.

I cried all the way to the storage facility. I had posted a prayer request online, and I sat in the car before we left the house, begging God to please help me.

He did. He always does. *Father, forgive me for doubting.*

As I usually do when my mind is churning, I started listening to the radio in the car. The first song or two didn't strike a chord in my memory. The tears were falling so hard, I probably couldn't have absorbed their message anyway.

Then God got my attention. The first song he used was "Chain Breaker" [8] by Zach Williams, which reminded me that when the chains of sorrow and pain weigh me down and I feel lost and alone, I know the One Person who can break those chains and shake me free from the prison of grief.

Well, I certainly have pain, and I've felt lost for two months. Hearing God remind me that He's bigger than all of that helped me to let go of some of the sorrow wrapped around my heart. Once God loosened my hold on it, my tears seemed to wash some of it away.

After God reminded me of who He is, He reminded me of who I am with the song "Move" [9] by Toby Mac. It challenged me to keep on keeping on even when I feel like I can't, to remember that I am a soldier. Soldiers don't quit.

Oh, I know the reality of feeling you have nothing left, like you can't take one more step. That's why I had put off this trip. But, you know, isn't that when God can do the most for us? When we can do the least for ourselves?

I did manage to stay almost exactly two hours by the grace of God and on the strength of your prayers. And the unit is sorted, at least until the possessions from my son's storage arrive. I didn't shed a tear while I was there, though there were many opportunities.

My son stored his memories in boxes as well as in his heart. It was both heartwarming and heartbreaking to see what parts of his life he kept close.

School trophies. Letters. Childhood photo albums. Old toys...

One of my mom's kitchen towels inside a small aluminum tin, because he said that kept it smelling like her house. And, while my husband stood by, I opened that tin and took a deep breath...and smelled my mom's house. I really did.

But in all of the work we did there, I think, in my heart, I was searching for something that I hadn't even fully realized. I think I was really looking for William there, among all the things that made up his home.

But he's not there. Or here.

He really IS home.

I can be - and am - sad about a lot of things right now. I think, like I once read, that my sadness stems from being an eternal soul in a temporal body. We weren't created to be separated by death. That's why it seems so unnatural to us, and so painful.

But there is a choice to be made here. In my grief and pain, I can either run *to* my Father, or *from* Him. I choose to run to my Daddy and tell Him I hurt, and rest in His arms as He comforts me.

Thank you all for praying me through this day.

Blessings with tears dried and peace in my heart,

Me

Today, some special friends of my son's put together a story line, complete with character interactions, for my grandson. They wanted his memories of his dad's upcoming birthday to be ones he could remember with joy, not just sorrow. My son and grandson were Comic Con fans, and they often attended these events. Below is my post to my son's memorial group page.

"I know you would have been there today if you could. In a way, you were, because the part of you that resides in the

hearts of all your friends put together an awesome adventure for your son. Thank you, Rob, for your offering of love for your friend."

October 30

Today we arrived at church a little earlier than usual. I should have known it wasn't an accident. When I walked into the sanctuary, I saw a young man working in the sound booth. He's one of the men for whom my younger son has worked the last two years.

He's also my older son's birthday twin.

Well, I was going to walk on by, but I just couldn't do it. I screwed up my courage and hunted for my hanky.

Guess who forgot her hanky today?

I wasn't going to let that stop me. I stepped up to the young man, and I asked if I could interrupt him for a second. He said, "Sure!" I explained that I needed a hug, and for the split second before I told him why, he looked a little surprised... and wary. Then I told him that tomorrow was my son's birthday, and, before I could say much more, he enveloped me in a wonderful hug.

God used that young man's servant heart to minister to me this morning. May God bless him with a wonderful birthday tomorrow.

A little bit later, just at the start of the first service, a dear friend walked in. She made a beeline for me, hugged me hard and whispered, "I know" in my ear. And, you know what? She really does...because she lost two precious ones shortly after their births after two difficult pregnancies.

There is purpose in this pain. There is power in His presence. There is peace in His plan.

Praise the God and Father of our Lord Jesus Christ, the Father of mercies and the God of all comfort. He comforts us in all our affliction, so that we may be able to comfort those who are in any kind of affliction, through the comfort we ourselves

receive from God.
2 Corinthians 1:3-4 HCSB

October 31

Today is my son's 33rd birthday.

But, praise God, he had another birthday.

When He was five years old, my son asked Jesus to be His Savior. Some call it being born again. Some call it accepting the Lord. Some call it salvation.

Now, if you knew my son as an adult, he might not have told you about this decision. But just as he can't "undo" being my child, he can't "undo" his adoption into the family of God. And even if he didn't give voice to his identity as God's child, you can't look at his relationship with his own son and not see the hand of God. His relationship with Oliver is a mirror image of his relationship with God. That's where he learned how to teach, how to guide, how to encourage, how to love, how to be a good father.

In honor of my son's birthday today, I'm asking each of you to examine yourself and where you stand with God. Not with church. Not with Christians. Not with religion. I'm asking you to examine yourself and where you stand with the Creator of your soul.

I'm not going to argue about whether you have a soul. You know you do. It's the part of you that makes you...you. It's the part that made my son who he was: adventurous, loving, creative, talented, introspective, procrastinating, smarty-pants. :)

It's the part of him that is NOT buried in that cemetery.

If you don't know where you stand with God, chances are you don't have a relationship with Him. He wants that to change. I know that, because on a day when I could be closed up in a dark room quietly crying my way through the hours, I am instead feeling a compulsion to share with you how you can reconcile with the One who made you who you are, the One with whom my son now resides.

The process itself is not hard. Do you realize that you're not perfect? (Neither is any other human being on the planet, by the way.) Can you be honest enough to admit that you've made bad choices, done bad things? Can you admit that you regret them, that you'd truly like to change, but that the power to do so doesn't reside within you? Do you realize there is no way you could ever be good enough, religious enough, generous enough to earn a home in heaven?

Welcome to the human race. We are broken. We are messy. We need help.

And God sent it. His only Son. He sent Him, knowing that the only way He could save us was to allow His Son to die in our place, to pay the price for all our mistakes, all our bad choices. Jesus was the only One who could do it, because He didn't make bad choices or mistakes. He was – and is - perfect. He took on Himself the consequences of our bad decisions, paid the price of death, and broke it's power over us when He rose from the dead.

In some ways, that's the theme of most of the superheroes my son enjoyed, isn't it? The world is broken. People are hurting. Enter the superhero to save the world. And perhaps the superhero stories resonate so strongly with us because, deep down, we know there is One.

And He did enter this world. And He does offer to save us. But He won't force you to choose what He offers.

I made the choice when I was 26. I recognized that I wasn't perfect. I realized that I couldn't do anything that would entitle me to live in heaven, and I knew I didn't want to go to hell. I admitted that I believed Jesus paid for my imperfection with His perfection, and I asked Him to be My Savior.

No bells. No whistles. No halo.

Just a still small voice within, One that whispered that my life had just been ransomed and that I would never be the same.

If you've never considered your life beyond this world, I encourage you to do so today. While you still have time. William had no clue that he would leave us so quickly. But, what happened to him could happen to any one of us. And once it does, there's no changing the decision you have or haven't made about Jesus. And, if you haven't made a decision to accept Him, then logic says you've rejected Him. There's no middle ground here.

Choose this day whom you will serve. Let my son's physical birthday become your spiritual birthday.

Because of my son's spiritual birthday, I'll see him again. If you've made the same choice we did, you will, too. And for those of you who never met my son, well, perhaps I'll be able to introduce you when we all get Home.

Prayers for you all,

Me

November 1

Saturday, after spending the afternoon sifting through my son's belongings, I came home to find that his insurance company had mailed me a check.

My baby made me his beneficiary. Now, I had been informally told this was the case, but that's different from finding out it's true. And worlds apart from holding a check in your hand that's supposed to represent the value of your baby's life. A check which incites an almost savage urge to tear it in pieces and scream. Loud. And long.

I'd return it in a millisecond to have him back.

Money has a nasty habit of causing friction in its wake, whether it's from the lack or abundance thereof. The love of money truly is the root of all evil. I didn't want this money. I didn't want to touch it. I didn't want to disburse it. I didn't want to administer it.

I wanted it to go away.

But it didn't. And it won't. It needed to be put in the bank as soon as possible, because having it in the house made my skin crawl. The next banking day was Monday.

My son's birthday.

Feather PILLOW moment.

I wish I could say that I made it through the whole transaction with grace and dignity. I wish, but I can't. I made blunders, unintentionally caused hurt, cried like a baby, whined. After I had already created a mess, I sought help from my brothers and sisters in Christ. They gave me wise counsel and prayed with me before I went to take care of business.

Once again, God showed up. *Lord, forgive me for being so faithless at times.*

The first instance occurred just as we sat down in the banker's office. While filling out papers and answering questions, I looked around for anything that would distract me from the process. My eyes landed on a tall shelf to the right of the banker's desk. There, on the very top shelf, was a plain, square curio. On it were four block letters that nearly covered the entire surface. Do you know what it said?

A gentle reminder from my Dad that I often feel ill-equipped for a task because I don't ask Him for His help.

Then, while the banker stepped out to retrieve paperwork, I received a text.

We've already discussed my cell phone habits, or lack thereof. The fact that it was charged and I actually heard it buzz are small miracles in and of themselves. But, the bigger miracle was who it was from.

It was an old high school classmate to whom I had recently sent a card.

This friend just recently underwent a heart catheterization. She is also battling cancer. A second time. After just recently losing her older brother to cancer. She's trying to arrange appointments and surgery while being at the mercy of others for transportation. And her prognosis at the moment is...challenging.

First, a message to pray. Then, a reason to pray.

My Father used this situation as an opportunity to show me something that I had missed in my journey thus far. How often are we so focused on our own troubles that we are blinded to the struggles of those around us? Just two days ago at church, a dear friend took the comfort she received from God at the loss of her two babies, and she shared it freely with me. Shouldn't I be looking for opportunities to do the same?

Yes. I should. I didn't look for it this time, so God showed it to me. Later last night, I texted my friend:

"Lord, I pray Your favor on my friend for all her appointments, doctors, treatments, and surgeries. I pray You will open doors to the treatments that will work, and shut firmly the doors to those that won't. I pray You will go before her in every decision she has to make, every ride she needs to arrange, and every step she needs to take. Encourage her by allowing her to see You working on her behalf. Fill her with Your peace that can't be explained, Your joy that can't be denied. Work a miracle here, Lord. In the mighty Name of Jesus I pray. Amen"

After that first text, we corresponded back and forth. I was able to share with my friend (who is not on social media and has no email) about my journey. I was able to tell her that because of what I've seen God do for me, I knew He could bring good out of her situation, too.

Did praying and sharing change either of our circumstances? No. But, I think, in the sharing of our struggles and encouraging each other, we might have changed our perspectives. I know that thinking about what my friend is facing has helped me put my challenges into perspective. And perhaps my friend feels a little less isolated, knowing that someone who has also suffered has reached out to her in love.

I don't know where my friend stands spiritually. We were no more than acquaintances in high school, and not much more than that now. Would you join me in praying for her?

November 2

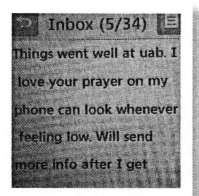

It's been two months since I buried my son. I expected today to be a hammer moment, and I was prepared for the blow. However, God has been merciful. Oh, there's no denying the thoughts that come, but they lack the intensity of pain so prevalent in past milestones. I admit to being curious as to why that would be so, but also relieved that, for the moment, peace prevails.

Instead of pain-filled memories, God gave me the opportunity to encourage my friend with cancer. He also gave her the opportunity to encourage me.

November 5

The two-month milestone for my son's burial service passed on November 2. It's not that I didn't think about it, but it didn't seem to be the hammer moment I was expecting. Perhaps it's because I spend so much time dreading the hammer moments that their arrival is less impacting than my anticipation of them.

It's the feather moments that are harder to cope with, because there's no anticipating when they'll come.

Like today.

My younger son is 20: responsible (mostly), reliable (usually), independent (well, he thinks so). This morning he and a friend were headed out of town to stay overnight with another friend about three hours away.

Easy peasy, right? Well, I thought so. We did the regular things: check this, don't forget that, what route are you taking, when will you be back. Then we said our goodbyes and our I love you's, and he went out the front door. The door had barely latched behind him when the urgency came on me. I bolted out the door, desperate to reach my son before he left...because he didn't hug me.

Sounds silly, doesn't it?

I caught up to him, explained I wouldn't get a goodnight hug tonight, and asked for one before he left. He's a special young man. He indulged his slightly frantic mom. I just hope he didn't hear the catch in my voice as I turned back toward the house.

Because in that moment, my thought was, *"I wanted to have that hug, in case you called him home today, Lord."*

I didn't want to have that thought. I didn't anticipate having that thought. I wish I HADN'T had the thought.

But there it is.

And feathers never arrive one at a time, do they?

We are in an election year, and I decided this year to take advantage of early voting. While standing in line this morning to vote, a feather memory drifted through my mind.

When William was small, I took him with me to the polls to watch me do my civic duty. We didn't make it a big deal or anything; it was just something I wanted him to see me doing. But, until that moment in line today, I had forgotten all about it.

I shook off the moment the best I could. It wasn't a moment I could have anticipated. And I agree with the girl who said they're worse than the hammer moments. Have you ever tried to defend yourself against a feather?

I thought I'd finally shaken the feathers off. Then, while running an errand at a local store, I wandered down the greeting card aisle. I needed some cards for long-distance friends, so I was skimming the racks, reading ones that caught my fancy. I read one with a really nice sentiment. I closed it to check the cover art, and that's when I saw it...in big swirling letters at the top of the card...

Son.

Why today, Lord? Why not three days ago, when I was prepared to do battle for my emotions?

Because today is not just about feather moments for me. It's about a hammer moment for my son's father.

My older son had another brother, his father's second son. If he had lived, he would be 25 today. Sadly, he died nine years ago.

Two sons. My ex-husband has lost both his children. And frankly, I'm not sure if he has the relationship with God upon which I have leaned so heavily during this entire journey.

Whenever you are feeling overwhelmed by your circumstances, keep in mind that, somewhere, there is someone that has a struggle equal to, or greater than, your own. Take a moment to inhale deeply, call on your Father, and request His strength for others going through valleys of their own.

Lord Jesus, this is a sad day for my ex-husband and his extended family. As they remember DJ and all he meant to them, help them to rest in the knowledge that he and his brother are celebrating with You. Give them peace in place of their pain, joy in the midst of their sorrow. Help them feel Your love and Your presence surround them. In the mighty name of Jesus I pray. Amen.

November 6

At church today, a group of talented women and young girls did an interpretive dance to "Eye of the Storm" [10] by Ryan Stevenson. I knew about the performance, because I saw them practicing before our first service. However, I had ministry commitments for the first two services, so it was the third service before I had an opportunity to see them perform.

I'm familiar with the song. It's been one I've repeatedly listened to, drawn strength from, worshipped with. I know it backwards and forwards. All of it.

I started the third service in the very front row, because I sign our worship songs. Up front I have less concern about hitting someone. (No joke. It's happened to my husband enough times that I've seen him glance at the lyrics of certain songs, then surreptitiously take a step away from me to get out of range.) After the songs, however, I moved back one row so I could see the dancers without craning my neck.

The song was beautiful, the dancers also. I was enjoying just being in the moment, with God's people, in God's house, praising God's name.

Then we came to the last verse, the second part, where the song talks about the maelstrom that breaks loose in your life when you lose a child to illness.

I don't know why I didn't see it coming...

I heard the words, and at first they didn't register an impact, sort of like a real feather just floating in the air. Then the dancers mimed holding a child in their arms, and that was all she wrote. I came apart, slowly at first, then with a flood of tears I really, really didn't expect.

I don't know what made me look around, but I did. Two seats to my left sat a woman in the same posture as me, weeping. I recognized her as a friend that lost her husband two weeks after I lost my son. It was just instinct to scoot down and hug her and mix my tears with hers. We hugged and cried through the end of the performance.

The feather moment ended there, but my journey does not. I've begun to see a pattern emerging. Maybe you see it in your lives, too. I have received God's comfort, not just for myself, but so that I can share it with others. This is just one instance. Just sitting here, I can think of at least five other instances in the last week or so where God has given me the opportunity to pray for or comfort others in need of help or encouragement. And it seems to me that God's comfort, like God's love, is multiplied when you give it away.

So, as the feather moments sneak up on you, look around. Perhaps there's

56

someone in your life that could use an encouraging word or a hug or a prayer. Share with them what God has offered you.

Be blessed, my friends and family.

Smiling through my tears,

Me

November 10

My son used to hunt up all the places serving Veterans on November 11 and go out to eat. I think Golden Corral was one of the places. I can remember going there with him and my parents when he was young. He used to fix my mom a dessert, I think, but I believe he might have ended up eating it.

My sincere thanks to all of his friends and family that served in the military. I hope you find a place tomorrow that will honor you with a heartfelt "Thank you for your service" and a hearty meal.

God bless you for your sacrifice for your country.

Yesterday a doctor friend of ours sat down with us and patiently explained our son's autopsy report.

Not a day I care to repeat. Ever. And while I have the relief of knowing the "how", I'm no closer to knowing the "why". I've tried to release that notion, the one that wants to question if there was something anyone could have done to change what happened. In the end, what good does that kind of questioning accomplish? My son is dead. God knew it would happen. God let it happen. And I am not God.

But the fact remains that going through that report made me think about things better left alone. Did he know? Did he suffer? Was he in pain? I didn't ask those questions, but they flutter around in my head like annoying little gnats. No matter how much I shoo them away, they keep returning.

I pray.

I listen to music.

I work.

I finally picked up a book to read, for a little distraction.

And God met me right there on page 226.

"Sometimes, you never get the answers to all the questions you ask...Sometimes there simply aren't answers. At least not the answers we're looking for. Walking through the fire forces us to face God. To strip our souls of all of the charades we play, until we see only Him. And in the end, we know Him better."
From *Hidden Agenda* [11] by Lisa Harris

November 11

Is anyone else finding comfort in some of the feather moments? As if God is saying to you, "Here's a memory for you, because I love you and want you to know I love William, too"? Because I had one this morning.

I try to start the day with God. I'm currently using Our Daily Bread's devotional booklet. This morning is already rife with memories of William because of his penchant for seeking out places where veterans would be appreciated on this day.

So...I pick up my booklet, read the scriptures and turn to the application story (http://odb.org/2016/11/11/seeing-well/). In it the writer speaks about their

58

dog, Raleigh. She also makes a passing reference to "*a comic book superhero*".[12]

I know I don't have to point out the superhero reference for anyone to get that connection, but there IS something that may not be common knowledge.

Raleigh was the name of William's childhood dog.

Thank You, God, for giving me a good feather moment. Tell William I love him.

I think I get why God gave me a good feather moment this morning. It was to encourage me through the tough one coming later. Many of you know my mom passed away just five days before my son. Before she died, she had passed on several boxes of books to me. One of them was full of Bibles. At the bottom of the box I found THE family Bible. Today, while shifting some things around, I found that box. I knew I needed to update the family Bible with my mom's death information. I pulled it out, flipped through it, and filled it in. While glancing at the entries my mom had made, I came across the "Grandchildren" page.

Tissue caution here. William was her first grandchild. She had penned his name in the space, and I can imagine the joy with which she might have done so.

That, itself, was tough, but it wasn't what struck me hard. What struck me was what's NOT there.

There's no line for date of death.

There was one for my mom.

There was even one on the "Children" page.

But not for grandchildren.

Sigh...

Thank You, God, for the good moment first. It helps to know You saw this coming. Tell Mom I love her, too.

Finished a book yesterday. Having feather trouble this morning, so I picked up another "light read" entitled *Take a Chance on Me* [13] by Susan May Warren. In the introduction was a precious word picture of what it's like to become a mother for the very first time. It beautifully described what an awesome, exciting, terrifying, painful journey it can be to watch your baby boy grow into a young man. It struck my heart.

It wasn't even on page one. It was in the preface to the story.

When I was blessed enough to get it in writing, I held on to it.

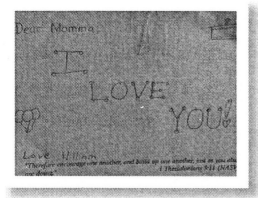

I will not cry.

I WILL not cry.

I will NOT cry.

I will not CRY.

November 12

When I picked up today's mail, there was a letter from a dear friend. Enclosed with it was a Navy challenge coin in honor of my son's military service. I only glanced at it at first. Then I took a closer look at the back of the coin. My friend, whom I haven't seen in many years, has no idea that a year ago our ladies' Bible study group completed a study by Priscilla Shirer called *The Armor of God.* [14] It was the first of two studies we did on prayer. God has used the things He taught me in those classes to help me through the last two months, and the ladies in

those classes became more than friends as we stood together against the enemy for our loved ones.

This coin was a gift from a friend, but, more importantly, a message from God. We are in a war, and our enemy is real. As a child of God, the enemy is powerless in his bid for my soul; his goal is to keep me so earthly-minded that I'm no heavenly good. What happened to my son left me with two choices: I could run FROM God, or run TO Him. I could isolate myself, lick my wounds, and percolate in my self-pity -- or I could open my heart to God and pour out my grief to Him, acknowledge His sovereignty, and invite Him to use this tragedy for His glory.

Some denominations speak of a "crisis experience" of faith...a place in life where you are confronted with an experience that is so life-changing and dramatic, that you feel as if your spirit is thrust onto a precipice. You can choose either to hold on to the things of this life with a tenacity and desperation that will leave your hands full but your hearty empty...or you can step off the precipice in faith, knowing that your heavenly Father has a plan, one that you cannot see but that you can trust is far better than anything you could ever think of or wish for.

Would I have chosen this path? No.

Do I trust my Father? Yes.

Is this easy? I am here to tell you that it is not.

I wish my son had not died. But I have to admit that I have seen God work in ways that were only possible through this journey. And I've lived long enough to trust that God is good, His plan is good, and He loves me far more than I am capable of loving Him. If I, who am only human, love my children with my whole heart, how much more does God, my creator and my redeemer, love me? Why would I believe He would ever mean me harm, any more than I would ever harm my own child?

This world is broken. That is a given. And because it's broken, bad things happen. God never promised us His paradise here on earth, He promised us His Presence and His perspective and His power. His power comes through the armor He has given us to protect ourselves and defend our faith.

Was it an accident that I was in a study that taught me the tactics of the enemy and the power of God to defeat them? No.

Was it an accident that the women in that study were knit together in love and faith and shared more than just a desire to study the scriptures? That, when the unspeakable happened, they banded together and prayed for me and cried with me and reminded me that God would see me through? Absolutely not.

Was it a coincidence that this coin, from a person over 100 miles away and unseen for 20+ years, contains not only the name of that particular study, but also the scripture reference on which that study was based, that it would land in my mailbox at the end of a week that I had suffered several "feather" moments that repeatedly knocked me down and had me struggling to find the strength to get up and keep moving?

No, there is no such thing as a coincidence. Nope.

Lord, thank You for the message of this coin, for the reminder of all You have given me for this fight I am in. Help me to stand my ground and plant my feet on Your promises. Help me to drench my shield of faith in the living water of Your Word, so that I can quench all the fiery darts of the enemy. Help me to stand with my sisters in Christ, shields locked together, to advance Your kingdom. In the mighty name of Your only begotten Son Jesus I pray. AMEN

Ephesians 6:10-18 NLT
The Whole Armor of God
A final word: Be strong in the Lord and in His mighty power. Put on all of God's armor so that you will be able to stand firm against all strategies of the devil. For

we are not fighting against flesh-and-blood enemies, but against the evil rulers and authorities of the unseen world, against mighty powers in this dark world, and against evil spirits in the heavenly places.

Therefore, put on every piece of God's armor so you will be able to resist the enemy in the time of evil. Then after the battle you will still be standing firm. Stand your ground, putting on the belt of truth and the body armor of God's righteousness. For shoes, put on the peace that comes from the Good News, so that you will be fully prepared. In addition to all of these, hold up the shield of faith to stop the fiery arrows of the devil. Put on salvation as your helmet, and take the sword of the Spirit, which is the word of God. Pray in the Spirit at all times and on every occasion. Stay alert and be persistent in your prayers for all believers everywhere.

November 15

There are days in this journey that pass without incident. They march slowly by to their conclusion. Thoughts of my son drift through my mind, but instead of grasping them and dwelling on them, I choose to let them pass through. Sometimes I don't have the energy to grieve. Sometimes I just don't want to.

That, for me, seems to be a danger. Because, most often, it's when we don't want to do something that we should press through and persevere.

My go-to escape from the trials of this life is books, mostly the happily-ever-after kind. That's where I was hiding today when God found me.

At first it was a gentle reminder of how I felt at the start of this journey.

"He had thought, for the past three years, that he'd suffered the worst life had to offer. But now he realized that he'd been mostly numb the whole time. It was like when your leg fell asleep. It felt dead and uncomfortable asleep, but it felt far worse when the feeling returned.

He was coming back to life now – feeling returning – and it hurt almost unbearably. He wanted to return to numb. He'd been trying for days now to get back to numb. But numb was gone. He was stuck with all this awful emotion. Inescapable." ---from My Stubborn Heart [15] *by Becky Wade*

Then, a nudge to let go of any anger or hurt I might be holding about having to deal with all of my son's personal effects and precious mementos.

"Resistance struck him with thudding force. He didn't want to do this. He didn't want to open any of these boxes and look inside and remember. He only wanted to shut the door, get back in his truck, and drive." ---from My Stubborn Heart [16] *by Becky Wade*

Finally, a gift of assurance that William is safe and secure with his Father.

"Beth hadn't deserved what happened to her. He looked upward. **She didn't deserve this!**

His only consolation had always been that Beth wasn't in any current pain. Despite his hostility toward God, he believed in heaven and he had no doubt at all that Beth was there.

Right?

This time a reply did come. He heard a steady voice deep inside himself speak for the first time in a long time. **She's with me now,** *it assured him.* **I've got her.**

Amazingly, tears did come to him then, blurring his vision. "Good," he managed to say, "Good then." ---from My Stubborn Heart [17] *by Becky Wade.*

I honestly didn't realize that I was hiding on those days that I opted out of the grief process. I am thankful that My heavenly Father did, and that He loves me enough to seek me out, even if it costs me a few tears.

Blessed are they that mourn: for they shall be comforted.
Matthew 5:4 KJV

November 18

Today is a hammer moment, the three-month marker since my mom passed away. She's been gone an entire season. It feels like years ago. And just yesterday.

In five days, there's another hammer moment coming. The day before we celebrate Thanksgiving marks three months since my son William died. I still sometimes shake my head in disbelief when I write or say that. My younger son Anthony gave me a word picture that described his feelings. It has stayed with me to this day. He said, "It's sort like you stubbed your toe really hard. It's extremely painful, breath-stealing, even. And then, while you're still trying to recover from that, someone punched you in the stomach."

That's it, only on a much larger scale.

How on earth do I celebrate Thanksgiving with these things on my heart?

By remembering that even in this situation, there ARE things to be thankful for.

I am thankful that my mother was called home first, so that I didn't have to tell her that her first grandchild had passed.

I am thankful that my sister and her family, who have lovingly devoted years to taking care of my mom, did not have to find her after she passed.

I am thankful that neither Mom nor William suffered protracted, painful illnesses.

I am thankful for all the years I had with both my mom and my son.

I am thankful that my grandson did not find his father gone, or helplessly watch him leave this earth.

I am thankful that William wasn't driving when he was called home.

I am thankful that William lived every minute of his life richly and fully.

I am thankful that both Mom and William had accepted Jesus as their Savior, so they were lovingly received into His presence when they stepped into eternity.

I am thankful that I have also accepted Jesus as my Savior, so I will see them both again.

And I am thankful for all of you, who have walked with me, and sometimes carried me with your prayers, through this extremely difficult season of my life.

I pray you all have a wonderful Thanksgiving. Even if you are experiencing difficult times, there are things for which you can thank God. You may have to look hard to find them, but that's exactly what you're called to do.

"In every situation [no matter what the circumstances] be thankful and continually give thanks to God; for this is the will of God for you in Christ Jesus."
1 Thessalonians 5:18 AMP

With tears in my eyes and thanksgiving in my heart,

Me

November 21

I've been thinking about this for a while, but I just didn't know what I could possibly say. Still don't, really, but I'm getting a sense from God that now may be the time; and, I'm praying that He will give me the right words, ones that will help all of us.

With everything that my relationship with William was, there was one thing that it wasn't: it wasn't perfect. There are things that I could have said or done better or differently or not at all. I'm wondering if you, like me and others I've spoken to, have also been tempted to dip your toe into the sea of regrets.

Please don't go there. The undertow of such a destructive exercise can quickly pull you out into that sea and drown you.

I want to encourage you (and myself) to stand strong against the temptation to indulge in "what if" or "if only". It's a pointless exercise and, at its core, sets us up to entertain the false notion that something we could or should or might have done would have changed what happened. That simply isn't true. We did not, and do not, have that kind of power. Yes, we could have made different decisions, but, in the end, they wouldn't have changed the outcome.

Is that a painful truth? You bet.

But there is another truth that helps me bear that pain, and that is this: God knew, from the moment William took his first breath, all the number of my son's days. From our human perspective, it feels horribly wrong for him to have preceded me in death, but I have walked with God for many years, have read and studied His Word, sung His praises, and worshipped at His feet. He has NEVER given me a reason to doubt His love for me, or His love for William. I have learned enough about Him to know that what we see in this broken, fallen world is a drop in the ocean compared to His infinite knowledge. I don't understand why William died, but I know my Savior. He loves me, and He loves William - more than even I, as his mother, ever could. After all, He sacrificed His Son Jesus so that William's life didn't come to an end when he left this earth. And God knew it would happen, He was ready for it, and He wants to help us through it.

So, that's what I'm doing. I'm letting Him help me through it. I'm leaning on Him, talking to Him, crying on Him. I give Him my sorrow. I give Him my pain. I give Him my regrets. And He gives me His peace. His comfort. His love.

And it's enough for me. I hope it is for you, too.

So, when those insidious thoughts come drifting across your mind, encouraging you to take a swim in the sea of regrets, remember that the invitation to jump in is not coming from God. Quite the contrary. Turn your back on those thoughts, and, instead, thank God for all the wonderful times He gave you with William. Post one on his memorial page. Play a song William liked. Watch a show he enjoyed.

Or text/ message/ email me, and we can shed some tears and seek God's help together. Just, please, don't beat yourself up over the past. William wouldn't want you to. I don't want you to. And God doesn't want you to.

If you were William's friend, you hold a part of my son's heart, and it knits me to you in a way I can't explain. I wanted to encourage you to stay strong and keep your head up. And don't hesitate to contact me if you need to talk.

Blessings,

Me

November 22

So, I'm finishing up a light read before the holidays, and I'm thinking to myself how this one actually turned out to BE a light read. The last few books that I've picked for distraction ended up having a message within them that came directly from God.

I should have known better than to issue a challenge like that "light read" thought, because, there it was, on page 354 - just eighteen pages before the end.

"Hard circumstances taught a person valuable lessons. The current circumstance was teaching Celia that even in the center of grief and confusion, God was enough for her." ---from *Meant to Be Mine* [18] by *Becky Wade*

Thank you, Daddy. Love you.

step 4

Resting in His Presence

And be sure of this: I am with you always...

Matthew 28:20b NLT

November 23

Given the proximity of this milestone to Thanksgiving, I didn't intend to post. However, the approaching holiday required some time on the road. As often happens when my hands are busy and my mind is free, my thoughts turned inward. Initially I chose to ignore them - even picked up another "light read" to while away a few miles. By now you'd think I'd have learned that God doesn't promise an escape from the trials of life on this broken planet. What He does promise is to work all things for the good of His children. So, there it was, on page 35. One of the characters describes another as the "Captain America type". Really. I'm posting the picture to prove it.

A Captain America type.

From *Twilight at Blueberry Barrens* [19] by Colleen Coble:

No pretending my way through this hammer moment, the day that marks three months since William died. So, while I watched God's creation stream past my car window, I pondered what God wanted me to learn at this juncture.

I have realized the truth of the cliché that part of my life ended when William died. There are blocks of time where our world consisted of just the two of us. There are experiences only we shared, and as long as I walk this earth I can no longer call him or text him and say, "Hey, remember when we...?" As I write this, I recall a verse about Jesus' mother, Mary. After the story of Jesus' birth at the beginning Luke 2, verse 19 (NLT) reads, *"But Mary kept all these things in her heart and thought about them often."* Did Mary know she would lose Jesus at a young age? I can't say. But I can say that she had the right attitude about her memories of Him. She treasured them.

I, too, have treasured up things in my heart about my son. I've shared some on his social media memorial page, like the "fence" post, voting, and the first haircut. There's a wealth of others, some of which are tucked so deeply in my heart that I suspect they will sneak up on me like feathers, drifting across my mind when I'm least prepared. Even though sometimes it hurts to remember, the pain is lessened when it's shared.

So, I think, when the memories crop up and God leads me to, I'll post them to William's memorial page that his ex-wife so thoughtfully created. In time, his son may want to read them. Who knows? William may have shared some of them with his son already.

And may I encourage you to do the same? You might not know William, but you certainly have friends or family who've lost a loved one. If, in your heart somewhere, you have a memory of that special someone tucked away, please share it with those who share your loss. There just may be someone who needs to hear it, and in the sharing, I think you'll be blessed as well.

With tears trumped by treasured memories,

Me

November 24

I have survived the first major holiday without William. If there is such a thing (and I'm here to tell you there is not), I would have to say this would be an "easy" one, because I haven't shared a Thanksgiving table with my son since he was in high school. Consequently, there are less memories with which to struggle.

We do travel to see extended family for this holiday, and we hadn't seen most of them since William died. I was apprehensive on what we might face as far as their reactions. We ourselves have been traveling this road for three months. I wondered if their grief would strike me as fresh and raw, and open wounds that were just beginning to heal. However, beyond an initial expression of sympathy and the occasional question about how I'm doing, the overall reaction was mild. It took me a while to realize that they just don't really know what to say or do. After all, they haven't been down this road before either.

Many of them don't have a relationship with Jesus, so they have no perspective on how I've weathered this storm in my life. As God gave me opportunity, I spoke of His steadfastness in walking with me. Please pray the seeds God allowed me to sow will fall on fertile ground and begin to grow.

The poem below was given to me by God while sitting and listening to the sounds of a family celebrating all that they're thankful for. I think it was His way of helping me see things from His perspective, and, really, isn't His perspective the only one that matters?

The Empty Chair

The food is on the table,
We've prayed a thankful prayer,
But no one's really speaking
About the one who isn't there.

China plates clink with silver,
Tables are filled with sumptuous fare,
Yet still no one is speaking
About the one who isn't there.

Delicious dishes fill their bellies,
Scents of pumpkin fill the air,
But no one seems to give a thought
To the one who isn't there.

Faces 'round the table,
Laughing, talking everywhere,
But not a single mention
Of the one who isn't there.

Don't hold it against them,
Or think that they don't care;
They just don't know what to say
About the one who isn't there.

Take heart that he's in heaven,
That he lives with Jesus where
It's now Thanksgiving every day
For the one who isn't there.

November 26

Lord Jesus,

On the back-side of the hammer moment of a holiday without William, many of us are struggling to get through the days without being sandbagged by memories or wishes or dreams. I, for one, feel more dread for the approaching holiday than anticipation. Help us to hold on to You through the tough moments. Help us feel Your love surround us. Help us feel Your peace fill us. Give us Your strength to remember William with joy and gratitude for the time we had with him. Comfort us with the knowledge of where he is and how much You love him and us. Thank You that he accepted You as his Savior. Thank You that if we have accepted You, we will see him again.

In the mighty name of Jesus I pray. Amen.

November 27

Some very talented young women performed an interpretive dance to the song "Blessings"[20] by Laura Story in church this morning. It's all about how the things that hurt us the most and wound us the deepest are often the very things that God uses to draw us near to His heart so that He can pour out His blessings in and through us.

It took the length of the first service for my husband's shirt to dry.

Didn't see that one coming.

November 29

I'm sitting here with tears slipping down my face and amazed and perplexed by how we all seem to ride the same waves of grief. I'm trying not to focus on Christmas because it's tough enough to manage the day I'm in right now. How on earth do you avoid it when it's EVERYWHERE you turn? Radio. Television. Stores. Neighborhood. Work. Memories of the few Christmas traditions we had keep ambushing me. I'm sure from the outside looking in, we're supposed to have "moved on".

Dear Father in heaven, please forgive me if I ever thought that about anyone!

This is less about "moving on" and more about "keep moving". In fact, someone asked me Sunday how I was doing, and I was honest about the struggle of this past holiday. He said something then that seemed out of sync with our conversation at the time, but it makes sense now. He said, "Well, the good thing is that you don't have to stay there." Perhaps I needed to share that with you. I'll be perfectly honest and say that it kind of sucks where I am right now, but the good news is I don't have to stay here. The best news is that I'm not here alone. God hasn't let me down yet. He's certainly not going to start now.

Heads up, friends and family. I love you, and I'm praying for you.

I would appreciate your prayers this holiday season. All the holiday hoopla is hard to escape, and the season brings up many memories that demand to be mourned so that I don't get stuck in one spot. It's really difficult to be where I am right now, but, as a wise man of God told me Sunday, the good news is that I don't have to stay here. The best news is that my Father is here with me.

Thank you for praying.

December 1

Today I read a poem all about what Christmas in heaven might be like. It wasn't exactly scripturally accurate, but God's point to me was clear. My son and mother are celebrating the birth of Jesus WITH Jesus! I can take comfort in that.

Lord, no matter how much I miss them, please help me never to wish them back into their life here and away from You. Help me balance my pain of missing them here with their pleasure in being in Your presence forever.

December 2

We took this picture in December 1991.

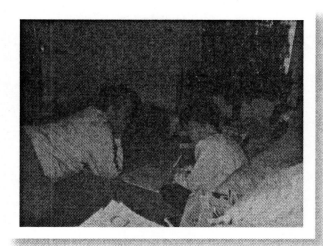

Who could have guessed that 25 years later, Mom and William would celebrate their first Christmas in heaven together?

We buried William three months ago today. I say "we" to include all of you, because those of you who knew him are right here with me, and those of you who know only me have prayed me through some extremely painful moments these last three months.

This holiday season will be a challenge for us. I think we can all agree that the enemy has worked hard to boot Christ out of Christmas. Let's not give him the opportunity to make this Christmas full of sorrow and if-onlys. If, like me, you're finding even the early days of December fraught with memories that wring your heart, then I invite you to join me in changing our focus.

Yes, let's remember William and Mom with joy. But, the minute your mind strays to those places where it's less about the memories you *do* have and more about the ones that will never be,

STOP.

RIGHT.

THERE.

We are not God. We do not have the whole picture. We need to trust Him, not only with what *has* happened, but also with what, now, never will. And we need to thank Him.

Yes, I said thank Him, especially at this time of year. God sent Jesus to save us from all this. He sent *His* Son so that He could save *my* son. Because of that baby born to a frightened young girl in a lowly stable, my son was able to choose God's forgiveness and salvation. Because of that first Christmas, I'll see William again.

Perhaps you don't have that assurance. I didn't, not until I was 26. Going to church won't get you that assurance. Reading the Bible won't do it. Being good won't do it. You simply need to admit that you are what we all are: broken, stained by deeds or words or thoughts that you'd like to undo, but can't. You need to acknowledge that you believe in Jesus as God's Son, and that He died and rose to life again to save you from your brokenness. And, you need to accept the gift He has offered to everyone who believes: salvation, the security of knowing that you will spend eternity in heaven with Him.

And with my son.

And my mother.

And me, too.

If you won't be there, I ask you to please re-read this and reconsider. You don't know the number of your days on this earth, but God does. If He's knocking on the door of your heart today (and if you're reading this, He is), you can be sure He has a plan and purpose for your life. Let this be the year you put Christ in your Christmas.

Blessings of the Reason for the season,

Leslie

December 3

I believe I've come to the first of the steep climbs on my way out of the valley of the shadow. I say this because each step takes strength and determination. You can feel the strain as you lean in and reach up, trying to get a firm grip so you can pull yourself higher.

Because today, I finished putting up a Christmas tree my son will never see.

It has taken me a week, but it's finally done. It's been a solitary task for me for many years. In the last two, I've used the time to pray over those that gave me the individual ornaments as I hang them, or for those whom they represent to me. There's one given to me by missionaries to Peru. I use it to pray for my missionary friends as well as all those who have sacrificed their holidays at home for the sake of the gospel. There's one given to me by my employer. I use that one to pray for all those I work with and for. There's one sent to me by a friend who has since succumbed to cancer. I use that one to pray for all those who've lost a loved one this past year and are coping with their first holiday without them.

Like me.

You get the idea. So, today I finally got it all finished, and I realized with a pang that there are no ornaments of William's on the tree. When he grew up and went out on his own, I lovingly separated out all the ornaments that were his and passed them on to him so he could share their memories with his family. Most are in storage now. It warms my heart that he saved them, but wrenches it at the same time. So many memories I've yet to mourn...

And the whole time I put up the tree, I was thinking how I do the same thing every year.

Same tree.

Same location.

Same lights.

Same ornaments.

Same ratty garland that desperately needs replacing but that I hold on to as tenaciously as I do the memories it carries.

Everything about the process is all the same...but it feels so completely, indescribably different...because I am different. My life is different. My family is different. Normal isn't normal anymore.

After I finished the tree, I sat down and idly scrolled through my social media site. I noticed a post from a friend who had tagged me. It was the video of a song called "Different Kind of Christmas" [21] sung by Mark Schultz. It's all about how different Christmas is after a loved one dies.

God used my friend to reach out to me and tell me that He knows that I'm struggling, and He loves me. He used her to let me know that He understands that things are different now, and that's okay. So many times and in so many ways, God has reached out to me in the hard places and held my hand, or, when I'm feeling overwhelmed, He's let me crawl into His lap like an injured child running for the safety of their father's arms. There's an intimacy there that I can't describe and that I couldn't fathom before my world, as I knew it, caved in on itself.

Later this afternoon, I got a message from my sister. She's facing a different kind of Christmas as well, because she and my mother were very close. Her message read: *"Went to Mom's today to take care of leaves and to go through some of the Christmas items to share with some young friends of my daughter's that don't have any Christmas decorations. I was fine in the house but kept getting hammered by memories as I walked the backyard with my grandson. Very weepy and I don't care for it. I'm so very thankful that my grandson will get to run around and play in the same backyard that we did. I found this in Mom's ornaments and I will save it for you. It's going to be a hammer and I'm sorry. I love you."*

Remember I was lamenting the lack of memories of William on my tree? My Father remembered, too, and He loves me so much, He has taken care of it for me. Just looking at that face, I can hear William's high-pitched laugh that always told me he was full of joy.

But I made a mistake today, one I think I've often made in this journey. I mistook the avoidance of mourning for victory over it. I was relieved that I survived the tree, the song and even the picture without crying. The picture was a near thing, and by the time I reached that point, I had an inkling that I had taken a misstep, but I didn't know what it was. My Father loved me enough to show me.

Tonight I attended a concert at church. A very gifted young lady was singing, as well as a band with whom she has performed in the past. The band played first. They're very good. The music was upbeat. It helped relieve the heaviness I had felt when I had received my sister's message.

About four songs into their set, the lead singer stopped to explain how he had come to write the next song. He told the story of a devoted church member that had consistently worked within the church in many capacities. He was 45, loved to run. Uneasiness began to stir in me. When he told us the gentleman had a heart attack, that uneasiness began to rise. It ebbed a little when he mentioned surrounding the hospital and praying for his healing. However, it reached tidal wave proportions when he mentioned that he died. I excused myself and darted as quickly and quietly as I could for the ladies' room. I stood in there, gulping air and trying to figure out why I managed to make it through all the memories and thoughts of the day, only to be slain by a song about a man I didn't know by band I'd never beard before. I pushed the uneasiness back down to manageable proportions and headed back into the concert.

Waiting at the door for me was a dear friend, arms open wide. I fell into them, and all the tears that I thought I didn't have flooded down my face. She held me while I poured out all the grief that had been building all day, like a storm percolating in the atmosphere. What I had mistaken for progress in this journey was actually avoidance of pain on my part. Mourning hurts, but my Father understands it's necessary to wash away the sharp edges of grief.

And because my Father loves me so very much, it wasn't just any friend holding me. This friend is the mother of one of William's birthday twins.

God is a good, GOOD Father.

December 4

God met me in a special way today. I don't say that lightly. It was so deeply, intimately HIM that I'm hesitant to share it.

In a Bible study on prayer earlier this year, we were encouraged to write out a prayer list for those closest to us. On that list we were encouraged to write their name and one word that would sum up our request.

I made out my list. There were ten people on it. I added that list to my daily quiet time, praying down it faithfully until I could actually do it without the physical list as a reminder.

Two people on that list are dead. One is my mother. One is my son.

Does that mean God didn't answer my prayer? No. It means that His answer was not my answer. But, who am I to question my Creator?

Once the initial shock lessened, I picked up the list again. However, I stuttered to a halt every time I got to their names. I couldn't do it. Not even without the list. Right or wrong, I laid the list down, and prayer for my family, while it continues, is not as regular as it once was. I wish that weren't so, but I'll not sugarcoat my shortcomings.

So, on Sundays there is a group of people where I attend church that devote one worship service to prayer. It is a small, but powerful group of prayer warriors who welcomed me into their fold about a year or so ago. They have stormed the gates of heaven with me and for me. If you've ever shared a prayer life with a group like this, you'll understand how spiritually close you become.

Today we were sharing in prayer the concerns and challenges of the church and ourselves as we normally do. In the course of praying and confessing, one brother shared the challenges he'd faced this year in the spiritual realm. It was obvious by his tone that he was struggling with issues that we all face at various times in our life, and just as obvious that the enemy was gleefully firing away at his faith with all the ammunition he could muster. As we went around the circle in prayer, I felt led to pray for him, to encourage him; but, as is often the case, words fail when feelings flow. It was then that God met me in that special way.

All of a sudden - and I do mean sudden - I had a thought of that abandoned prayer list tucked in my Bible. I thought about how, time after time when I tried to restart it, my heart was wrung when I reached my son's name, and I would give up.

But my God didn't give up. And right there, in that tiny room, with a handful of people bowing in prayer, God shone His Light into my darkness, and, I hope, into that young man's despair as well.

Because that devout young man, struggling to hold onto his faith in the face of the enemy? That young man bears my son's name.

I believe it's time to make a new prayer list.

———————————————

When I am overwhelmed by the circumstances of my life (such as the emotionally charged time in prayer this morning), my escape of choice is what I have termed "Cinderella fiction". You know the type I mean. Boy meets girl. Drama. Intrigue. Suspense. Boy gets girl.

That's where I was today, hiding out in the land of Happily Ever After.

I should know better than to hide from God. You should, too. No matter where you hide, He'll lovingly pull you out and help you see that in your attempt to escape, you've robbed yourself of the blessings that often come only through the pain.

"God had led her through rough patches exactly this way countless times in the past. Just when she was about to have a meltdown, a neighbor would knock on her door, a friend would invite her out for dinner, a loved one would call. Then and now she recognized these small interventions for exactly what they were: God throwing her a lifeline through the words and hands of His people." ---from *Undeniably Yours* [22] by Becky Wade

I can attest to the truth of the quote above. Early on in my journey, a neighbor did knock on my door, and she spent a couple of hours just chatting with me. It helped me to focus on something besides the pain. Another dear friend has invited me out for lunch a couple of times, just to check on how I am doing. In some of the toughest places, my cell phone would buzz with an encouraging text from yet another dear friend who would share her prayer for me in the situation I was currently facing. Sometimes, instead of escaping, perhaps we should stop and pray for all those that have carried us through a part of our life through which we didn't have the strength to walk alone.

On the page following the above quote, a character references the initials on a work shirt. The initials were WCH. I don't suppose I have to tell you that those are my son's initials. God wanted to make sure that I was paying attention while He was speaking to me. That's another lesson I'm still learning, to look for God's message in the everyday and the mundane. Because, there are messages there. A great number of them. I often miss them because I'm too busy listening to what's happening instead of Who's in charge of it.

"Faith is moving ahead in obedience, dear. Just moving ahead one step at a time, trusting Him, until He shows you what's next. Just wait on Him and then do what He says. That's truly your only responsibility. He'll take care of everything

else." ---from *Undeniably Yours* [23] by Becky Wade

Sometimes on this journey, one step is all you can see. If you look up and see how far you have to go, you can be overwhelmed by the enormity of the journey. So you close your eyes, put your hand in Jesus', and let Him lead the way.

Difficult?

Absolutely.

Necessary?

Positively.

The last quote from this "light read" was a prayer that echoed in my soul.

"I'm so thankful for You, God...No matter what, You are still on Your throne. You're good, and mighty, and full of grace. My heart's broken, my body's wrung out, my mind's drained, but I have You and no one can take You away from me. I'm grateful for my blessings. I worship You with my whole heart. I trust You with my life." ---from *Undeniably Yours* [24] by Becky Wade

December 7

I can't decide what hurts most: days where the loss of William rides my every thought, or days when it doesn't, and then I suddenly remember, and it's like it has happened all over again. Is there anybody else experiencing this?

And I still can't bring myself to listen to Christmas music. Can't figure that one out.

Sigh...

December 10

As a token of their love for my son, several of his friends collected digital pictures of him and produced an hour-long video photo montage for the reception after his funeral.

Before last night, I had never made it all the way through it.

It's not that I didn't want to watch it. I had, in fact, seen the first half the night before his service. But it was painful. So very, very painful. I know, physically, they are just images on the screen. Emotionally, each one is a moment in time that is fixed in my heart. Watching him on that screen, so full of life and love and, yes, sometimes, himself and knowing that he's gone...well, I just couldn't do it. I physically couldn't do it. The montage ran throughout the reception after his service. I steadfastly kept my back to it. I suspect I hurt the feelings of those that worked so hard on it, and I'm eternally sorry about that. The fact of the matter is that I was merely trying to survive a tragedy that no mother ever wants to face. It came down to having to pick my battles, because I didn't feel strong enough to fight them all. I suspect that God had a hand in making those choices, helping me to set aside those that could wait in order to give me the strength for those that wouldn't.

But the enemy knows a weakness when he sees it, and he saw this one and took full advantage of it.

Because somewhere along the way, in the past three months "can't watch it" morphed into "don't want to". It wasn't a conscious decision, but I recognize now one of the pitfalls on this journey. This IS a journey. I'm supposed to keep moving. Resting to gain peace and strength for the journey? Fine, great. Camping out because you're tired and it just feels good to stay where you are because it's familiar and comfortable? BEWARE.

In Psalm 23, David talked about walking THROUGH the valley of the shadow of death, not taking up residence in it. I know it's probably a theological stretch to view it this way, but I do see this as if I'm walking through the valley of the shadow of my son's death. If I'm to walk THROUGH it then it follows that God does not want me to live IN it. I'm supposed to be a sojourner here, not a citizen.

So, late last night, I put the DVD in the computer, set up a live feed on my son's memorial page, and sniffled my way through a photo history of his life. It was painful, yes, but it was beautiful, because just viewing it showed me so much about the ones who put it together and how much they love my son. God bless you all. As painful as it was for me to watch it now, I can't even imagine the pain you experienced to put it together at a time when all our hearts were still raw from the blow of William's unexpected death. Your sacrifice makes the gift so much more meaningful. I can't thank you enough.

And, please forgive me for waiting so long. I am so sorry.

I was leisure-reading *It Had to Be You* [25] by Susan May Warren today, and I came across some lines about the enemy of our souls and his primary goal of destroying our faith. Although he can't have our souls, he can render us ineffective... BUT he can't do that without our permission. We have to choose our focus when tragedy strikes. Do we run to the safety of our Father's arms? Or do we run away?

I have seen the truth of this in the last few months. The enemy is not stupid. God has never created anything stupid. While I am trying to navigate my way through the morass of emotions that surround a sudden loss like this, the enemy is lurking, biding his time while he looks for any cracks or weaknesses in my armor.

One of those cracks is emotion, feelings. There are days when I don't *feel* like doing anything. Quite the opposite. The exhaustion of fighting my way through this valley often feels so overwhelming, I feel like just staying in bed.

I go to bed tired. I wake up tired. At least that's the way it *feels*. The enemy would like me to swallow the lie that sleeping the day through is what I need. Yes, he would really like that. But I have chosen a different route.

I am trying to continue on, doing those things that need doing. There is some comfort in the routine and the regular. And sometimes, someone else needs to see that, in spite of what I have suffered, the enemy remains defeated and God remains exalted. Once in a while, God will urge someone to speak words of encouragement to me, words that help me to know that I am still on the right path through this valley. I am thankful that God has shown me how He has used this to bring others into a deeper walk with Him.

So, for me, there really is no choice. Why, after all God has done for me, would I allow the schemes of the enemy to separate me from the One who loves me most?

December 11

A dear friend sent me a package earlier this year. Among other things, it contained three copies of a statement encouraging us to persevere in the path of righteousness and doing right, patiently waiting for God's work in us to come to fruition, holding fast to the faith that nothing that has happened to us will ever be wasted, and not giving up on the threshold of His blessings to us. I couldn't find a source and didn't want to quote without permission, but it was very inspirational.

Coming on the heels of today's nudge from God do take a leap of faith, it has spoken to my heart.

Because, if you're reading this, today has been instrumental in making this book a reality. I had been approached about publishing early on, but my journey's not yet finished and at the time I couldn't see beyond surviving it. A little distance has granted me a better perspective, and I have allowed the person who approached me to plant the mustard seed of faith in the possibility that God wants this to happen.

That was Tuesday. On Wednesday, I approached another party to ask their opinion. They agreed with the first person. Fast forward to Sunday. Aside from the message that spoke directly to me, there was a third party - totally oblivious to what had happened earlier in the week - who walked up to me, hugged me, and whispered in my ear, "I think you should write a book."

Never underestimate God's ability to use your brokenness. This is not a journey I wanted to take. I'm not even comfortable recording it for others to read. But, if what happened to me helps just one person find their way to my Father, then this journey will not have been in vain. God promises to use what's meant for evil to bring about His good. I cling to that promise, and, in your darkest moments, I hope you can, too.

"God often chooses to move through our prayers to accomplish His work...God wants us to join in His work through humble, persistent prayer. Regardless of our human limitations, God may choose to move through our praying in amazing ways. When we make it our aim to serve God through praying faithfully as Elijah did, we're taking part in a beautiful privilege--where at any moment we may be given a front row seat to a miracle!"[26] ---from *Our Daily Bread*, December 11, 2016 (https://odb.org/2016/12/11/serving-god-with-our-prayers/)

Prayer, true prayer, involves an intimacy with God that cannot be faked. My Creator is not fooled when, on the outside, my head is bowed, but, on the inside, my spirit is distracted or downright defiant. True prayer begins with submitting in humility everything *I* want to the authority of my Father. It is not about changing God's mind. It's about agreeing with Him. I should always pray, if not verbally, then certainly spiritually, "Thy will be done." Does that sound like a copout to you? Perhaps it rings truer in the more modern phrase, "Nevertheless, You know what's best in this situation." Not an easy way to pray, submission, but it is certainly the best way. When you acknowledge that God is infinitely wiser than you and there is no reason to question His ways, it makes the deeper parts of this valley easier to tread, because you know, deep down where it counts, that you can trust Him in those dark places.

I did not intend to share this here. I had left a short note to myself from which I wished to write an altogether different thought. But, as has happened on more than one occasion in this journey, God has figuratively grasped my shoulders, turned me toward *His* will and whispered, *"No, not there. Here."*

In this case, I'm truly stepping out in faith, because not many people knew about this beforehand -- most still don't. About two years ago, I began to pray quite fervently for William to find a warm, loving church where he could share his incredible talents. William, however, was resistant. I won't say he was without reasons for his dislike of organized religion. (Who of us hasn't been disappointed or hurt by a brother or sister in Christ at one time or another?) Still, I wanted him to find the comfort, love, and support of a good church home. In the past, I had nagged, cajoled, advised (without being asked for advice), and all the other things mothers try in order to bend their children to their wishes. It only annoyed him and frustrated me. I wasn't far into my continual prayer for William when God nudged me. I didn't hear an audible voice, but I clearly got the message. In essence it was this: *You need to step out of My way and let Me work. My own Son's ministry didn't start until His mid-thirties. It will all be worked out by the time William is 33.*

So, I did my best. I learned to bite my tongue, take a deep breath, do just about anything to keep from overstepping the line God had drawn for me. I did ask for permission to answer any question William asked, and I was granted that privilege. However, that was it, and no more. I wasn't always perfectly obedient, but I did try.

And God kept His promise, but certainly not in the way I expected.

Because, just three months and eight days before his 33rd birthday, God called my son Home.

I trust my Father. I don't always understand His will, but I trust Him. That's the beauty of intimacy with my Father. Even when life looks its bleakest, I know He loves me, I know He sees my pain, and I know He will use it for His good purpose.

December 13

Season's Greetings

It's no longer my practice to write a Christmas newsletter, but I'm choosing to make an exception this year. I hope you are enjoying this season as we prepare to celebrate the birth of our Savior.

My husband continues to use his retirement to volunteer in various organizations, such as Habitat for Humanity, the public library, and of course, our church. He also spends time helping my mother keep up with her house and yard work.

I still work full time at the library. I have been in my new position for a little over a year now, and I am still learning all its aspects. I've been told that I will be having a hand in this summer's children's program. I'd appreciate your prayers for me. It's been several years since I planned any children's events.

My husband's daughter still lives in Indiana. She recently changed jobs, and is enjoying her new work. She's dating a nice young man, whom we met at Thanksgiving.

Our younger son continues to live at home and work toward his associate's degree. He works part time at the college and for a local sound production company. He's still looking at options for a four year degree. He and his girlfriend celebrated two years together in November. She's a wonderful young woman with a lovely family.

That was the normal part of our year. Normal ended for us in August.

My mother suffered an infection with serious complications in August. She made an amazing recovery, but two days into rehab, she passed away peacefully in her sleep. While we knew she had chronic health challenges, we were caught by surprise, because she had been doing so well.

Five days later, my older son William, joined her in heaven. It was sudden. It was unexpected. And, it was devastating. Many of you have been walking this journey with us. We are so grateful for your support, encouragement, and prayers. We are still sorting out all the details, and God is helping us every step of the way. I honestly don't know how anyone else walks this path without Jesus. I really don't.

So, life looks different now than what we expected. We spent last Christmas with William. We had hoped to start a new tradition, but not the one we will be starting now. Still, we are coping and God has been teaching us so much. We've been blessed to be able to watch Him take this heart-wrenching tragedy and bring many good things out of it. We still have tough days, but we have easier ones, too. God is good on both kinds of days, and we trust Him fully.

William's son now lives with his mother and stepfather, and he is doing well. He earned straight A's on his report card and also won a leadership award. In October, William's friends created an awesome adventure for his son at the local Comic Con event. It was a beautiful tribute to how much they all love William.

If there's anything I can say to you this Christmas, it's to please consider the first and greatest Christmas gift ever given: Jesus. If you don't KNOW that you know Him, have acknowledged your inability to be good enough to go to heaven on your own merits, and asked him to be your Savior, please consider what might happen if your next breath is your last. I don't say that to distress you - quite the contrary. Christmas means so much more when you're on intimate terms with Reason for the season. Please, open your heart and ask Him to come in. He loves you, and he's waiting for your invitation.

Blessings of the season,

Me for the Family

December 15

Yesterday was our city employee luncheon. Today was our staff breakfast. They were much the same as years past.

I am not.

Although I am doing a lot of the same things, I am different. It's like the day after you get new glasses. The important things seem so much clearer, the trivial things have been delegated to the background, where they should have been all along.

The gatherings, for me, have become a celebration of friendship and camaraderie. Sitting together, enjoying the company of friends and coworkers. Sharing stories. Laughing together. The gifts and games become important only in their ability to further the fellowship.

Christmas shouldn't be lost in the rush between plays and parties, writing cards and wrapping presents.

Stop.

Take a breath.

Enjoy your friends and family while you have them.

You never know which Christmas will be your - or their - last.

December 18

Dear William,

About two weeks ago, I received an email inviting me to take part in our church's Christmas skit. I imagine you got a kick out of suggesting that to God. Only you know how far outside my comfort zone the limelight is. Well, I was all ready to snap off a resounding, "Thanks, but NO thanks."

I was.

I really was.

But, something happened. I couldn't seem to come right out and say "No", so I said nothing.

Then, a second email.

Then, a text.

A message down the church grapevine through your brother.

Still, I didn't WANT to do it, but I couldn't say "No". I just couldn't.

So I said, "Yes." I qualified my acceptance with how bad I stink at acting. I was assured it was a small part with no lines. I guess you knew that, if they'd asked me to speak, I'd have quit on the spot.

Thank you for that, at least.

It really was a small part, praise the Lord. A few steps, a little acting out the narration...perhaps a few tears. (I nailed that part, by the way.)

Somewhere in the midst of the second service, I was reminded of you in "Hark, the

Herald Angel". It came to me that although I was trying to do something totally different this season so that I would have less painful reminders, you asked God to help me come full circle. Because from the moment I thought of you in that second service, you were uppermost in my mind the rest of the morning. And I know YOU were the reason I couldn't say "No." For some reason that I'm sure God will reveal in His time, I needed to do this for you. In memory of you.

You were always such a natural on stage.

But enough is enough, Son. Have some mercy on your mother. Because, while I survived all three shows without tripping, fainting, or barfing, I have not the slightest desire to do it again.

So, next year, could you pick someone else? Please?

Love you for always.

Love you forever.

Mom

On the four month milestone of my mother's passing, I stepped outside my comfort zone and did something I haven't done since high school. In the grand scheme of things, it's a small step, but not for me. And, when I accepted the task, I neglected to notice that date on which it would fall.

That seems to be becoming a habit. Milestones that at first were dreaded and fretted over now sometimes pass without a whimper. Then, afterwards, I feel almost guilty because I didn't spend the day curled in a ball just wishing it were over.

It doesn't make sense, I know. There are a lot of things about the past four months that don't make sense from my perspective. That's why I am so blessed to have a heavenly Father that I can - and do - trust.

It's in the hard, incomprehensible places in your life that you learn the truth about your faith. Without a doubt, we all trust God when we see Him work the way we want Him to. But, what happens when He allows something that you never imagined would happen to you in your life? Where is your faith then? Do you cling to it tenaciously, allowing it to hold you together in the face of unendurable grief and shock? Or do you cast it to the four winds and shatter into a million pieces, while those before whom you've talked that faith wonder where it is, now that you really need it?

Friends have asked me how I have managed this journey thus far. I am not being overly humble or just quoting a trite phrase when I respond that I am living and breathing and moving by the grace of God. In those moments where the enemy wishes me to drown in my worldly sorrows, I wrap myself in the faith of all I know my Savior to be, and I rest in His arms. When I am tempted to steep myself in sorrow and, yes, self-pity, I remember all that God has done for me to show me how much He loves me.

It is possible to experience both pain and joy at the same time. (Ask any woman who has given birth and she will tell you it is true.) I think I am learning to embrace both. Sometimes with happy tears. Sometimes with sad ones. But always with my Savior.

December 19

"Do you think any of this took God by surprise? Do you think you have the power to change what He's ordained and set in motion?" ---from *Mermaid Moon* [27] by Colleen Coble

One of the greatest comforts God has given me on this journey is His knowledge. He knew this was coming. He was ready for it. He didn't allow it to happen by accident or as a punishment. There was nothing I could do to change what was going to happen. It is comforting to know that God knows all and sees all.

I have to admit to curiosity about God's children who choose to rail at Him when bad things happen. Do any of us really think we have that right? That we, who are God's children by adoption, should escape suffering when His own Son volunteered to suffer? In our place? Do we really think that we know better how things should happen than the One who created us and knows our end from our beginning? How can we doubt His love for us, when He has even counted the very hairs on our head? Do you love your children enough to number the hairs on their heads?

When I feel the enemy tempting me to be angry, I remember that my Father loves me. Just as we, as parents, can't always explain situations so that our children will understand, God knows that I can't comprehend all the whys and wherefores of this tragedy.

I choose to trust Him, just as I hope my own children would trust me.

December 20

Early this month I visited the local Hallmark store. I was searching for an ornament for some family members to celebrate William's life. My desire was for a Captain American ornament, and I did find it, but they were all sold out. They didn't even know if they would be getting any more in. Rather than leave empty-handed, I bought a smaller, animated version.

Today, William's best friends posted a picture of *their* Captain America ornament. It looked close to the one I had wanted, so I posted a picture of the one I had purchased.

Shortly after that, another friend of the family posted that she'd bought one like mine for my sister.

God knows how much I'm hurting, and He continues to show me His love through His children.

step 5

Experiencing His Joy

*For I have given rest to the weary and
joy to the sorrowing.*

Jeremiah 31:25 NLT

December 23

Four months. It's so hard to be here on the eve of a major holiday, especially this holiday.

Because one year ago tomorrow, my family broke all sorts of familial traditions and obligations and started one of our own. We spent the day with my son and grandson.

Unless your kids are grown, you might not understand this next part. When you visit them in their own homes, you often wonder if it's going to feel like you're a guest or you're family, especially if you've lived far apart for a good portion of their adult life. I am blessed to say that William's home felt like my home. We enjoyed our time together so much; that's why we hoped to make it a new tradition. That won't happen now, at least not on this side of heaven. But, I'm so grateful that we had last Christmas together. So very, very grateful. I know it was God's gift to me.

If you don't acknowledge the true Reason for this season, I have to tell you that you're missing out. Let me tell you why. Oh sure, you'll get gifts and cards, have parties and sing carols. But, because you can't see past the wrapping, you'll never get the gift God has waiting for you beneath it. Let me explain.

About a week ago, on December 15, the library where I work had our staff Christmas breakfast. At the breakfast we always do a small gift exchange, just for fun. This year, the gift I was randomly (*Hah! You know how I feel about that!*) assigned was a box full of smaller gifts. Among those gifts was a tall glass cylinder candleholder.

Two things you should know about me: First, I burn candles rarely, and then only in or on the fireplace. (Blame it on having had boys all my adult life. When your house can spontaneously become a paper-plane airport or a football field at any given moment, open flame is NOT your friend.) Second, I am not a fan of cutesy knickknacks. If they hold meaning to me, yes, I'll enjoy them. If they're stuff I don't need or want, or can't use, somebody else is going to be unwrapping them at some later date. You've heard of re-gifting? I wouldn't be surprised if I'm the reason they had to give it a name. I've been doing it long before it was a "thing". My kids know this about me, and they love me anyway. They also make sure to give me stuff I need, want, or can use. :)

Back to the story. So, I'm sitting at this breakfast, looking in this box and wondering what on earth I'm going to do with this candleholder, or who I can give it to that would really appreciate it. After work that day, I took the box home, tucked it under the tree and forgot about it.

Fast forward to two days ago, the 21st. I'm linked to a social media page for a local group of people who've lost loved ones, especially children. At lunch, while scrolling through that site, I came across a link on that page for memorial shirts, hoodies, and coffee mugs. The saying caught my eye: "My Heart Wasn't Ready...Even Though Heaven Was". However, the items themselves didn't appeal to me personally. In my own heart, there is a fine line between a memorial and a shrine. It's a line I don't want to cross, because I don't feel it would be healthy for me. These particular items seemed to ride that line for me, personally, but I did like the sentiment.

When I got home from work that day, I hiked up to the mailbox. Stuffed inside it was a box and some letters. I grumbled under my breath about the box, figuring it was another package my husband had ordered. The joke was on me, because it was *my* name on the box. I didn't recognize the return address, so I went ahead and opened it. When I began pulling back layers, I saw a tag from my new "adopted" son and his wife, William's friends. I'll admit to the selfish thought of setting it aside to avoid the pain that I knew would

come when I opened it fully, but I hope I have learned something from the "video" incident. You make sacrifices for the people you love. So I opened it, and it took my breath away. Nestled in layers of packing were two candles. One has a picture of William on it. The other has this: "Your Wings Were Ready But My Heart Was Not - William C. Hotalen 10/31/1983 - 08/23/2016".

At first I was just overwhelmed by the love Matt and Ashley show me. This isn't an isolated incident. They have taken their love for William and shared it with me countless times in a myriad of ways. I am so grateful that William has friends like them. Then it hit me. The sentiment on the candle - it was so close to the one on the other items I had seen on social media earlier that day. God had given me the gift of Matt and Ashley's love, and just to show me He loved me too, He made sure I got *His* message through *their* message.

And, as I've said before, if the story stopped there, it would be amazing. Wouldn't you agree?

But Daddy really enjoys things in threes.

Because, about 30 minutes later, there was a knock on the door. My younger son answered it, and a young boy handed him a package. Anthony, in turn, handed it to me. Now, the package came from UPS, but Anthony says the boy looked too young to have been working for them. Where was it between the time UPS dropped it off and the time the boy brought it to us? I don't know. What I DO know is that God wanted it to arrive just after Matt and Ashley's gift, so He made sure it did.

This time, I did recognize the return address. It was William's girlfriend. I knew it, too, would have the power to reduce me to tears, but like I said: when you love someone you make sacrifices for them. So I opened it. Tucked inside the packing were three things: a Cracker Barrel gift card, a ribbon candle, and a letter. I'm not sure if Kim was aware that one of the last times William came out to our house, we went to Cracker Barrel to eat. Also, William had discovered that I *will* burn a ribbon candle, and the last couple of times he bought me gifts, they were ribbon candles. (I'm seriously hard to buy for. When the boys find something that works, they tend to stick to it. They love me so much!) As much as the card and candle meant to me, it was the gift in the letter that meant more. It was full of Kim's treasured memories of William, and it truly warmed my heart. One of the things she shared was this: *"He loved candles in general, so, anytime I light one now, I always think of him. I remember, after he would clean the apartment, he would light every single candle he could find...those were things that always brightened Wil's day."* Kim's memory of William's love for candles arriving directly after the memorial candle? More proof of my Father's love for me.

So, the tag that came with the memorial candles is going to become an ornament on my Christmas tree. In fact, I wouldn't be surprised if the Cracker Barrel card, once it's used, ends up on the tree as well. Two more loved ones that I will pray for when I set up and take down the tree each year. Two more memories to treasure in my heart.

One of the memorial candles will be displayed in the candleholder from my work gift exchange. Just yesterday, the person who bought that gift called me at work, so now I know where I can get a matching holder. But, you know what? I think I better wait a bit. Maybe, just maybe, God is sending the other holder through someone else.

So there it is. In less than a week God brought together three gifts from three people in three different states. He did it to show me He's still at work, bringing good out of a bad situation. *This* right here is what you miss if you don't know Jesus. The gifts themselves were individual blessings - no doubt about that. But the three of them: their arrival, their timing, and the way they all fit together? That, my friends, is my Father. HE'S what you miss when you celebrate Christmas without Christ.

With tears in my eyes and love in my heart,

Me

December 24

Last year, we drove out and spent Christmas Eve with William. It was great. We all enjoyed it so much, we hoped to do it again this year.

I wish I had words to make this better for all of you.

I don't.

Just yesterday, while driving out of town to do some shopping with Sherman, I was singing along to my music playlist. I got sandbagged when I realized, halfway through one tune, that I was singing the song I had signed at the funeral. I strangled on the words, and my husband reached over and grasped my hand. We just hung on to each other through the rest of the song, crying. I felt my heart crack when Sherman whispered, "Does it ever get any better?" I answered as truthfully as I could, "No. I think it becomes different, but not better."

I hope I'm wrong.

I want to be wrong.

Dear God, please, let me be wrong.

A gift from my Father in my devotions this morning:

The people who walked in darkness
Have seen a great light;
Those who dwelt in the land of the shadow of death,
Upon them a light has shined.
Isaiah 9:2 NKJV

Cried my way through the carols at first service. Then received a "Christmas hug" meme from one of my sons' friends. Thank you, Father.

December 25

I went looking for a special gift from William the other day. It was a sheet of paper torn from one of those small desk calendars. On it William had written, "Momma, you are so pritty and I love you." I have treasured it for years. I wanted to post an encouraging note today about gifts that truly matter.

But God had other plans.

Because, as hard as I have looked, I can't find it.

What I *did* find, buried in a file in a box, was an email William sent me in June of 2004. Not only do I not remember receiving it, I don't remember printing it or keeping it. I'm attaching pictures, but I'm going to transcribe it here, just as he wrote it. As you read it, hear William's voice in your head, not mine. These are HIS words, and I don't believe I found them at this time of year by accident. I believe God let me find this email as William's gift to all of us.

Life

by Wil Hotalen

What is life? Well first and foremost it's a powerful opening question for a small scribbling such as this. But above all else it's a question that has plagued man for centuries. Opinions on life vary depending on the person you ask. To the young adult, life is friends, boyfriends or girlfriends, parties, and all around "living life". To the older, more experienced adult, life is providing for family, having kids, jobs, houses... everything we grew up associating with being a grown-up. What is life to me, as a young adult? Well I have to say that until this moment, my life was your normal 20 year olds view on life, much like I mentioned before. But upon deep personal reflection on this subject, I have realized a few things. Life is not merely a sequence of events, sum of friendships, good times, and worthwhile memorable moments. Life is experiences. Not just the good "party on" times. While maturing, one must learn to accept the good times with the bad, the awkward with the comfortable, the painful with the breathtaking. Only recently through a deep emotional and personal loss, have I realized this fact. It occurred to me that not only is life a bed of roses, like the old saying goes, but rather the entire rosebush. Only through learning from, and respecting the thorns, can one realize the beauty of the rose. It is unfortunate that, for those such as myself, sometimes it takes a few more pricks with the thorns than for others to realize not only the beauty of the rose, but the purpose of the thorn. The size and painfulness of the thorns vary, but they are, and always will be present in every one of our lives. Some problems, however are bigger than your average thorn. There is no quick fix to a deep-seeded problem. It's like a giant weed you can't seem to rid from your garden of beautiful roses. You can cut off the top of the weed, but the roots will remain, and the problem will return. You can also beat yourself up all day, thinking you found the answer, thinking through your own strength you can overcome your own emotional, and sometimes physical turmoil. But only one person can pull up the roots. And it's not you. But when you go to bed thinking that you have figured it all out. Thinking that through your own god-like situational awareness and control that you have devised the solution to your problems, you'll find yourself waking up with the same weed you thought you rid yourself of the night before. A man much wiser than I once told me that "to gain control, you must lose control." In some cases, the loss of control is not completely brought on by a conscious act to do so. Recently, I, myself, have learned this firsthand. In my case, much as in the case of others, the concept of losing total control of a situation is preceded by a time of denial in which the person attempts to convince themselves that he or she is in total control. Practices of this vary, however "I am better than this situation, I am not worried, I can fix this, and watch me fix this," are all too common. And all too frequently, this is followed by an unhealthy coping by associating one's self with people and situations which boost ones self image. i.e. Partying, drinking, smoking, unhealthy relationships etc. This practice, as I mentioned before, is unhealthy to say the least. Please do not get me wrong. I am not saying that a person should not feel good about themselves. There are, however, healthier, but most of the time more time consuming and sometimes painful ways to come to such a self realization. No one can wake up and all of a sudden, genuinely feel good about themselves after having had circumstances cause them to belittle and short come themselves. Life is not a movie, although sometimes it can feel like a scene from a bad one. You can't fast forward, or skip to the good part. And you definitely have never seen this movie before. Now is the part of my little soapbox sermon where I am supposed to dish out all the answers to all of your questions. After all isn't that why you are still reading? All of this applied to you in some way, and you think "If he knows this, he must have seen the end of this movie already." But I have an urgent news bulletin for you. You're movie isn't out yet. Most of you haven't even seen the previews. There is no quick fix to a problem. You're not the only one without a quick fix. No one has it. Let's say you're driving down the road of life and your car breaks down. You pop the hood only to realize that you are missing a bolt that is vital to the operation of your car. You think to yourself "I have a huge box of spare bolts in the trunk" so you retrieve them, only to find you don't have the exact one you need. There are plenty of substitutes. But none of them will withstand the amount of pressure you are going to be putting on them. Only one person has the replacement bolt. But he wants more than you want to give him. So you put in the wrong bolt, only to break down again further down the road. But the man's offer still stands. No human being can give you this bolt. I can't give it to you, no psychiatrist or therapist can. You can't find it at the bottom of a bottle of beer or in an empty cigarette pack. Only in the pages of your bible can you find the way to retrieve this vital bolt. Maybe your bible is like mine used to be. Collecting dust on a shelf, or replacing a leg on your coffee table. Just remember this. You must fix the problems that cause your instabilities. How you decide to do this is up to you. Just fixing what causes the problem isn't enough. You have to confront the problem itself before any type of closure can be reached. The missing bolt isn't your problem. It is one of the smaller problems caused by the fact that you don't know this road very well. You have no map, and you've never driven this way before. All you need is this one bolt and you can be on your way. But there's still the problem of the dealer's price. He's not asking for any type of monetary reimbursement, only that you let him drive your car. Not just around the block, but for the rest of your trip. Look what happened when you were driving. The man promises you he knows the best way to drive this road. But what do you do? Will you let him drive, or spend your entire time on the side of the road watching the traffic go by? This time you have the choice to lose control. Will you take the chance, or go on in life wondering what could have happened if you did?

December 28

Dear Lord,

Please let next Christmas be a little less painful. I know it won't ever be easy. I'm not asking for the impossible. Please let joy flow more deeply than sorrow next Christmas. Help us celebrate the memories more than we mourn the loss. Help us laugh a little more and cry a little less. Thank You for William. Thank You for all the years he was with us. Thank You that he's safe with You now. Thank You that we, Your children, can look forward to a beautiful reunion with him one day. In Jesus' name I pray. Amen.

December 29

I believe I may have hurt someone's feelings today. She asked a perfectly innocent question for someone who's unaware of my journey.

"Did you have a nice Christmas?"

I don't know why it stung this time, except perhaps because the wound is still sore, and it has been poked and prodded a great deal this holiday season.

I've had quite a struggle over this question. You see, honesty is important to me. I've been in a quandary each time someone has innocently asked me this. Do they really want to know? Is it wrong to say "Fine", when nothing feels fine? And is there a way to politely say, "No. I did not have a 'nice' Christmas. But, praise God, I survived it."?

Well, that's the gist of what I told my friend. First, I tried to shrug the question off so I didn't have to answer. When that didn't work I said, "I lost my mother in August, and my older son five days later. So, no, I didn't have a 'nice' Christmas, but, God got me through."

Shame on me for throwing an innocent friend under the bus. It's not her fault we haven't seen each other since the summer. I could have handled that better. I wish I had.

I am, obviously, still a work in progress.

I say that to let you know, that although I am striving to follow God throughout this journey, I am human. I get distracted. I get frustrated. I slip and fall.

But God is gracious. He forgives. He restores.

When I ask.

If you'll excuse me, I believe I have a fence to mend.

December 31

Today marks the ends of 2016.

In one way, I'm fairly happy to see the back of it.

In another way, I'm really not.

Because, when 2016 ends, it will be taking a good-sized chunk of my heart with it.

There'll be many folks counting down the minutes today, reflecting on the past year while looking forward to a fresh, new year with hope and anticipation. Some will start with resolutions to "do better" than past years. With all the attention and meaning we give this day, I think much of it should be refocused...

...on the One who gave it to you.

You are living and breathing right now by the grace of God, the One who gave you life and breath. You may only resurrect a countdown of hours once a year, but there is a constant countdown in your life that started with your first breath. It will end with your last, and the only Person that knows how much time is left on that clock is the One who set it. Use it wisely, my friends.

I'm still heartbroken over my son's loss, but I am grateful to God for the way He created William. William loved to experience things. He loved making memories, especially with Oliver. He spent his life doing just that. All of his friends are connected to each other by the memories of William that they share.

But William had something far more important to share. Maybe, while he was alive - while his clock was still counting down - maybe you weren't ready to hear about it.

Well, tick-tock, my friend.

William asked Jesus to be his Savior when he was just five years old. And I've already shared with you the email that he wrote at twenty (*see the December 25 post - it was God's gift to me and perhaps His call to you*). Because of what Jesus did by dying on the cross to take our punishment and rising again to conquer death, William still lives. Not just in my heart and yours. He lives in heaven.

You don't have to be in church to ask Jesus to be your Savior. You don't have to clean up before you ask Him in. You just have to do like William said and let the One who made your "car" drive it. Admit that you are not and never will be perfect (*welcome to the human race*). Accept the fact that Jesus lived a perfect life and gave that life up on the cross to do what you couldn't. Ask Jesus to be your Savior. There's no set prayer to say - your decision will be as unique as you are.

Please, if you feel God tugging at your heart today, don't delay. All our clocks are ticking. Some of us are counting down to the end of our past. But some of us are really counting down to the beginning of our future.

William would want to see each and every one of his friends again. I know that's true. He loves them all. And he was put in their lives by a Person for a purpose.

Tick-tock, ladies and gentlemen.

Countdown

The day is here.
The year's near done,
But it's seemed over
Since you went home.

I know you're happier
Where you are,
But your leaving here
Left my heart scarred.

The year's near over.
We're counting the minutes.
Can the new year be happy
Without you in it?

Happy is fleeting,

Here today, gone tomorrow.
But, perhaps, this new year
Will lessen my sorrow.

Your memory's wrapped tightly
'Round my pained heart.
A whole new year
Where we'll be apart.

It is a great comfort
To know where you are,
Celebrating a new year
With the Bright Morning Star.

A whole year with Jesus
In heaven above!
Happy New Year, baby,
With all my love.

January 1

Heavenly Father,

As we begin a new day, a new week, a new month, and a new year, may You be at the forefront of them all. Give us Your eyes to see the opportunities You place before us to share what You've done for us. Give us Your words to say to those in need of You. Give us Your wisdom on when to speak and when to keep silent while You work. Thank You for Your many blessings, especially those we often take for granted. We love You, Lord. In Jesus' mighty name we pray. AMEN

In the season of resolutions, even we, God's children, seem to focus on what we can do for ourselves. May I suggest a different perspective? This year, what is God calling you to do for others? Give? Pray? Help?

How about joining a church? I don't mean just attend, I mean join. Become a member of a Bible-believing church, where you will have the opportunity to serve as well as be served. God gives His children unique talents and abilities - gifts, if you prefer. Do we really think that He gave them to us only for our own benefit? What if your gift - whether it's praying or teaching or encouragement, or something else - is desperately needed by one of God's children? What if they're sitting in church right now, crying out to our Father and waiting for His answer. What if YOU are that answer?

But you aren't there. You've been wounded. Or offended. Or you don't feel it necessary to be in God's house or a member of His established church to worship. Well, you can certainly worship God wherever you are, that's true. However, He also calls us to help our brothers and sisters in Christ. If He's given you the gift of teaching, where better to share it than a Bible study or Sunday school? If He's gifted you with encouragement, where better to use it than to build up the church? If He has called you to pray, where better than His house, where countless souls convene to seek His help and encouragement? God's gifts aren't meant to be hoarded. They're meant to be shared.

This is the voice of experience speaking. Over the last few months, I've been the recipient of the gifts of God's children in countless ways. Prayer. Encouragement. Admonition. Teaching. Helps. Service. God has never failed to put in my path a friend in Christ with the exact gift I needed for the moment. N-E-V-E-R.

Perhaps you think that lets you off the hook. After all, God doesn't *need* you to accomplish His will. That may be true, but He *wants* to use you. He wants to use you because He knows it will benefit you as well as those you serve. He also knows that it will deepen your relationship with Him as you learn to love and forgive others.

So, this year, consider a resolution that will bless you, honor God, and help others. Ask God to show you the church where He's called you to serve. Then GrOw.

If you're already a member of a church, then thank you. You, or others like you, have helped me on this journey, walking with me where I could not walk alone, leading me when I was blinded by tears, and carrying me by prayer when the pain was so great that each breath hurt. May God bless you abundantly for all that you do in His name.

Blessings without tears,

Me

January 2

There was a very real temptation this past holiday season to retreat into a cocoon of tears and weep my way through December. In truth, tears are never far from the surface. Remember the play I was in? Cried all three times, right on cue.

For me, I've found that my tears now come in two types. One is the spontaneous, oh-my-goodness-I-didn't-see-that-one-coming kind. They seem to be the kind that soften the sharp edges of my grief and help me heal a little.

The other type is what I call the alas-woe-is-me kind. These are the ones where I've begun to dwell on all the things that are done and can't be changed, or on all the things I wonder about that I should just let go of. They're the ones that tend to attack when I'm tired, stressed, cranky ---generally when my eyes are on me and not on God. These kind do _not_ make me feel better. In fact, sometimes the more I cry these kind, the more I want to cry. They do not heal and they do not help.

With God's strength, I am learning to identify and resist the type-two tears. They do not serve my Father's purpose of healing and learning to move forward. The only one interested in keeping me trapped in a bubble of sorrow is the enemy. He has no power in my life unless I relinquish it to him. Instead of giving in to the temptation to melt into a puddle of grief for myself and all I've lost, I begin to pray for someone else, and I pray until the temptation passes, or at least eases off until, with God's help, I can resist it.

Please don't think that resisting these tears is easy. You all know that it's not. And I'm not speaking about anyone's tears but my own. I just wanted to share my experience with you in the hopes that you find comfort in knowing that you're not the only one still crying.

January 4

January 2 marked four months since we buried William.

I passed a milestone without even realizing it. I feel conflicted about that.

On one hand, I feel a little guilty that I "missed" a milestone. However, I know that guilt is one of the enemy's tools, so I'm dropping that hot potato right here. If any of you out there are still playing the "If only I had done this or said that..." game in your head, please...let it go. I know it's not easy, but you need to let it go. You are not God. You are not in charge of life and death. You are not guilty of saying or not saying, or doing or not doing, anything that would have changed where we are now. That's the enemy trying to hold you down to keep you from your God-given purpose here on earth. Don't give him that kind of authority in your life, because you will have an immense battle on your hands to get it back.

On the other hand, I am relieved. I didn't relive that awful event in my mind. I didn't spend the day sitting around moaning over what I've lost. I didn't try to rewrite the past in my head to make it come out differently. I simply didn't think about his funeral at all.

Instead, I had this inexplicable urge clean. Not Formula-409-and-Mr.-Clean clean, but use-it-or-lose-it declutter clean. I cleaned out desk drawers, shelves, my closet. I got rid of stuff that has been cluttering my physical home that has value but does me no good.

And it wasn't until today, when I read my "adopted" son's media post, that I realized what God is doing. He's helping us all turn a corner here. We've all been moving along, living and breathing, putting one foot in front of the other, just trying to get through this pain. Now, like Matt said, it's time to move forward with purpose. While a part of us is buried with my son in that plot in Suffolk, God left us here because we still have work to do. Now is the time to figure out what that is, and get to it.

If you don't have any dealings with God, that is your first step. Find out who He is. Learn what He's done for you. Accept what He's offering you, so He can equip you for the purpose He has planned for you.

If you already have a relationship with God, take it deeper. Join a Bible-believing church. Get involved in serving there. Already in a church? Someone there may be going through something like you have and need to hear your story of hope for coming out on the other side of their grief. Look for them, either in a small group or a ministry, or even ask the pastor.

Saying goodbye isn't ever easy. And I'm not saying there aren't still some milestones looming that are going to be mighty painful. But God has given us a message through my "adopted" son and his wife today.

Yes, we took a hard blow in August.

Yes, it knocked us flat.

But it's time to get up.

Dust ourselves off.

And get back in the game.

I may not know you all by name, but if you loved my son, then a part of him resides in you. Because of that, I can say that I love you all. Thank you for sharing your memories on his memorial page. May God bless you as we continue to walk through this mourning and into His joy.

January 5

Have you read through the entire Bible? Or do you wonder why some people read it through over and over and over? I've read it through in several different translations. For me, it helps to clarify some areas and it gives me experience on which to base an opinion, if someone asks me to recommend a particular version.

I find something new and insightful each time I read through the Bible. I've never doubted that the Word is living and active, and that's why it's always so fresh. But just today, I had an epiphany about why God and His Word remain the same, but I always seem to discover something different.

It's because I am different.

I'm not the same person I was a year ago.

This year, I've chosen to read chronologically. That, in itself, is a nudge from God. I prefer to go cover to cover. I just had this nudge (thanks to a sister in Christ's encouragement) to do it differently this year.

So, here we are, January 5, and I'm a few chapters into Job.

You remember Job? The man who lost everything in the span of a day?

Oh, yes, I am different, because I've not felt a great deal of compassion for Job's friends in the past. I sided with Job when he called them "miserable comforters". Yes, they made some mistakes. Yes, their words weren't particularly helpful. But, really, what can you say to someone who's lost so much? It took them seven days before they could say anything! And they sat with him for s-e-v-e-n days. That, right there, shows their love for him.

I have been blessed in the people that have spoken into my life in the last few months. Not a single time do I remember someone saying something unhelpful. Some have quoted the lines we all hear at funerals, but God has blessed me to be able to see beyond the remark and into the heart of the one who spoke it.

If I may offer any word of advice in approaching someone suffering a severe loss, it's this: Tell them the truth. "I'm so sorry." "I don't know what to say." "I love you." "I'm praying for you." They already know all the platitudes, the socially correct responses. Say them only if you sincerely mean them. Your presence, a hug, a shoulder to cry on - they often mean much more than anything you could say.

There's not enough time to tag all those that have helped and continue to help me as I walk through this valley, so...

From the bottom of my broken, healing heart, thank you all. I love you. God bless you.

Me

January 6

Earlier this week on my son's memorial page, we were talking about moving forward. The conversation sparked a memory. In high school, William adopted the phrase "*carpe diem*". I don't know where he came across it, and I don't know why it struck a chord with him, but it did. Looking back, if I had to choose two words to sum up William's philosophy of life, that would be the two: *carpe diem* - seize the day.

William lived most of his life making memories. For me. For his son. For his extended family. For his friends. He could turn anything into an adventure. I remember as a child, he didn't cry or get upset when something broke. No! His face would light up and he'd say, "This is broken! Can I take it apart?" I'm not privy to all his adventures beyond his youth - **Thank You, Lord!** - but I know he built his beloved K.I.T.T. car (partially in my back yard), went skydiving, tried a sensory deprivation chamber, drove a Ford Mustang, went overseas in the military, visited Disneyland, went to New York. Everyone who knew him can attest to the fact that William didn't waste of minute of his life.

Perhaps God allowed him that sense of adventure because he would need to pack a lifetime of experiences into 32 short years.

God gave me that memory, and I have to say it was a most unexpected gift. But, while the gift is mine, the message, I think, is for us all. Seize *your* day. Start right now. Use every moment God has given you to live your life to the fullest. Stop fretting about what's missing in your life, and start praising God for what's there. Keep short accounts with both God and man. If you goof up, 'fess up and move on. If you're stewing about something or someone who has wronged you, let it go. Live your life on purpose - not *your* purpose, God's purpose. If you don't know His purpose for you, make it your primary goal to find out.

Then, get to it.

January 7

It's snowing here today. Earlier in the week, forecasters waffled on whether it was going to. Then they disagreed on how much it was going to. Then they debated when it was going to. When they finally nailed down the day, give or take a few hours, I made a note to ask my husband to fill the bird feeders. Unfortunately, he caught a bug going around and hasn't felt up to it.

Well, I remembered yesterday, the day before the big event. It also happened to be a day I had to report an hour early for work. And, did I mention that I can't *reach* our bird feeders without a ladder?

I was determined to put out a good amount of seed so the birds could "stock up" before the bad weather arrived. So, I threw my husband's big black winter coat over my pink fluffy robe, and I trudged - in the dark, flashlight in hand - out to the bird feeders. Since I couldn't reach them, I did the next best thing: I peppered the ground under and around the bird feeders with seed. With the dire predictions being made about snow and single-digit temperatures, I was very, VERY liberal with the seed.

Then off I went to work.

I live close enough to come home for lunch. I looked forward to seeing how many feathered friends would be enjoying the bounty I had laid before them. Once I arrived home, I headed to the kitchen to wash my hands, and, as I did, I looked out the picture window.

One (very happy) squirrel. One bird.

What?! Where were the flocks? Why didn't that little fellow tell all his friends what he'd discovered? I checked with my husband. No, he hadn't noticed many birds. I checked the weather report. Yes, the snow was still coming. Aren't birds supposed to have a God-given sense about things like this? I've seen them do it in the past with hurricanes. Were they already hunkered down to ride out the bad weather? I went back to work. Checked again when I got home. Nothing.

So, I rise this morning to a veritable winter wonderland. It is snowing even as I write. Unless the reports have changed, it's not expected to stop until mid

afternoon. I got up, did all the usual
stuff. Once it got light enough, I opened the
blinds on the back of the house. I started
with the picture window in the kitchen. I
raised the blind, looked out, and there they
were.

A flock of birds, all shapes and sizes and
colors. *On* the snow. Pecking at it to reach
the seed *beneath* it.

Really?! I actually got a little huffy,
standing there, looking out at them. I made a special effort to put that seed out
there BEFORE the weather got bad so that they would be prepared and ready. Why
did they wait until it was well and truly awful out there before they sought it?

That's when it hit me. Don't we do the same thing with God? Hasn't he put
everything we need before us in His Word to prepare us for the storms in life?
Isn't it available now, when things look rosy and we're at peace in our little corner
of the world?

And He paid a far higher price for what He gave us than I did just flinging
bird seed in my p.j.'s. Why, *why* do we wait until we are in the midst of a storm
of major proportions before we seek Him out in His Word? Why don't we "stock
up" for the bad weather that eventually comes to all of us?

I don't know your church situation, but if there is a Bible study in your church,
perhaps you should be in it. Our church has small groups, and being in such a
group encourages me to dig into God's Word. If you attend where I do, I highly
recommend that you consider joining one in the next round. I am speaking from
experience here. In the two groups God led me to attend prior to August, we
did studies on prayer. We studied scripture. We prayed. We bonded. We became
a family. We shared burdens and we shared joys. The ladies in those two groups
are knitted into the fabric of my heart, and I am so grateful for each and every
one of them. Because I was open to God's leading to join those small groups, He
was able to equip me for the storm that struck in my life in August. I may have
been knocked flat, but God had given me His strength in those studies to keep
my eyes on Him, to seek the help of others - many of them those same ladies - and
to use what He had instilled in me in those studies to point others to Him.

Please don't misread this.

I HAVE NOT ACCOMPLISHED ANY OF THIS IN MY OWN STRENGTH.

I have walked this path with God's strength, not mine.

I have written it out for His glory, not mine.

I want it to serve His purpose, not mine.

One of the purposes may be for me to point *you* to Him. Perhaps you're already in the storm. It's not too late! Some of those birds are out there, even as I speak! The wind has picked up, the snow is swirling, but they continue to look for provision. You can, too! In the midst of the storm you may have to dig deep to find it, but the provision is still there. God put it there for *you*. He wants a deeper relationship with *you*. He wants to equip *you*. But He won't force your hand.

The ball is in your court. Pass or play, my friend.

January 8

We were planning a trip to the coast to see family yesterday. We had set this date by conferring with several families and several schedules, working to make it possible for us all to come together. When the weather reports first forecast an inch or two of snow, I didn't change our plans. My husband caught a nasty cold, and I didn't change our plans. Thursday morning he felt really bad and was running a fever, and the forecasters had raised the number of inches of snow and dropped the forecast temperatures. I conferred with my sister, and we changed our plans.

To be honest, I'm a little relieved, because we had decided, extremely reluctantly on my part, that we should stop by my son's gravesite on the way. It's not that I haven't thought about going before now, because I have. However, each time I've thought about it in my head, my heart has skittered away from the pain of such a visit.

And it will be painful. Of that, I have no doubt. The last time I was at that cemetery was the day of my son's service. Seeing that marker will just be one more confirmation that my life is forever changed. If you've had a "forever changed" moment in your life, you'll understand that feeling.

Sometimes God reveals that I am ready to take a step in this journey - usually a painful one - but I just don't want to. I thought that was what this was--one of those things that I was just avoiding. But I don't want to get trapped in the valley of the shadow because I refuse to move forward. I was going to take this step because I thought I was ready, but just not willing.

In this instance, however, I think God wanted me to just be willing, even if I wasn't ready. In His infinite mercy, perhaps God used this bad weather to spare me an experience for which I really am not ready. And, apparently, I won't be ready next week, or the week after that, because God has made sure that I have other commitments that will keep me at home.

How about you? Is there an area in your life where you might be running ahead of God, willing to take a step for which you believe you're ready, but He knows you're not? Are you, like me, trying to drag God into your will because you just want to "get it over with"? Have obstacles been thrown up in your way, blocking your every effort to do what you think is right? Stop, pray, and listen for that still small voice. Whether He's saving you *from* something or *for* something, God is on your side. If you are willing to move forward with Him, you need to be willing to wait with Him, too.

I don't know when I will visit William's gravesite, but I am keeping myself open to God's leading. I don't want to run ahead of Him. He'll hold my hand either way, but I'd rather have Him beside me than behind me.

January 10

Work was cancelled today. I decided to take advantage of the time to catch up on reconciling bank statements. I slogged through the savings. It was when I started on the checking that my heartstrings were plucked.

There's an outstanding check to my son on the account.

There's a story behind it, of course. It was his birthday check from several years ago. Bless his pointed head, he never mentioned not receiving his card/ present until I asked him (several months later, after another long session of reconciling bank statements) why he hadn't cashed it. I replaced it but told him if it ever showed up, cash it.

That won't happen now.

It's this kind of memory, the one that sneaks up on you and catches you with your guard down, that used to undo me very quickly. Today it didn't. Oh, it wrung my heart all right, but it didn't lay me out flat. That puzzled me for a bit.

Then I realized that I am, indeed, moving forward. You all are, too, or you should be. Moving forward is not forgetting. Not at all. For me, it's dwelling more on the gifts of memories I do have and less on those that I never will. It's acknowledging the tug of them on my heart without allowing them to pull me under. Sometimes they're a joyful celebration of the gift of William's life. At other times they're a breath-stealing blow to the chest. As each day goes by I have more of the former and less of the latter. I recognize that as a gift from God.

But moving forward carries a pain of its own. My mother's heart feels like I'm abandoning my son by letting him go. I know it's not true. William will always be a part of me, but losing someone so suddenly - there is a temptation to set up a shrine to them in your heart. That is not healthy. It's a temptation from the enemy to prevent you from fulfilling God's purpose for your future by keeping you trapped in the past.

William is a permanent part of my life and my heart, but my heart rightfully belongs to the Father who lent William to me for thirty-two fantastic, frustrating, exhilarating, exhausting, forever memorable years. William's work here is finished. Mine (and yours) is not. We are all still here for a reason. Some of us know what that reason is. Some of us are still searching for it. No matter which camp you're in, keep pressing forward. God will reveal all in His time.

And, please, keep sharing your memories. They warm my heart.

God bless you all.

Me

January 12

Sometime in November or December, a patron at the library asked me to crochet a bonnet for the daughter that her daughter was expecting this month. I said yes, she wrote out her name, number, and what she wanted, and I set it aside, figuring I'd get to it eventually. When I think about how long I put off what amounted to an hour or so of work, it's embarrassing and a little shameful. I had no valid reason for procrastinating, no pressing engagement or task that swallowed all my extra time. I also can't explain, in human terms, the compulsion I felt to finish it this weekend. Believe me, there were a hundred other tasks calling my name, but I felt a need to make those bonnets.

So, I whipped them up this weekend. I set them aside to take to work, but I couldn't find the note where the patron had written her phone number. I searched off and on for a couple of days. Nada. At lunch today I looked in the same places again, and - voila! - there it was.

After lunch I returned to work. Early in the afternoon I picked up the piece of paper and phoned the patron to tell her the bonnets (I made two because I felt a little guilty for taking so long) were done, and she could pick them up at her convenience. She said, "That's great....

because my granddaughter was born about thirty minutes ago!"

I know you're wondering what this has to do with my journey. For me, it was a reminder that things happen in God's time. Nothing surprises Him. Nothing "gets by" Him. If it happens, there is a reason. Sometimes we are allowed to see the reason - like calling that patron thirty minutes after her granddaughter was born - and sometimes we don't. I'll likely never know (at least on this side of heaven) why William's life here ended before mine. But the God that breathed life into a new little girl today is the same God that called William home in August. If I want to thank Him for the former, I must trust Him with the latter.

Perhaps you're facing a journey like mine. A death. A miscarriage. An injury. I know it's hard to hear, but God is with you. I've been there. I know the truth of this. When you learn to trust God completely, - in the good and the bad - you'll be able to see Him working within your circumstances. You'll be able to see the small, everyday miracles that those outside His family call "coincidence". And you'll learn to recognize them for what they are: messages of His love for you.

Like my mother's memorial magnet and my son's medallion magnet holding the same message.

Like William's memorial candle and his girlfriend's story about his love for candles arriving on the same day.

Like phoning a grandmother about her granddaughter's gift just thirty minutes after she entered the world.

I may be a few steps ahead of you on this journey. Let me encourage you that there is hope. There is healing. There is joy, even in the mourning.

January 14

There was a prayer conference at church today. I've been looking forward to attending for several months. Of course, I caught a nasty cold three days ago. But I persevered. I warned everyone to stand back, I slid into a seat in the back, and feasted on a message from a prayer warrior filled with the Holy Spirit.

When we broke for lunch, I went home. While I was there, I saw a post on William's memorial website from his childhood best friend. It was a picture of William in his basketball uniform in elementary school. His uniform number, as you can see, is 32.

William was 32 when he died.

This was another of those feather moments for me, the ones that sneak up on you. But the enemy had an ulterior motive here as well. In addition to keeping me trapped in the past, he also was hoping to keep me from stepping into the future.

This afternoon's session was on intercessory prayer. As a child of God, I believe we are all called to some type of intercessory prayer. The banquet of information provided by God's servant was so bountiful that I've yet to digest it all.

How sad if I had missed it because I had stayed home and given in to the temptation to indulge in a session of weeping and lamenting.

I believe moments of sadness over loss are inevitable. It's almost like a release valve for all the pent up grief that comes day by day as you adjust your thinking to your new "normal". That's as it should be. In one sense, it's an expression of gratitude for the gift God gave me in William. I wouldn't miss him if I didn't love him. There is nothing wrong with that, but there is a temptation inherent in anything God designs for our good. That is the temptation to overindulge.

Self pity usually comes to us wearing a disguise. That's because that little sin knows we wouldn't touch it if we could recognize it for what it truly is.

This next part may sting. Perhaps a lot.

Self pity is nothing more than selfishness. Plain and simple. It wrenches your focus from God, where it should rightly be, and aims it all at yourself where the enemy would like to keep it. Beware this slippery slope. There are usually warning signs that alert you to this danger. Most of your thoughts begin with "I" (I miss him, I'm so sad, I just want to cry all the time, I can't eat, I can't sleep, I can't go on without him). Your bouts of sadness may begin to interfere with your life. At that point, it's time to step back and look at yourself objectively. For whom are you really crying? Your lost loved one? Or yourself?

My best remedy for self pity is to pray for someone else. And believe me, I have used this remedy quite a bit the last few months. I encourage you to do the same. It will not only help you readjust your focus to your Father, it will bless the person for whom you pray.

Please understand that I am speaking of *my* journey here, of what I have observed as I have traversed this difficult valley. I am not speaking about depression or mental illness or anything other than the journey on which God has sent *me*. If you have problems of that nature, I pray God will direct you to the best source of help available to meet your need and give you the courage to seek it out.

January 15

"Every loss leaves a space that can be filled with God's presence." [28]

The quote above was from the today's entry in the devotional booklet, *Our Daily Bread* (http://odb.org/2017/01/15/losing-to-find/). It struck a chord with me. Oh, the sentiment is nice, but there is one little word that made all the difference to me.

"Can."

That one word says a great deal. The quote is a fact. Loss *does* leave a space - in your heart, in your family, in your life. And what you fill it with is up to you. By *not* choosing, you are, in essence, choosing to hold open a void, a wound, if you will. It will scab over, but will never heal until you intentionally seek out restoration.

I made a conscious choice early on this journey that this whole process would be filled with God's presence. Since He would be the one to pick up my pieces and help me start anew, then I was going to point everyone to Him as the source of my strength and comfort. I chose to fill the loss in my life with the presence of God.

With His presence, I made some hard decisions.

With His presence, I gave my sleepless nights to Him in praise, even if I had to do it with tears streaming down my face.

With His presence, I spoke more boldly for Him than I ever have.

With His presence, the flotsam and jetsam of life have taken their proper place on my list of His priorities....right at the bottom.

In this exchange of my emptiness for His fullness, I have learned so much. Try as I might, I haven't been able to list it all down. There is an intimacy in my relationship with my Father that I did not have before. Might it have come to me in some other way? Perhaps. But the path it took to reach me went through my Father's hands first. I've often *said* I trusted Him. This journey has given me ample opportunities to put feet to my words.

January 20

I've had several books recommended or given to me along this journey. Most are meant to encourage, and they do. However, the ones that hold the most weight are the ones written by those who's path has led through tragedy. Their voices ring with a truth that just can't be duplicated by someone on the outside looking in.

One of the books recommended to me was *One Light Still Shines: My Life Beyond the Shadow of the Amish Schoolhouse Shooting* [29] by Marie Monville. Marie was the wife of the man who, in the grips of something we will never comprehend, barricaded himself in an Amish schoolhouse and committed the shocking, unspeakable act of taking the lives of innocent children before turning his violence on himself. In the wake of his horrific acts, he left behind broken hearts and wounded souls, including those of his unsuspecting family. The book is Marie's story of how God stood faithfully by her, her family, and the families of the girls who lost their lives so senselessly.

After I finished reading her book, I wrote her the following letter.

Dear Ms. Monville,

A precious sister in Christ shared your book with me. She wanted me to read it, because she (and several others) believes that God is calling me to share my experience in print as well.

You see, in August my 84-year-old mother died. She had been ill, but had rallied and was actually in rehab. She'd spent the day with my sister and her family, then died in her sleep just hours later. While we were surprised, we weren't shocked. She had a heart condition that often complicated any illness she contracted. And, as sad as it is true, we expect to outlive our parents.

Five days later, out of the blue, my 32-year-old son, her oldest grandchild, joined her in heaven.

I tell you that so you understand my perspective on your journey. It resonated strongly with me, and I shed tears more than once. You might think I was crying for me, but no. I was crying for you, because, in a small way, I know what it feels like to be pushed into the valley of the shadow without warning.

I want to thank you for sharing your journey. I want to thank you for sharing the signs and miracles that God shared with you. I, too, have a long list of what the world would call "coincidences", but I know to be my Father at work. And I think I recognize in you a sister, who, like me, has discovered that there is an intimacy in your relationship with God that came by way of the trials you had to suffer. I've not found anyone that understands what I mean when I say that, unless they, too, have suffered through something where only God could comfort and console them.

If I have the dates correct, you have just passed the ten-year milestone. That encourages me, because I am only at the five-month mark, and some days the wound feels so fresh, it's as if it's still bleeding.

Thank you for sharing your story. It can't have been any easier to share than it was to live. I pray it reaches into the hearts of many, and plants seeds of God's grace, mercy, and love.

I hear the strength of our Father in your words. God bless you.

Sincerely,

Leslie Harder

January 22

One of the thoughts I admit to was that I would change places with my son if I could. Yesterday, when I had that thought, God gave me a different perspective on it. Would I *totally* trade places with William? Would I really want him to be standing in my shoes right now? Would I want him to bury his mother and son in the same week? ABSOLUTELY NOT!

Heavenly Father,

Thank You for revealing this to me. Thank You for showing me the futility in this kind of round-robin thinking, and the selfishness in thinking that I know better than You how our lives should play out. You know all. You see all. And still, You love me anyway.

I love You, Lord. I trust You, especially when it's hard, because I know it would be harder still if I didn't. Thank You for keeping me in the shelter of Your arms for the hardest parts, and for encouraging me in the parts where I needed to walk in the strength of my faith in You. If anyone reading this is facing a similar journey, let them feel Your presence and understand that Your help and Your hope is only a prayer away. In Jesus' name I pray. Amen.

step 6

Sharing His Comfort

He comforts us in all our troubles so that we can comfort others. When they are troubled, we will be able to give them the same comfort God has given us.

2 Corinthians 1:4 NLT

January 23

One of the many ways that sisters and brothers in Christ reached out to me in the early days of my grief was with books. They wanted to help, and while I wouldn't feel like reading anytime soon, they knew that the day would come when I'd be ready to hear how others had coped with losses like mine. One of the books shared with me was *Have You Felt Like Giving Up Lately?* by David Wilkerson.

When I started reading the book, it was out of respect for the precious sister in Christ who lent it to me. At the time she brought it over, just days after William died, she shared with me why she thought it would be helpful. The words are lost to me, drowned in a sea of grief. There was a bookmark in it, too. It might have been marking the passage. Alas, the enemy snatched it out, and I couldn't remember the page where it had been tucked.

I did, eventually, finish the book. Just this month, actually. All of it is good, but much of it is not relevant to my current situation. However, I have learned a thing or two about my Father's messages to me. Sometimes they are in-your-face, straightforward, look-at-Me-when-I'm-speaking-to-you messages. Those are hard for me to miss. But, there is a second kind of message, one that often is left, not "hidden-I-dare-you-to-find-it" hidden, but rather hidden in plain sight. It is there. It is for you. But you must seek it out. You must be looking, in faith, for when and how God will speak to you. This was one of those messages. It was toward the back of the book, just five pages from the end, in a chapter entitled "The Ultimate Healing".

"Did someone you love break out of his shell? Were you there when it happened? Or did the news reach you by phone or telegram? What kind of horrifying feeling rushed through your mind when you were told, 'He is dead!' or 'She is dead!'?"

"Certainly it is natural to mourn and weep for those who die. Even the death of the righteous is painful for those left behind. But, as followers of the Christ who holds the keys of death in His hand, we dare not think of death as an accident perpetuated by the devil. Satan cannot destroy a single child of God. Satan, though permitted to touch Job's flesh and afflict his body, could not take his life. God's children always die right on His schedule, not one second too soon or too late. If the

steps of a righteous person are ordered by the Lord, He orders the final one, too."
---from *Have You Felt Like Giving Up Lately?* [30] by David Wilkerson

This is true, but it is a hard truth, one that I realized at the time of William's death. I spoke to very few people about it. Many weren't ready to hear it. Some, perhaps, still are not. If I hadn't been in a season of walking and praying and staying in God's presence at the time He called William home, I would have had a harder time accepting it.

Please understand that I am not saying it is easy. Not by a long shot. And I am not saying that it was God's will that William die. It was God's will that man never taste death at all. After all, in the garden of Eden, which tree was prohibited to us? The tree of life? No! It was of the fruit of the tree of the knowledge of good and evil that God told us not to eat, and He told us that because He *didn't* want us to die. God planted both trees in the center of the garden (Genesis 2:9), and when He told Adam he could freely eat of fruit of the trees (Genesis 2:16-17), His only stipulation was about the one tree that would do us harm.

So, no, I'm *not* saying that it was God's will for William to die. What I *am* saying is that God knew it would happen. He was not surprised. He was not shocked. He was not unprepared. He was ready, and He walked my child into the most joyful home he'll ever have. William's with the one Person who loves him even more than I do, the only One who's known him longer.

If I can trust Jesus with my life - and I do - then I can trust Him with my child's death.

It has taken five months to be able to say that, and I don't say it lightly or without tears. But my trust remains in the only One worthy of it. It's still painful. And, yes, there are still days it hurts to be breathing when I know my child is not.

Are you facing a difficult journey in your life? I invite you to join me in keeping your eyes on God and your heart open to His healing. Call to Him, and He will answer you and show you great and mighty things which you did not know (Jeremiah 33:3).

Dear William,

Five months ago today, you slipped into eternity. Your absence has left a gaping wound in the hearts of your friends and family. To say you're sorely missed is so inadequate, it's laughable...when we're able to laugh, that is. Many of us are trying to celebrate your life now, instead of mourn your death. It hasn't been easy, but then, life around you rarely was. You touched our lives in ways and places that we have forgotten, until they rise up to smack us right in the kisser when we least expect it.

A candle.

A song.

A snowfall.

Most of us haven't travelled this way before. We don't know where to look for those rabbit holes that will trip us up and bring us down. Some of us are unprepared for how to get out of these snares, especially for how painful and how much strength it sometimes takes to break free. Of course, you know exactly Who has the strength we need. Still, I wish it wasn't because you've met Him face to face.

I've tried to think if there was anything important that I left unsaid between us. Praise God, I don't think there was. Even if there had been, the one thing I didn't leave unsaid was the most important one.

I love you, William. Tears flow as I type. The moments where I feel the searing pain of having you wrenched from my life do not diminish in intensity; but God has been merciful by allowing the span of time between the pains to lengthen. It's almost like labor, but in reverse. Instead of welcoming you because you've come into the world, I am in the process of releasing you because you've left it.

But, oh, the pain. People claim that women forget the pain of labor in the joy of a new life. Not me. I remember the process, enduring the pain, feeling my body move inexorably toward your birth. You were coming, whether I was ready or not.

You left the same way.

I was so very, very not ready.

From the outside looking in, we're all getting by. The path's not smooth, but we're learning to navigate the dips and curves. In some ways, your leaving has shaken loose from our lives the unimportant stuff. On the flip side, it's helped us to focus on the things...and people...that truly matter. I hate that you had to go in order for these revelations to come.

I am no closer to understanding your death, but I do have a deeper understanding of your life. Remember that man who prophesied that you would be a minister? You might have thought that online thing "qualified", but I have news for you. I've read what your friends say, how you helped them, encouraged them, supported them, invested in them. You, my child, ministered to a great number of people, whether you ever called it that or not.

The only thing I know the future holds is life without you here. No more long discourses on the philosophy of life. No more phone calls on long trips because you're fighting road hypnosis. No more fussing that we change the message on the answering machine just to mess with your head. Thirty-two years never seemed so short until you left.

But, life will continue. I will laugh. I will love. And I will live in joyful expectation of the day I once again get to see your face.

Love you, baby.

Momma

It has been a difficult milestone today, for some reason more difficult than the previous one. My Father knows that, and He's showed me His love through His children once again.

Schedules, weather, and circumstances have made it impossible for my sister and I to get our families together to exchange Christmas gifts. Since my husband had to travel to her area today, he dropped off our gifts for her family and picked up the ones she'd left for us at our mother's house.

The gift to me was in a recycled box. (It's a family law for us: always open the box because it hardly ever contains what the packaging says.). There was a card attached in an envelope that said "Please read AFTER opening." I set it aside and opened the box. This was inside.

The card read:

Dear Leslie,

We had this made from a vase that contained flowers at Wil's service... Madeline's artist friend hand-painted it with symbols that reminded us of Mom and Wil. I pray that you'll be able to enjoy the vase within your own time.

I love you.
                Mary

Go ahead and cry.

I did.

January 24

If you remember back, I put up our Christmas tree on December 3 and realized with a pang that there weren't any ornaments from William on there. That same day, my sister found an ornament of him in 1987 among my mother's decorations. God provided.

The only snag is that we live hours apart, and as the holidays progressed it looked more and more like we weren't going to be able to mesh our schedules to meet. We messaged back and forth, trying to decide the best way to get the ornament from her hands to mine. Our mom's mailbox? Risky. The mail? Less risky. So we chose the mail. It was small and flat. It wouldn't pose any problems - wouldn't even require a trip to the post office - just stamps and a small padded envelope.

So my sister mailed it from work. That was December 15.

Then we waited.

And waited.

And waited.

We'd text back and forth.

"Did you get it?"

"No. Is it maybe still in the outbox?"

"I'll check."

Then we waited some more. And texted some more.

So, when would you have given up?

One week?

Two?

Three?

At about three weeks, on January 6, I had to go to the post office for work. While there, I explained the situation to the distribution clerk. He kindly went in the back and checked for the package. Nothing.

By now, I think my sister was breathing fire on the postal clerk that serves her workplace. Calls were made, but, if you've ever tried to reach a living, breathing entity at the post office, you'll understand what an exercise in futility it can be.

By January 15, I think Mary had lost hope. By the 20th, she was heartbroken, apologizing, and offering to use the picture she'd taken when she originally texted me, and get the ornament reproduced. My answer? Straight from the text:

"It's fine, Mary. Don't worry about it. It may still show up. We've seen God work out bigger problems."

Today is January 24. I came home late. (I work late Tuesdays.) When I get out of the car I almost always do two things. First, I collect the newspaper. Then, I get the mail from the mailbox.

Are you ready?

The marks you can see on the envelope are all that there is. No post mark. No barcode. Just some numbers and initials.

How did it get here? Where has it been for almost six weeks?

I can't answer either of those questions (though I do plan to revisit the post office to see if they can shed some light on it). But I can answer the more important question.

I know Who made sure it reached me.

Now, this might seem a small thing to you. Inconsequential. But it wasn't to me. It certainly wasn't to my sister. And I imagine, by tomorrow afternoon, most of the people where Mary works (and where I work, for sure) will be hearing a testimony of God's love for His daughters in the shape of one small, padded envelope.

Luke 16:10a HCSB says, *"Whoever is faithful in very little is also faithful in much."* God may have been talking about us, but it speaks volumes of Him, too. When we know He's faithful, even in the little things, we find it easier to trust Him with the big things.

January 27

I am reading through the Bible this year using a chronological schedule. In today's reading I came across this verse.

"And if I must bear the anguish of their deaths, then so be it."
Genesis 43:14b NLT

This is Jacob speaking. He's been cornered into having to send his youngest son, Benjamin, to Egypt in order to rescue his family from famine and his son Simeon from the Egyptians. He's lost one son already, because Joseph has been dead to him ever since his brothers produced Joseph's bloody robe. Benjamin is especially precious to him, because he is Joseph's only full-blood brother and the only other child of Jacob's beloved wife, Rachel, who died shortly after giving birth to Benjamin.

What kind of faith does it take to make a statement like this? Did it take all the struggles Jacob had faced up to this point in his life to prepare him for it? Did he say it with faith and confidence? Or fear and trembling? Or resignation and defeat?

Have you ever been in a position to make a decision that might be fatal to your family? Or has someone else put you in that position? Where did you go for wisdom? Where did you find strength? Hope? Comfort?

I know where you can find it. Jacob did, too.

"While the people of Israel were still at Rephidim, the warriors of Amalek attacked them. Moses commanded Joshua, 'Choose some men to go out and fight the army of Amalek for us. Tomorrow, I will stand at the top of the hill holding the staff of God in my hand.' So Joshua did what Moses had commanded and fought the army of Amalek. Meanwhile Moses, Aaron, and Hur climbed to the top of a nearby hill. As long as Moses held up the staff in his hand, the Israelites had the advantage. But whenever he dropped his hand, the Amalekites gained the advantage. Moses' arms soon became so tired he could no longer hold them up. So Aaron and Hur found a stone for him to sit on. Then they stood on each side of Moses, holding up his hands. So his hands held steady until sunset. As a result, Joshua overwhelmed the army of Amalek in battle."
Exodus 17:8-13 NLT

Grief can become your enemy. If you don't control it, it might just control you. That's a place where you don't want to find yourself. It's like a hamster wheel. You go and go and go, but you never get anywhere; you never move forward. It's exhausting. Even when you know the Lord will win, you can feel like victory is never coming, or, if it does, you won't be around to experience it.

There is much to be said about the power of two or three gathered in His name. When we, in our grief, don't feel like we have the strength to go on, it is God's gift of brothers and sisters in Christ that pull us through. They prop us up and hold up our hands in the battle, so that we can endure until the victory God has promised is ours.

Thank You, Lord, for the gift of friends, deeply committed brothers and sisters in Christ, who have lifted me up again and again in the battle against overwhelming grief. Thank You for their perseverance. Thank You for the victory I know is coming.

January 28

Today William's best friend Matt posted a link to the video of his and William's skydiving adventure. It wrings my heart to see them so happy and healthy and excited. They truly enjoyed that day.

Toward the end of the short video, William reached back and deployed his parachute. The wind filled the chute and he was swept up into the sky.

And my tears began to flow.

Because as William zipped up into the air, it brought to mind the feeling that his sudden death had very much the same effect, as if a cord was pulled and he was suddenly ripped from our lives. It's a whisper of the enemy, of course, an insinuation that William has been removed from his rightful place.

The truth is, he has actually taken his rightful place in his Father's house.

Lord, the enemy often attempts to make me feel cheated and angry. Help me to recognize his plots and refuse to engage in them.

January 28

Yesterday I got a message from someone who just heard about William's death. It was his half-brother's mother. DJ preceded William in death by almost ten years. He was just fifteen.

It felt surreal to message with DJ's mother. We have both trod the same path, but at different times. We were both married to the same man. We both had a son by him. We both were divorced from him. Now, we've both lost our son.

I think she initially contacted me out of shock and curiosity. I thought someone would have told her months ago, for I had no way to contact her.

We didn't have a long conversation. She offered her condolences. I offered mine. She told me how she has moved on. I told her what a comfort God has been to me during this time.

It was just a couple of messages, really. I wonder if my pain is still so raw that perhaps it brought hers back to mind. She wasn't abrupt or rude, but I could tell she didn't want to linger over the conversation. I also wonder if she knows my Savior. My mention of His help seemed to close the door on the conversation, when I thought it might open it wider. I hope I've planted a seed there. God certainly has given me an opportunity to pray for her.

Lord, if you put people in my path who are thrust into circumstances like mine, please give me courage. Let me be brave enough to delve into the hurt and pain and shock that You've pulled me through, so that I can offer them the comfort You offered me. If I flinch from their pain, remind me that You didn't flinch from mine.

January 30

Circumstances made it necessary for my workplace to close today for maintenance. I thought, "*Hooray! A day off!*" Then, this morning, God tapped me on the shoulder.

Well, He'd been nudging me all weekend, but - shame on me - I just rationalized it away. But today, well, I couldn't ignore Him without being outright disobedient, so I submitted. He called me to spend the day at church in what we lovingly call the "War Room". It's a tiny room, only big enough for eight chairs and a small sofa table. We meet there on Sundays to pray. Today, God planted me there to pray and worship and pray some more. I didn't go with an agenda, but I did go with my tools: Bible, pen, paper, and a device full of worship music.

It was an amazing time. I worshipped. I cried. I prayed. I listened. I waited.

And waited.

And waited some more.

Early in the afternoon, I took a break, I waited to see if I had been released, but God sent me back.

As I was journaling, I realized God sent me back to pen a letter to a good friend who just had to make a decision that broke her heart and changed her future. The death of her relationship is no less real than the death of my son. Grief looks different on everyone.

I thought that was it. It was about 1:30 in the afternoon. I'd been praying off and on since about 9:30 in the morning. I was ready to leave, but I when I checked my spirit, I just didn't feel released to go. So, back to the "war room" I went.

At about 3:05 p.m. or so, I took a break and I checked my phone (in case my husband had left a message). Even though my phone was in my purse and I should have heard it vibrate, I hadn't, but there was a message on it. It had come in just minutes before, at 3:01. It was from an old high school friend I mentioned earlier in my journey, who has had surgery to remove a cancerous tumor in her throat. God put me in a position to be able to encourage her as she faces some serious health challenges. She had contacted me because she was feeling overwhelmed by the enormity of what she's facing. She has to have all her teeth removed. She has to have six to seven weeks of intensive radiation treatment. She has to keep her calorie intake up or she will have to go back on a feeding tube. All this, while juggling employment issues, transportation issues and trying to learn to talk after having her vocal cords reconstructed.

How likely is it that (1) I would be off on a weekday due to a maintenance closure of my place of employment, (2) have felt the urge to go to the church and spend my day off in prayer, (3) check my phone because my husband might be looking for me (he could have called the church office, plus my phone's usually dead), and (4) just "happen" to check it literally minutes after my friend left her frantic message?

You are not at this point in your life by accident. Your present circumstance has a purpose, whether it's to teach you something now, prepare you for something later, or put you in a position to help someone else. No matter how hard it is or how long you've been there, God is there, and He is working.

If the cacophony of life is drowning our His Words, may I make a suggestion? Get by yourself. Remove yourself from the chaos that is life on this broken planet, even if it's just for ten minutes. I've been known to sit in the bottom of my closet. Go in the bathroom (when you have boys, sometimes it's the only place they don't follow). Step out on the back porch, or sit in your car. It doesn't have to be fancy or far away. Just back away from the noise of life so that you can hear the voice of God. He speaks to us all the time, but we often can't hear Him above the din that so often surrounds us.

If possible, get away for a day, even if it's just to spend it in a small room at the back of your church. You will be amazed at what God can show you and how He can use you when He has your full attention.

What God wants you to hear may not change your circumstance, but it sure will change your perspective.

God has listened to you. Are you willing to listen to Him?

———————————————————

This is part of what came from my time with God today.

Whatever the loss you're facing, it is, in a sense, a death. It might be the death of a loved one. It might be the death of a relationship. It might be the death of a dream due to tragedy or illness. We are all so different that our losses are as unique as we are. You will grieve: sometimes loud and long, sometimes in brief showers of tears that will go as quickly as they come, and sometimes quietly in the deepest part of your soul where only God can hear or see.

Many people will offer what they believe to be kind words. Some will help. Some will feel like salt rubbed right into the wound in your heart. Resist the temptation to speak from your place of pain. Instead, take a deep breath and pray for God's eyes to see past their words to their heart's intent. They mean well; they don't know what to say, because there isn't anything they can say that will help. Just know they speak out of love for you.

As the days and weeks go by, you'll feel an almost imperceptible shift take place. The milestones - birthdays, holidays, special occasions - will pass, some with ease, others as painful as the blow of a hammer on an unsuspecting thumb. Accept both kinds, praising God for the former and crawling up in His lap as you tearfully endure the latter. In both, seek reasons to praise God. You might have to dig deep, especially on "hammer" days, but - you're breathing - so, start there. If you know Jesus as your Savior, you have even more for which to praise God. Start there and work your way out of that pit. Don't give the enemy a victory by laying down and wallowing in it. (It won't make you feel better anyway.)

Time will not heal the gaping wound left by your loss - only God can do that. Just like any good doctor, you will have to give the Great Physician full access to your wound and trust Him as He works. Healing doesn't always come without some pain. Don't flinch from it. Trust Him, because He can and will do great things in you, for you, and through you. Watch for them. Expect them. Write them down. Your faith will grow as you see His faithfulness in small things, and you'll find it easier to trust Him with big things.

You are not alone in your grief. Your family and friends will experience it from a different perspective, but one that is no less real to them. Draw strength from God when their grief overflows onto yours, and keep in mind they wouldn't hurt so much of they didn't love you so dearly.

If you are my brother or sister in Christ, there is no need to remind you of God's promises. You know where to find them. They will be your true source of comfort. Immerse yourself in them. Meditate on them day and night, and they will fill you with our Father's peace and hope.

You are not alone in your grief, even if it feels as if you are. As I write this, I am praying for you. I pray God will reveal Himself to you in a way you can't miss, that you will see His power and feel His presence like a blanket surrounding you. I pray, even in the midst of your pain, you feel His peace.

February 1

A friend from high school lost her 25-year-old son yesterday, right out of the blue. The autopsy revealed he died of a massive heart attack, that three of his heart valves had blockages, and he had a minor case of pneumonia. Just like that, her life changed in an instant.

How well I know that feeling.

I've reached out to her, but I well remember the maelstrom of grief and shock and pain of the first few days. She won't be responding any time soon. That's probably a good thing, because it may take me a while to fully grasp the reality of sharing my experience with someone who's behind me on this journey, not ahead of me. Up until now, I have been receiving comfort, hope and help from those that have trod this path before me. It looks like I may be on the verge of stepping into a new place in this journey, one that will require God's strength. It will not be easy or painless to empathize with someone who is just starting out on their journey in this valley. God may not have called me to speak to this friend in particular. He may just be calling me to be open to His leading in this area.

At this point, the idea of it is...not welcome. Emotionally, it feels as if I'd be tearing my shirt open and exposing the scars on my heart, scars that are still tender and sometimes feel almost raw. Answering questions that I would have posed at the beginning of this journey would feel like someone poking at those scars - hard. It will hurt. I will cry, and not just for my friend, but for me, too.

After my prayer on January 27, I can see the hand of God in this encounter. I also see yet another reason He had me fast and pray on Monday. I know in my own strength I cannot do this.

Thank you, Lord, for preparing me for the possibility of sharing Your gift of comfort and peace with others behind me in this valley. Hold me close so I can feel Your strength flow through me.

February 2

It's been five months since I stood in a pavilion in a military cemetery and faced a sea of faces that mirrored the shock and grief on mine. Five months of trying to figure out how to live with one of my children in a world separated from mine. Five months of trying to reorient myself to speaking about him in the past tense in order to avoid awkward questions from well-meaning people who misunderstand me when I speak of him in the present tense. Five months of having to adjust my thinking to my new family dynamic.

It just feels so wrong. Even now, I find myself stopping and forcing myself to remember that this is not a dream. This is reality. And it is harsh. And it hurts. And while more time elapses between bouts, when the grief does hit, it hits with almost the same intensity as when this journey began. Sometimes it comes with a warning. Most times now, it does not. Sometimes it's dropped in my lap.

Like hearing from DJ's mother this week, who hadn't heard about William. It was almost like living it over again.

Like discovering a friend whose relationship has died a death no less real and no less painful than my loss.

Like hearing a high school friend lost her 25-year-old son Tuesday from a sudden and totally unexpected heart attack.

Perhaps it's the combination of these three events that has me on the verge of a meltdown of major proportions. I dare not surrender to it. It would be one of those crying jags that would benefit me little and suck me under even more.

So I'm choosing life. I'm enjoying the memories. Reading everyone's posts on my son's memorial site about their experiences with him and memories of him. Hunting up pictures that evoke happy times. I'm focusing on the 32 years we had William rather than the five months we have not. I know that this urge to melt into a puddle of sorrow is just one wave in this sea of grief. If I keep treading long enough, it too, will pass. Then the sea will even out once more, and I can once again swim through it without drowning.

Blessings from a mending heart,

Me

February 7

Grief is not my friend, especially today.

Today is my grandson's ninth birthday.

It's strange that the celebration of my grandson's birth is, in my heart, steeped in the grief of his father's death. Strange, how my heart seems able to contain both at once. I'm not enjoying it one bit. I suppose that's why God has put some distance between me and my grandson. He knew long before I did that this day would come. He knew I would struggle. He knew my grandson didn't need to watch me do so.

A good portion of the pain stems from all memories of my son's birthdays assaulting me. We were never ones to go all out, but we would try to make the day a celebration - not too difficult when you're born on a holiday. The important thing to me was that we spent it together, the way he and I spent his actual "birth" day.

Perhaps that's a small grief all mothers share, when their children reach the point where they no longer want to spend their birthday celebrating with their mom. I know it's been bittersweet for me with both my children, watching them mature into young men, knowing that that same maturity that is drawing them away from me is drawing them toward their future.

A smaller portion of my grief stems from all the memories I know William was looking forward to making with his son. Did William have plans for today? A place they would visit together? A trip they would take? A movie they'd see? Would they just hang out and enjoy each other's company?

Funny, how the smaller part of my grief offers the larger temptation to indulge in sin. Asking the questions and surrendering the pain they bring to God is good. Dwelling on them is not. That is a slippery slope upon which I do not wish to plant my feet.

Lord, I thank You that You know our end from our beginning. I thank You that William was able to enjoy raising his son for eight years. I thank You that I was able to enjoy William for 32. I thank You for his son's ninth birthday today. Please draw him near, plant Your Word in his mind and the desire to be Your child in his heart, so that he might soon celebrate a rebirth-day. In the name of Jesus I pray. Amen.

February 8

"*...the greater the love the greater the grief, and the stronger the faith the more savagely will Satan storm its fortress.*"
---From the introduction written by Douglas Gresham to *A Grief Observed* [31] by C.S. Lewis

When Mr. Gresham penned this line, I'm sure he was speaking of his stepfather, C. S. Lewis' love for Mr. Gresham's mother. I can't speak with any authority on the death of a spouse, but I can speak with experience on the death of a child. Unwanted experience, but experience nonetheless.

If there is a love stronger than a mother's, I can't imagine it. You've shared more with a child you carried beneath your heart than you will ever share with anyone else: breath, blood, health, sickness. You literally know them their entire life: the good, the bad, the ugly. No matter what they do or where they go, they will always be your child. The bond may begin in our physical bodies, but it soon takes root in our hearts. If you are a mother, you will understand.

Have you ever noticed that there is no designation for a mother who's lost a child? There's one for those who've lost spouses (widow, widower). There's one for those who've lost parents (orphan). But there isn't one for parents who lose a child.

Do you wonder why that is? I've decided it must be because it is not the natural order of things. We expect to outlive our parents. We expect, at some point, that one spouse will outlive the other. We do not expect to outlive our children. Giving the condition a name would seem to validate it in some way that, I think, we find repellant.

With a love this strong, it's only natural for grief at the loss of it to be just as strong. Even though I didn't always see eye to eye with my son, that never changed my love for him. (Sounds like another relationship, doesn't it? How often does our Father shake His head at our choices, but He continues to love us?) The first part of Mr. Gresham's statement makes perfect sense.

It was the second part that snared my attention, because it articulated a truth that I faced early on in this journey.

For the last few years I've attended a women's Bible study at our church. Each successive study drew me closer to the women in the class, as some members drifted in and out, but a core group remained throughout each session. Each successive study also drew me closer to my Father. The effect of the two together was a spiritual growth that I had not experienced heretofore. In the months preceding William's death, we completed two different studies on prayer. I learned a great many things in both studies that helped me exercise my faith and strengthen my prayer life.

I did not know it at the time, but my Father was preparing me for what was to come. To say that the enemy was displeased with my spiritual growth would be a gross misstatement. His opening volley was fired when my grandson's mother called me to tell me William had died. She was distraught. She was nearly hysterical. She was close to a meltdown, and she still had to pick up my grandson and tell him he'd lost his father. While she's falling apart on the phone, my husband and younger son are eavesdropping on my conversation, they have deduced what has happened, and they are in their own freefall trying to comprehend the incomprehensible.

And there I sat on the floor, phone in one hand, grieving family on both ends of it, and I feel like someone swung a two by four at my head and made a solid connection.

In the moments before my life erupted into chaos, I heard in the deepest part of me a whisper with the strength of a shout.

"You've talked the talk for many years. What will you do now? Will you live out what you have spoken? Trust Me with even this? Or was it just talk?"

No it wasn't audible, but it was all the more powerful for that reason. And I knew the Speaker. Oh, yes, I knew Him. And I knew what He was asking, and I knew how hard it would be.

But the alternative was not an option.

So, I took a breath, spoke peace into my ex-daughter-in-law's heart, and, probably less than a minute after hearing the hardest news of my life, I offered to pray for her as she prepared to deliver the hardest news of her life. I can't remember the words, but I can remember the peace and strength they brought us both, peace and strength we would both need as we delivered our news and dealt with its aftermath.

Yes, I have encountered the enemy when he stormed the fortress of my heart. But more importantly, when he breached the walls of my soul, he encountered the Holy Spirit.

Praise God.

Thank You, Lord, that no matter what we face here on earth, we have Your Spirit in our hearts and Your Son in heaven interceding for us. Thank You that Your love is greater than our grief and your peace is greater than our pain.

February 11

A group at church had two meetings this week. I didn't have to go to the second one, held this morning, but I wanted to. So I did.

Oddly enough, I was the first one there. I had one of those "twilight zone" moments, where you think back, check your watch, and try to remember if you have the place and time correct, or if everyone is somewhere else wondering why you're absent.

Anyway, the youth pastor was the first to show up. He was carrying some things in his hands, so I held the door for him into the building, and then into the sanctuary. The lights in the sanctuary were dimmed, but you could see how to get around. My eyes naturally drifted toward the stage.

That's when I saw it. Flowers in vases. Flowers in arrangements. A plaque. And a picture of a handsome young man, engraved with his name...and two dates.

A sister in the church lost her 33-year-old son in a fire Sunday morning. His funeral is today.

Out of respect for this sister in Christ, I walked to the front and looked at the arrangements and the display. The scent of the flowers drifted across me. I noticed one arrangement in a blue vase. Memories floated to the surface of pictures another young man and another flower arrangement in another blue vase.

It was too much. It was too soon. I sometimes wonder if it will ever *not* be too much and too soon. I suspect it will always, to some degree, batter me to see a sister in Christ walking this path behind me.

My younger son was attending this meeting, too. He was behind me by enough time for me to go through several tissues, but he was right on time to give me a hug and pat my back while I tried to collect myself and put my grief back into the compartment of my heart where it usually resides.

Our church is large. I'm not well-acquainted with this sister, but I am well-acquainted with the shock and sorrow that will fill her days and nights for the weeks to come.

Lord, I lift my sister in Christ to You today. She will need every bit of Your strength and Your comfort to get through the next few hours. Surround her, Lord, with Your presence in the days and nights ahead. Speak to her in the deepest parts of her pain, and fill her mind with Your peace.

Shortly after I posted the above to my social media page (in great indecision about whether or not I should), I received a reply from a friend I know through homeschooling. Though I know her to be a sister in Christ, she doesn't attend my church. Her reply: *"Thank you, Leslie for sharing your thoughts. This young man was my nephew. Somehow sharing your grief helps."*

God is with you always, even and especially in the hard places. I knew when I saw those flowers that I didn't want to go near them, but I felt in my heart that it was what my Father wanted. I obeyed because I want to walk where He sends me. I thought His purpose was to teach me something, and He did, but certainly not in the way I expected. The farther I travel in this valley, the more my journey becomes about others and the less it becomes about me. Look around, my friends. Is there someone in your life that needs to see you trusting God through your tragedy? Do they need to see that you can trust even when you're burdened with grief? Do they need to see your pain in order to be able to trust your Source of peace? If you step out in obedience to God, He will, indeed, show you things that you did not know.

Father, thank You for encouraging me, especially in the hard places. Thank You for allowing me to watch You work good out of my grief. Help me to keep my heart open to Your leading.

February 14

Valentine's Day. The day of hearts and roses. Candy and cards. Love.

For a little boy, his first Valentine is usually his mother. We are the blessed recipients of paper hearts and handmade cards inscribed with X's and O's that fill our eyes with happy tears and our hearts with love.

Oh, yes, we treasure those hand-crafted gifts created and presented to us with joy beaming from our little boys' faces. Pictures done in a kaleidoscope of colors. Hearts - always red, NEVER pink! - painstakingly pasted on dainty doilies. Glitter-covered cards filled with love in the childish scrawl of those energetic bundles of joy we call sons.

Much as we love and appreciate these gifts, there are other gifts that reach deeper into our mother-hearts. These are the ones given spontaneously at random moments across the entire fabric of our little-boy-turned-young-man's life, not on a prescribed holiday or a result of art class. They are the true expression of a son's love for his mother. Sometimes boisterous and extravagant, sometimes quiet and introspective, but always from their hearts and precious to ours.

A hastily printed memo-calendar page: "Momma, you are so pritty and I love you."

A flower picked from the yard presented in a chubby hand by a small boy with a big smile.

An out-of-the-blue hug, especially in the teen years...and in public!

Exchanging goodnight greetings, no matter what the hour.

Checking in a little more often and sticking a little more closely to home when your mom is trying to find her balance after a stunning life's blow.

Spending a day celebrating memories of your childhood friend.

Stepping in to do and be for your best friend's mother what he no longer can.

The last three may seem unusual, but they are all the more precious for that very reason. They were gifts from grieving hearts offered to a broken one, all bleeding from the loss of someone who loved and lived enthusiastically. The first is my younger son, my precious gift from God who has been constant in his love and care for me (even when I'm driving him crazy). The second is the son of good friends, lent to me on a day when I wasn't even aware of how badly I needed his presence. The third is the newest son of my heart, planted when its soil was churned by grief and watered with tears. These three young men are gifts from God, and I am grateful that God loves me so much He has allowed me to be a part of their lives.

Thank You, Lord, for sons - by birth and chosen. Thank You for Your love that flows from their hearts to mine. Thank You for allowing me to be a part of their lives. Thank You for Your strength that I see residing in each of them. Thank You for drawing them to You, for their acceptance of You as their Savior. Bless them as they walk through their lives with You as their Lord. Give them wisdom as they lead their families. May they see their children and their children's children come to know You as their Lord and Savior. I ask that You do these things - or something even better - in Jesus' name. Amen.

Happy Valentine's Day to "my" boys. God bless you all. I love you.

February 15

For the third time in two weeks I have encountered a mother who's lost a child. She is one of my sister's good friends. I remember her from our teens. Her daughter was 33, and was not ill or injured, as far as I know. Her daughter didn't wake up Sunday morning and was rushed to the hospital. My sister's friend had the additional burden of her daughter being an organ donor.

For the third time, I have followed God's leading and offered my condolences. I expected much the same result as with the other two that I recently learned of, as we are no more acquainted than the other two mothers who have fallen into this valley. There was, however, one difference. This "mother in loss" knew of my plight and had prayed for me. When I reached out to her, she responded. We've been messaging back and forth ever since.

I am learning daily the truth of 2 Corinthians 1:3-4 NLT.

All praise to God, the Father of our Lord Jesus Christ. God is our merciful father and the source of all comfort. He comforts us in all our troubles so that we can comfort others. When they are troubled, we will be able to give them the same comfort God has given us.

Lord, my heart overflows with thanksgiving for Your loving care and comfort throughout this difficult journey. I thank You for using it to strengthen my faith and open my eyes to Your constant working in the lives of Your children. I thank You for the opportunity to share with others the peace and comfort and encouragement that You shared with me through Your Word and Your children. Thank You for allowing me to see You work wonders with what the enemy meant for evil. All blessing and glory and honor be unto You, Father. Amen.

February 18

Today we're going to visit William's grave on our way to visit with Oliver. It doesn't promise to be an easy day. I started the day with time with God, using the *Our Daily Bread* devotional booklet. Today (https://odb.org/2017/02/18/the-lighthouse/) the Bible reading was in Isaiah:

The Spirit of the Sovereign Lord is upon me, for the Lord has anointed me to bring good news to the poor. He has sent me to comfort the brokenhearted and to proclaim that captives will be released and prisoners will be freed. He has sent me to tell those who mourn that the time of the Lord's favor has come, and with it, the day of God's anger against their enemies. To all who mourn in Israel, He will give a crown of beauty for ashes, a joyous blessing instead of mourning, festive praise instead of despair. In their righteousness, they will be like great oaks that the Lord has planted for His own glory.
Isaiah 61:1-3 NLT

Part of the devotional included two questions

1. "In what ways has Jesus responded to your own hurts and needs?" [32]

Quickly. Wholly. Generously.

2. "In what ways can you respond to the needs of those around you who are hurting?" [33]

On January 31, a friend from high school lost her 25-year-old healthy son to a sudden heart attack.

On February 5, a woman that attends our church lost her 33-year old son to a house fire.

On February 14, one of my sister's close friends lost her 33-year-old daughter to unknown causes.

Three women that God has placed within my orbit in less than three weeks. This is not a turn I expected, and while my desire is to follow where He leads, I did not expect Him to ask me to turn around, and to go back, as it were. The journey was so painful the first time. Can I do this? He wouldn't call me to unless He was going to equip me for it. And we are called to share with others the comfort He has given us.

Shouldn't we respond to Jesus' call the way He responds to ours?

Quickly?

Wholly?

Generously?

Today for the first time since September 2, I walked the grounds of Alfred G. Horton Jr. Memorial Veterans Cemetery. I have felt the obligation to go for a while, but God used logistics and distance and even illness to keep me away. However, it's been almost six months and I knew it was time.

I so very much didn't want to go. That was my sign from God that I needed to, before I got so comfortable that I never did.

I want to thank you all for praying for me. I surely needed those prayers today, because the tears began to well in my eyes when we hit the Suffolk city line. I managed to hold most of them in check, even after we arrived at the cemetery.

When William was buried, the service was held in a pavilion on the cemetery grounds. We could have waited while he was buried, then have been directed to the site. However, we were all so wounded at that time that the service was all we could manage. We were given information about the section he was in, and as we passed the cemetery, we saw an open site that we thought might be for William, but we didn't stay to find out. We just couldn't.

Today we drove to the area we suspected was his final resting place. We didn't have a map or a plot number, nothing. Just God. There was a rock path that was obviously used for transport to the sites. I took a deep breath, looked up the path, and started walking. Even in something as simple as that, God looked out for me. I can't ever remember a finer February day.

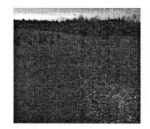

I started up the hill with my mind blank on purpose. Any mother would. Just because almost six months have passed hasn't changed the pain. Though I feel it less often, it's just as sharp and raw when it hits.

And it hit when I reached row 4. There, right

at the edge of the path, straight in front of me, was the marker indicating my son's final resting place. I called to my husband to direct him to it. Then the pain hit. It literally drove me to my knees, and I wept harder than I have since William breathed his last. I prayed and I cried and I clawed at the ground and I prayed some more. And though the tears kept coming, I leaned my head against the marker and I prayed again and surrendered it all to God. The good. The bad. The ugly. The pain. The sorrow. The tears. And I thank Him now for sending only my husband with me. Our own sorrow was all we could handle today.

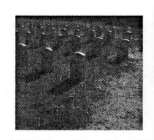

Lord, what You called me to today was hard, but You are faithful. You promise to walk with us through the valley of the shadow of death and to comfort us, and You did. I am so grateful. Thank You that You never change. Thank You that You are always with me. Thank You that you love me enough to sit with me on hill far away at the foot of a six month old grave in cemetery filled with brave men and women who put their lives on the line so that I could live mine in freedom. Thank You that no matter how much I mourn, You are greater than my grief. I love you, Father. In Jesus' name I pray. Amen.

February 19

Last night I was too spent to do more than get the first part of yesterday down. Today, as Paul Harvey would say, I deliver the rest of the story - or at least the story to this point, because God is still writing it.

Well, I was a mess after visiting William's grave, and since I was, I decided to go to Mom's grave, too. After all, I buried them close together. It seemed only right to visit them together, too.

I didn't cry at Mom's. To be honest, I expected, at some point, to outlive her. Not at the point that I did, but certainly (unless Jesus returned for His children first) at some point in the future. We spent a few quiet moments at Mom's gravesite, admiring the flowers my sister had put there.

When we left we were headed for a family gathering at my parent's home. My grandson and his mother were meeting us there. We hadn't seen them since September, and we had Christmas and birthday gifts for my grandson. We arrived early so that we could gather ourselves and process being in a house void of my mother's presence, but full of her memory and the pain of her absence. My husband had an errand to run, so I opted to stay at the house and try to compose myself while he took care of his task.

After he left, I sat for a minute, just breathing. It wasn't too long before I realized something was different. It took me a minute to realize it was the silence. Total silence. No television. No heater. No clocks ticking. I can't ever remember it being silent like that. Almost like everything is still waiting for her to return. But she won't be. After a minute or two, I pulled out my phone to check to see if my younger son was on his way and to tell my grandson's mother we had arrived. That's where God met me for the second time that day, because on the phone was a message from my friend that I've mentioned earlier in this journey, who's on a journey of her own being treated for cancer. Just this week she had oral surgery and two trips to the hospital for "hiccups" in her recovery. In addition to health issues, she has had transportation issues, finance issues, and insurance issues. Her message?

"Hey, Leslie, haven't heard from you. Everything okay?"

Here I sat feeling a bit sorry for myself and trying not to, and here's a friend with more than enough on her plate, yet she's concerned about me?

Thank You, God for showing me, through my friend, the best way to combat the poor-pitiful-me syndrome is to reach out to someone else who needs an encouraging word. Thank You for allowing me the opportunity, three times in the last two weeks, to pray for mothers suffering the sudden loss of their adult children. Thank You for giving me that chance to share Your comfort, peace and strength with them. And for the third mom, who has the impossible task of bidding her daughter goodbye today at 4:00, I pray and ask everyone who reads this to pray for her and her family, including her 11-year-old granddaughter, as they endure one of the most painful moments life on this broken planet can bring to mothers. In Jesus' name I pray. Amen.

February 20

This weekend was hard. In addition to all that transpired, I had agreed to join with another young woman to sign for one of the songs at our special "Awaken" evening service. A band was coming in for a special night of praise and worship, and they were going to do some of the music from their new album. Within their set, they were also doing some songs with which I was familiar. When I was asked to pick one to sign, I actually picked several and was going to ask the young woman who was signing with me to choose the one she wanted to do.

Bless her heart, she got the flu. However, the worship leader asked me to go ahead without her. Out of the songs I had picked, there was one called "I Surrender" [34]. I selected it because it was the oldest song in the set, so I'd done it more than the others and was more familiar with it. (This is important when you have terminal stage fright and, from the minute you face an audience, you clamp your eyes closed and don't open them again until you're done.)

I had no idea, at the moment I chose it, that God was going to bring me literally to my knees on my son's grave and remind me that I need to surrender all the grief and sorrow and loss and chaos and heartache - the whole beautiful mess that is me right now - to Him and stop camping on the what-ifs and the if-onlys and all the things that still need to be done that circle my head like vultures. He reminded me that if I don't surrender them to Him, then I'm handing them to the enemy as ammunition.

So I come home Saturday night, and I sit down and I think about the words to this song, and I know I have a problem. When I sign, in my heart I'm singing to God with my hands. I don't know how to separate worship from performance, and I knew there was a very good chance that I would end up in tears with this song. I contacted the worship leader after Sunday morning services and explained my dilemma. Wise woman that she is, her response was *"That's okay. Tears are a part of worship."*

So, Sunday afternoon, I show up at the church just before the band (Resound Live) does. They come in and begin setting up, doing voice checks, mike checks, and headset checks. While they're doing this, I'm looking at my watch and wondering when they'll have time to practice. There were eleven songs in the set, the one I was signing was number seven, and I did the math. There was no way they'd get to it, and I didn't think I could sign a song with a strange band without even one run-through.

Yes! This was my out! I now had a valid reason to tell the worship leader that maybe I better just stick to my seat in the front row. The relief I felt was prideful and selfish, because I was more worried about how I'd look on stage rather than whether or not I should be there.

But God had a plan.

After the band tweaked everything and got ready to play, the leader looked down at his music stand, and I kid you not, folks, he said, "Okay, let's do 'I Surrender' [35], just because that's the song in front of me." And they did. It was the *only* song they ran through.

"I Surrender." [36]

I sure did.

I climbed those steps during the service that night and took my place and signed that song. Perfectly? No, but it wasn't about perfection, it was about obedience and surrender. It was about sitting on that hill leaning against that tombstone and emptying myself of everything that's not working for my good, because it's not from my Father. It was about filling the space left behind by moving out all that "junk" with God: with His Word, with His worship, with His presence.

What do you need to surrender?

February 21

"In time they all served as lovely remembrances, not just painful reminders."
---from *The Visitor* [37] by Lori Wick

Today was my late day at work. I worked until 7:00 p.m. On my way into the house I stopped by the mailbox. Among the pieces of mail was a large manila envelope. When I saw that it was from the Department of Veteran Affairs, I had a strong suspicion it would have to do with William. I was right. I wish I hadn't been.

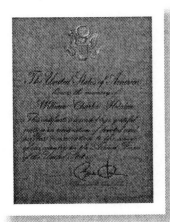

It was a Presidential Memorial Certificate, issued in recognition of my son's service to our country.

In two days, it will have been six months since William died. And he died on a Tuesday, my late day, and I found out something was amiss just after I came home at 7:00 p.m. that night.

As painful as receiving this was, I know my Father meant it for my good, to remind me that He's aware of the days when I struggle to keep my eyes on Him and off the wave-tossed storm that is life on this fallen earth.

Heavenly Father, help me. Thank You for showing me the quote in Lori Wick's book. Help me apply it. Help me take what the enemy means to be painful reminders and, in Your strength, turn them into lovely remembrances. In Jesus name I ask for this or something better. Amen.

February 22

I recently read someone's post to a friend who has suffered a loss. In essence the message was, "Don't worry. It'll get easier." I realize the words were written in love. I do. But, please, *please* be careful how you speak to a grieving mother. Even though the words weren't intended for me, they pierced my heart afresh, and the pain that followed brought with it an anger for which I'm still repenting.

Easier? A piece of my heart has been brutally amputated without benefit of anesthesia, and you say it'll get easier? Well, it isn't easier from where I'm standing. It's been nearly six months since my son breathed his last. It's not any easier to say and it's not any easier to live. Easy, for me, is buried on a hill in a veteran's cemetery.

step 7

Heeding His Call

*Therefore, whenever we have the opportunity, we
should do good to everyone...*

Galatians 6:10a NLT

February 23

I am reading through the Bible chronologically this year. Today, as I began the book of Numbers, I read this introduction.

"What gift is God holding out to you right now that you have been refusing to receive? What marvelous opportunities has He sent your way that you don't want to consider because they don't fit your agenda or because they seem too hard or too frightening?" [38]

For the last three weeks, God has let me cross paths with three women who have suddenly lost their adult children. He has given me an opportunity to reach out to each one, though doing so comes with a price. But, if it makes just one day of their lives a little easier, then in God's strength, I will do it.

For the last four or more months, God, through one of His gifted daughters (more than one, actually) has been encouraging me to put this journey on paper and consider publishing it for the benefit of my sisters that are behind me in this valley. I have been more reluctant than Moses and more timid than Gideon to even consider this. God has given me this incredible gift, this ability to pen what I'm feeling, and I thought it was just how I process things, how I go about life. Until approached, I never considered a book. Even now, the words in that introduction, "too hard and too frightening" resound in my head like a gong.

Lord, I want what You want, but I can't see what You see. Forgive me for my lack of faith in this area. Thank You for being so patient with me, for showing me over and over that You want me to share the comfort You've given me with others through the medium of print. Your will be done in Jesus' name. Amen.

It's been six months today. Sometimes it feels like six minutes. Sometimes it feels like six years.

It always feels wrong.

I don't know who it was that decided it

would get easier with time. It hasn't for me. Easy doesn't seem a word that would ever apply to having a part of your heart brutally amputated without benefit of anesthesia. No amount of time will heal it either.

That's not to say that I haven't experienced joy in the midst of the sorrow. I have. But it's just different. It's all so different. And so hard to describe. Perhaps C.S. Lewis has come the closest:

> *"I suppose if one were forbidden all salt one wouldn't notice it much more in any one food than in another. Eating in general would be different, every day, at every meal. It is like that. The act of living is different all through."*
> ---from *A Grief Observed* [39] by C.S. Lewis

That sums up my life for the last six months. Absolutely nothing is the same. Oh, I work the same job, live in the same house, attend the same church. I eat the same foods, read the same books, listen to the same music.

But throughout it all, even when I don't say it or think it, there is an invisible thread running:

He's gone.

It colors everything, and I know I'm not explaining it well. I fear unless you've walked through this valley, there just isn't a way to explain it. C.S. Lewis' words will have to do.

It all sounds so terribly hopeless, doesn't it? That's the beauty of my Father. When the whole world around me came crashing down, when everything I thought I knew about my life was turned on its head, and when everything inside me was screaming in agony...

God was WITH me. God IS with me. GOD is with me.

The Creator of the universe, the One who fashioned my mother and my son, and the One who gave me 55 years with Mom and 32 glorious, happy, aggravating, heartbreaking, breathtaking, frustrating years with William has not for a single second left my side through all of the last six months.

Not at the funerals.

Not on the birthdays.

Not during the holidays.

Not at the graves.

He has never left my side.

He never will.

Does He walk with you? If so, then you know how I have managed to survive what any mother will tell you is unbearable pain.

If He doesn't, please hear me when I say that He wants to. In fact, He wants to so much that He sent His Son to pay the price for you to be able to do just that. Do you have any idea how much He loves you?

I have.

He sent His Son to DIE in your place. He didn't die suddenly or unexpectedly or by accident.

He died willingly in an agonizing manner, to pay what you couldn't. And He did it knowing that you may never want the gift He paid the ultimate price to give you.

That's how much He loves you. That's how much He wants to walk with you.

Heavenly Father, I am humbled by Your love for me. I'm thankful for Your presence in my life, especially over the last six months. Thank You for revealing Yourself in so many ways through so many people and in so many circumstances. Please reveal Yourself to those reading this that haven't accepted Your gift. Open their eyes to the truth of life without You and their hearts to the joy of life with You. In Jesus' name I pray. Amen.

Dear William,

This arrived in Tuesday's mail.

As if visiting the graves Saturday wasn't enough of a blow.

Or the six month mark for Mom on Saturday.

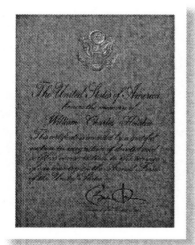

And you today.

When will it stop feeling so fresh? Ever? I'm still running into people who don't know, or who just found out, which rakes up all the places in my heart that were finally beginning to settle.

I still think of calling to tell you goodnight sometimes.

You're my first thought whenever I'm stumped by a tech question.

Seeing your son brings tears to my eyes. He's so you. In him I hear your voice. I see your smile. My heart cracks a little. I know you'd be amazed at the young man he's becoming.

I don't know who started the saying that it gets easier. I see no evidence of it. But I am learning to live with it. I am learning to trust God and watch the beauty He can create from the ashes of my grief.

I miss you, William. I knew you your entire life, even before you were born, when you still lay nestled beneath my heart. You know I trust God to know best, but it doesn't change that fact that it feels so wrong for me to have buried you.

You have amazing friends. You'd be pleased, I think, to see how they've reached out to me and shared their parts of you with me to ease my pain a bit. God blessed you in your friends. And I know to have such good ones, you had to be a good one, too. I've never doubted you were. Even as a child, you never met a stranger. A legacy from my daddy, perhaps. And yours.

We are surviving, William. We're finding comfort in messages, pictures and videos you've left. We're sharing our memories of you. And our grief. I am relieved to say that the former are beginning to outweigh the latter.

But no one save the Lord will ever be able to fill the hole in my heart left behind when you died.

Good night, my child. I love you. See you when I see you.

And I WILL see you.

Love,
Mom

February 24

I woke up this morning still feeling the effects of yesterday's milestone. My first order of the day is time with God using a small devotional booklet called *Our Daily Bread*. After whining to God the minute my feet hit the floor that I didn't feel like making nice with people today and would rather crawl back in the bed and sleep for the next hundred years or so, this was His reply. (http://odb.org/2017/02/24/the-land-of-what-is/)

"Even all these years after losing our seventeen-year-old daughter Melissa in a car accident in 2002, I sometimes find myself entering the world of 'What If.' It's easy, in grief, to re-imagine the events of that tragic June evening and think of factors that—if rearranged—would have had Mell arriving safely home.

"In reality, though, the land of 'What If' is not a good place to be for any of us. It is a place of regret, second-guessing, and hopelessness. While the grief is real and the sadness endures, life is better and God is honored if we dwell in the world of 'What Is.'

"When we do face hard times, our greatest help comes from trusting God.

"In that world, we can find hope, encouragement, and comfort. We have the sure hope (1 Thess. 4:13)—the assurance—that because Melissa loved Jesus she is in a place that is 'better by far' (Phil. 1:23). We have the helpful presence of the God of all comfort (2 Cor. 1:3). We have God's "ever-present help in trouble" (Ps. 46:1). And we often have the encouragement of fellow believers.

"We all wish to avoid the tragedies of life. But when we do face hard times, our greatest help comes from trusting God, our sure hope in the land of 'What Is'." [40]

February 25

This morning, I woke up with one of William's friends on my heart. I can't explain why. We've all had these feelings before. I've learned to use them as encouragements to pray, and sometimes I feel led to let the person know I'm praying for them, sometimes not. However, I don't have a way to directly contact this person, so I wrote them this note and asked my new "son" to get it to him. I may never know why I felt like I had to do it, but I can rest in the knowledge that I answered God's call.

The next time someone just lands on your heart for no apparent reason, pray for them. You never know what blessings or what comfort you might be sending their way.

Dear Rob,

This is William's mom. I woke up this morning with you on my heart. I don't know why. But then, I've spent a lot of the last six months not knowing why about a lot of things.

I have to shamefully admit that I don't remember meeting you. I know you were at the service and I see your name in the reception book, but I just can't recall speaking to you. If I did, I'm sorry I don't remember, because William chose his friends carefully and well and I've enjoyed every one I've ever met. If I didn't then I'm doubly sorry, because to miss meeting you is to have missed the part of my son that you carry in your heart.

And I know you carry a large part of him there. You wouldn't have done for Oliver what you did, if that weren't true. I want to thank you for that, for taking a time that would have truly sucked for him and turned it into a celebration of everything he and his father enjoyed. I could see by the posts all the work that went into it, and your gift for creativity is astounding. I know it really blessed Oliver, and in doing do, it blessed me. You did for him what his father would have, if he could. I'm eternally grateful for that.

Like I said, I don't know why you were on my heart today, but after last August I have found myself following William's high school motto, carpe diem. I thought of you, and I wanted you to know.

Thank you, again, for what you did for Oliver. Your love for William clearly showed in your efforts to comfort and encourage his son.

God bless you, Rob.

Leslie

March 2

Six months ago today, we buried my older son.

Some of the days of these last six months have been pure torture. Everything I put my hand to, every task I try to complete, every step I attempt to take toward closure, is thwarted by the enemy. I will not pretend it is not disheartening. And disappointing. And frustrating. The enemy would really love me to dive right into the pool of self pity and anger and enjoy a nice long swim. And it is tempting, sometimes very tempting, to do just that.

The enemy is sneaky that way. Getting me all tangled up in Martha-knots because of all the tasks that remain unfinished, all the loose ends that fray when a loved one dies unexpectedly and unprepared, poking at me relentlessly until I'm desperate to finish just one task so I don't have to revisit it again and again and AGAIN. Before I know it, I've taken my focus from where it should be and hand delivered it to the one entity that is sure to abuse it.

But I'm learning. Before I open my mouth or do something stupid, I try to remember to stop. Take a deep breath. Pray. Ask others to pray. Seek the counsel of brothers and sisters in Christ whom I respect.

And I wait.

Sometimes a short time.

Sometimes not.

But God always comes through.

He is never late nor early.

So put down YOUR time table.

Lay aside YOUR agenda.

Take a deep breath.

And let God do what He does best.

None of us is good at His job. Best we get on with our own.

Lord, thank You for bringing to light the dark places in my life that still need work. Thank You that no matter how many times I'm ready to give up, You never do. Thank You that Your ways are higher than my ways. Thank You that Your thoughts are higher than my thoughts. Thank You that You are never late and never early. Thank You that You never change. Thank You that You always come through. Give me the determination to wait on You to renew my strength. Let me run this race of life and not be weary. Let me walk and not be faint.

Teach me, Lord, to wait on You.

Amen.

Six months ago today we buried my son. That is not an easy thing to say, much less do. And I'm certain that it's a situation that he, and possibly many of you, his friends, have never taken into consideration.

Out of respect for your friend and my son, I'm asking that you do consider it. And before you go there, no, thinking about is not inviting it to happen.

For the last six months, in addition to grieving a gigantic hole in my heart, I have been attempting to settle my son's affairs. Doing it at all is the one of hardest things I've faced, but doing it with one hand tied behind my back has made it doubly so.

You are the children of the "net" generation. There are, most likely, millions of affordable resources out there to make a will and get it put in place in case something unexpected happens.

Do. It.

I know it's not pleasant to think about and I know you're busy and I know that your relationships and wishes change.

Do. It. Anyway.

Please, please, don't put your parents or your spouses or your significant others through the added pain of having to "figure it all out" if something happens to you. Mourning you would be hard enough on your family. Do what you can to spare them some pain.

Please.

March 6

Last week a situation arose. In the process of trying to untangle the knot, I was caught in the crossfire between two grieving souls. It wasn't the situation itself I wanted to review, but my reaction to it.

I know for a fact that the parties involved did not intend to hurt me. In my head I know that. But my first "gut" reaction to the pain they innocently inflicted was really ugly. And I didn't like it.

I didn't like me.

I'm disappointed that my first thought was for my "self" - *my* pain, *my* wants, *my* agenda. After all I have seen my Father do in the last six months, it is humbling to see how quickly I try to usurp His position in my life. I am ashamed of how quickly I succumbed to the enemy's attack. Apparently, I have not surrendered all of the anger that comes with grief. There was still one bitter root hiding beneath the surface, and this situation was just the fertilizer it needed to spring forth its ugly shoots.

One of the first things I did was seek the counsel of two strong sisters in Christ. They have helped me see this situation from two other perspectives, and, like iron sharpening iron, they are helping me to smooth the rough edges of my response and see in this opposition an opportunity to share my Father's love. It has not been easy, but we were never promised that life here would be easy.

"I have told you all this so that you may have peace in Me. Here on earth you will have many trials and sorrows. But take heart, because I have overcome the world."
John 16:33 NLT

My two sisters in Christ have done more than give me wise counsel. They have helped me see as God sees, looking beyond outward appearances and into the heart. I am grateful that God pointed me in their direction before I did or said something that would hurt others and dishonor Him. Because, from the moment I believed in Jesus as my Savior and surrendered my life to Him, it stopped being all about me.

Now, it's all about Him.

March 9

For in grief nothing 'stays put'. One keeps emerging from a phase, but it always recurs. Am I going in circles, or dare I hope I am on a spiral? But if a spiral, am I going up or down it? How often - will it be for always? - how often will the vast emptiness astonish me like a complete novelty and make me say 'I never realized my loss till this moment'?
---From A Grief Observed [41] by C.S. Lewis

C.S. Lewis was baldly honest about his journey after the loss of his wife. His observations were written, not for publication, but for his peace of mind. I believe he processed his emotions by writing.

There's a great deal of truth in what he says. Just when I think I have a handle on my grief, that I have it boxed into its little compartment and labeled neatly, it either bursts free and explodes in my face, or it wriggles out and slips up on me unexpectedly.

It also changes form, so that I'm sometimes overcome by it before I even realize it. One moment I'm enjoying a pleasant memory. The next minute I'm awash in tears and the realization that nothing in my life will ever be the same. I know the truth that can set me free, but so does the enemy, and he's had eons to perfect his skills of attack. If I am to have any chance at victory, I must walk closely with my Father and daily put on my armor for the battle that is life on this broken planet.

A final word: Be strong in the Lord and in His mighty power. Put on all of God's armor so that you will be able to stand firm against all strategies of the devil. For we are not fighting against flesh-and-blood enemies, but against the evil rulers and authorities of the unseen world, against mighty powers in this dark world, and against evil spirits in the heavenly places.

Therefore, put on every piece of God's armor so you will be able to resist the enemy in the time of evil. Then after the battle you will still be standing firm. Stand your ground, putting on the belt of truth and the body armor of God's righteousness. For shoes, put on the peace that comes from the Good News, so that you will be fully prepared. In addition to all of these, hold up the shield of faith to stop the fiery arrows of the devil. Put on salvation as your helmet, and take the sword of the Spirit, which is the word of God. Pray in the Spirit at all times and on every occasion. Stay alert and be persistent in your prayers for all believers everywhere.
Ephesians 6:10-18 NLT

I've mentioned that our ladies' group at church completed Priscilla Shirer's Bible study, *The Armor of God* [42]. It details each piece of spiritual armor with which we are equipped, its purpose, and its uses.

Belt of Truth - God's Word is truth. The more you know it, the less room the enemy has in your life to work his wiles.

Are you daily girding yourself with God's Word?

Breastplate of Righteousness - Our own righteousness is no more than filthy rags. It will not protect us, but will only hasten our fall into the clutches of the enemy. The only righteousness that can protect our hearts is Christ's righteousness.

Are you daily confessing your shortcomings and asking God to forgive you and cover you in the righteousness of Christ?

Shoes of Peace - God calls us to walk this earth in His peace. The shoes of a soldier often had nails driven down through the soles so that, in the heat of a struggle, he could plant his feet firmly and hold his ground. Our enemy hates the peace of God.

Do you daily don your shoes and plant them firmly, so that no matter what our enemy throws at you, you will not be removed from God's peace?

Shield of Faith - A Roman soldier's shield was made to protect not only him, but, when linked with fellow soldiers' shields, could be used to protect a fallen comrade. The soldiers would surround the injured and hold their shields side by side to protect him and themselves. But, the enemy knew the shields were wooden. And what fights wood better than fire? Enemy arrows were often set ablaze so that their impact could be increased. That's why the Romans drenched their shields in water.

What about your shield of faith? Do you know how to wield it effectively? Is it drenched in the living water?

Helmet of Salvation - A soldier's helmet was a vital part of his armor. If he were injured or knocked unconscious, his life might very well be forfeited in battle, and the rest of his armor rendered ineffective.

Do you wear the helmet of salvation? It's the only helmet that will withstand the enemy's attack.

Sword of the Spirit - Most of a soldier's armor was designed for defense, to protect him from attack. His sword, however, was designed for offense, to increase his opportunity for advancing, for taking ground from the enemy. To use it he had to understand it, have the strength to wield it, and keep it ready. Our sword is the Word of God.

Do you understand it? Do you study it so that you can wield it? Do you memorize it so that you have it ready?

Prayer - Prayer wasn't part of the Roman soldier's armor, but it's a vital part of the Christian soldier's. It's what gives him - or her - the breath and strength to don the rest of the armor and step into the fray.

Do you pray at all times? On every occasion? In the power of the Spirit? Are you alert? Persistent?

You may remember the biblical account of David and Goliath. King Saul urges David to wear the king's armor for the battle. David refuses.

> *Then Saul gave David his own armor—a bronze helmet and a coat of mail. David put it on, strapped the sword over it, and took a step or two to see what it was like, for he had never worn such things before.*
>
> *"I can't go in these," he protested to Saul. "I'm not used to them." So David took them off again. He picked up five smooth stones from a stream and put them into his shepherd's bag. Then, armed only with his shepherd's staff and sling, he started across the valley to fight the Philistine.*
> *1 Samuel 17:38-40 NLT*

You cannot wear someone else's armor to your own spiritual battle. If you want to be spiritually victorious, you must wear armor that fits, armor that you are comfortable in, that you KNOW.

Do you know your armor?

March 11

I'm following a chronological Bible-reading schedule this year. Today I started Deuteronomy. In the introduction to the book, I found these lines.

> *"Or perhaps you are simply facing a new challenge or a new direction in life. Read the book of Deuteronomy and find out how God can prepare you to face any new challenge you might encounter."* [43]

The last six months have seemed to be one challenge after another, but the author of this introduction is correct. God is more than enough to meet any challenge we face. And, once you've faced the challenge of coping with the death of a child, most every other challenge pales in comparison.

I'm noticing a new direction in my life, too. That's only natural, I suppose, because my life can never be as it was. There is a "before", and there is an "after". Even if I traveled the same direction, the journey would be different, because William wouldn't be with me.

March 12

This afternoon there was a ladies' reception at our church - just a gathering to promote fellowship and bonding. The pastor's wife shared a few words about what God has shown her in her own life, and she felt led to speak them over us as well. She spoke about how God cared for Hagar when she had run away from Sarai in the account in Genesis. It was her conclusion that struck me:

"You are pregnant with purpose."

This sister in Christ has walked with me through the death of my son, so she's aware of a great deal of the struggles that have taken place. She's even aware of the suggestion of publishing my journey with God through this valley. What she is not aware of - what no one is aware of - is that almost exactly three months ago (December 11), I handwrote a draft of the lines below. At the time I couldn't see how it fit into the story of my journey in the valley (that's why I never typed it up), but God used this incredible woman of God to show me where this piece would fit.

A dear friend of mine learned about my son's death about a month after he was gone. In an effort to fill her in, I organized my social media posts up to that point and emailed them to her. After she read them, she asked to use what God has done for me to encourage some friends. The thought that God could use my pain to bring others peace brought me comfort, so I agreed, and she and her daughter organized the story into a small file.

But my story wasn't - isn't - finished yet. The following month, I had amassed an equal number of pages filled with everyday miracles I had seen God perform. I shared them with my friend, and she saw more than just my story. She saw a message. When she told me what she thought, I wasn't convinced, but I asked close friends to pray that God would show me His will for this story.

And God continued to work, so I continued to write.

After I shared a third installment with my friend, she invited me to meet with her. Thinking she was tiring of the barrage of words, I was caught by surprise by her enthusiasm and her vision. Where I saw a way to process my pain, she saw a message of hope and encouragement to others - a book.

A book?! Me?!

I'm more than willing to be used by God, but a book? I'm just trying to process my own grief!

A book, Lord? I wouldn't even know where to start!

But my friend? She's a published author.

So, after praying with my friend, I sought my pastor's advice. After reading the first installment, he added his encouragement to my friend's.

Still, I remained doubtful. (I make the disciple Thomas look like an intern in the Department of Doubt.)

The Sunday following all of this, my pastor preached the second message in a Christmas series. The first message had already convicted me. It had been about Elizabeth and Zechariah and how, despite an angel's announcement of their miracle baby, Zechariah doubted and asked for a sign.

Ouch.

This Sunday, the message was about Mary's response to her visiting angel's announcement. Aside from curiosity about the physical mechanics, Mary voiced no doubt. Instead, she simply submitted. When the pastor quoted her response from Luke 1:38 NLT, I felt the Holy Spirit stirring in my soul: "I am the Lord's servant, and I am willing to do whatever He wants. May everything you said come true."

Could I do that? Step out in faith? Trust and believe? Speak those words?

Then the pastor began wrapping up his message. "God is so ready to choose and use anyone who puts their hope in God, who trusts in Christ and is ready to be launched into the purposes of the Kingdom of God."

That seems to seal it up right and tight, doesn't it?

I'm ashamed to say that there's a lot more Zechariah in me than there is Mary. Do I want to be the Lord's servant? Yes. Do I want to see His Word fulfilled? Certainly. I just don't know what His will is concerning this.

Shortly after the service ended, a dear friend approached me. She has been instrumental in helping me over the tougher spots in this journey. She has walked with me, prayed with me, cried with me. She has been the hands and feet of Christ to me. Today was no different.

This dear friend walked up to me, embraced me, and murmured in my ear, "I think you should write a book."

Wow. Just like that, this literary "child" was conceived. And, in His amazing way, God timed this message. It was given on December 11. In eight and a half months, on August 23, it will have been a year since my son died. On September 2, almost nine months, a year since we buried him.

This whole story began because I needed to process the fact that though I do the same things and celebrate the same holidays, everything is different.

Because I'm different. Some things in my life have gained meaning. Other things that used to seem important now seem petty and superfluous. But through it all, one thing has remained and will always remain the same.

God's love.

Is this a sad story? In some ways, yes. But please be encouraged by what God is doing for me. He's taking the broken pieces of my life and putting them back together. He's leaving the cracks so that His light can shine through them, and while my story is different from yours, our God is the same God. He can do for you what He is doing for me.

Let Him.

So, there I sat, listening to the pastor's wife talk about the message God had given her in January, just a month after He spoke to my heart.

"You are pregnant with purpose."

And just like when you think you're pregnant, but you have to make sure, God sent me a follow-up message.

He does seem to like doing things in threes in my story.

Later Sunday night, I received a message from my sister's friend who lost her daughter. I had shared with her all the installments of my story because she has found the path as difficult as I did, and I wanted to encourage her that she's not alone. This is what she said:

"Hey Leslie. I have found much comfort in your writing! I'm just feeling so lost tonight, it will be a month on the 14th, and sometimes it feels like yesterday and it feels like forever! I just find it so hard to believe she is gone!! I'm so confused I feel ok sometimes and then feel bad for feeling ok. What do I do? I pray all the time and I know that our Father knows what he is doing. I'm sorry to bother you though, thank you for all the words of kindness and wisdom. I appreciate you! And I feel connected to you too."

I suppose congratulations are in order.

Because I am pregnant with purpose.

And you know what? You just might be, too.

March 13

"Stay on the path that the Lord your God has commanded you to follow."
Deuteronomy 5:33a NLT

Sometimes we're called to a difficult path. One we'd not tread if we weren't commanded to. I certainly wouldn't have chosen this path on my own, but I *have* chosen to trust God. He loves me. He loves William. He loves you, too.

Today a friend of William's posted a picture of a server at Chili's that could be William's double.

I was reduced to tears.

It sounds ridiculous, but just seeing an image that looked like William, hale and whole, struck my heart like a fist. The temptation (and that it truly what it was, straight from the pit of hell) to question and rail and rage rode me hard. I wanted desperately to indulge myself, but I didn't. It wouldn't solve anything. It wouldn't change anything. And it would have been straying from the path that God has commanded me to follow. And, since this is the path He has for me, then I will stay on it. And I will follow Him.

I won't stand still.

I won't retreat.

March 15

A few days ago a patron came in to where work. She lost her mother a year and a half ago. When she mentioned all the details with which she's still dealing, I was reminded of some of the trials with which I've been struggling. I shared my losses with her in an effort to tell her that I understand her challenges.

Her response was quite consoling. She asked me to come from behind the counter so she could hug me. She held my hand. She looked me right in the eye (something I've noticed some people avoid, probably to avoid my pain) and told me how sorry she was and how she understood. And I knew she really did. She asked questions that I'm sometimes asked out of curiosity, but she was genuinely concerned. She told me her name, and she said she'd be back.

She came back today. I was called to the front desk at her request, and she presented me with a grocer's bag and said, "I've made something for you." I opened the bag, and inside was a beautiful sashay ruffle scarf in blues and

greens. She had no way of knowing my favorite color is green.

But my Father knows.

It's this kind of small miracle that helps me smile in spite of the maelstrom that is sometimes my life these days. It's like a kiss from my Father. A sign of His love. A reminder that no matter what the enemy throws at me, God is there to catch me when my knees buckle. He is not uncomfortable with my tears.

He simply loves me.

March 16

Two days ago, our worship leader approached me about teaching a song in sign language to the children in Kid's Church. She wants to do it for Easter.

That's in four weeks.

I really wanted to say no. After all, it's another milestone, and a hefty one, because last Easter season, we all got together and spent the day at Mom's.

I tried to rationalize my resistance. After all, I work full time. I'm involved in two other ministries. I'm currently encouraging two others who are mourning the loss of their children. Not to mention the ongoing dealings with two estates. And a challenging upcoming work project.

I just couldn't escape that I was supposed to say yes.

So I did.

Then I woke up this morning. My first thought was a panicked one.

What on earth have I done?! I haven't taught children in eleven years! And this is different from any other teaching I've done. What was I thinking?!

Then I read this morning's devotional in Our Daily Bread (https://odb. org/2017/03/16/spilling-through-my-fingers/). The final line put paid to all my panic.

"We can trust God to handle things that overwhelm us." [44]

So I'm trusting God to work through me to bring glory to His name with this song and these children.

After all, He is more than able.

March 17

Before I became a member of this "club", I always assumed that death happens, you grieve, then you move on.

My daddy was right about the word "assume".

Death does happen. You do grieve. And you do move forward. But the grief moves forward with you. At least it has with me. I can't outrun it. I don't have the choice to leave it behind. There's no escaping it. When I've tried to hide from it, God has sought me out and made me face it. My favorite escape is reading. Time after time, God has put a message in my path from what I'm reading. He loves me enough to make certain I stay on the path to healing.

Grief isn't just a process for me. It's a permanent scar on my heart, one that - for me - is still raw in places. Writing about that process drains the wound and helps me heal. It has been a gift from God.

How about you? Are you facing a loss? Or running from one? There is nowhere you can run that your loss will not find you. And when it catches up, it just might bowl you over.

March 18

Today is the seven-month milestone of my mother's death.

I've been invited to take a CPR class this morning.

My first thought was N-O. Not on this day. Not me. No way.

Then I prayed. And I thought. And I prayed. And God answered.

What better way to honor Mom than to take a course that might prevent someone else from walking in my shoes? What better way to honor her life than to learn how to help others keep theirs?

And, to make sure I understood Him, my Father gave me confirmation last night.

For the last few years of her life, my mother shared with me her love of crosswords. Her daily newspaper came with two. She would joke that she'd do the "easy" one and save the "hard" one for me. When we visited her, she would have a stack of newspaper sheets sitting on the piano bench for me to take home. I was often months behind her, but I did do them. I would just arrange them in date order, stack them on a shelf, and pull one down when I had a chance. I was months behind when she died. I still am. Strange as it sounds, I find some comfort in seeing her writing on the page, knowing that what is in my hands was once in hers.

Just before I went to bed, I picked up the next puzzle in the stack, (It's dated 1/15/16, and that is NOT a misprint. Like I said, months behind.). I could see that my mother hadn't finished her "easy" one, so I started scanning it to see if I could complete it. I'm attaching the picture so you can see 13 across.

Yes, right there, in my mother's own hand, is "CPR".

So, I'm going to the class. I may cry. I may have to step out. I may not make it through the class if I think too hard about what could have been. But I'm going to show up and let God do what He does best.

Have you been asked to do something, but you think you're incapable?

Good.

That way, when you do it, you will give God all the credit.

March 20

Have you ever awakened in the morning just as tired as when you went to bed?

One of my coping mechanisms these last few months is to work hard all day so that I can sleep at night. Laying awake while waiting to nod off has lost its appeal. When my mind is untethered from a focused task, it wanders willy-nilly and can sometimes get mired in all the what-ifs and if-onlys that I otherwise studiously avoid. The downside is that I can do too good of a job of it; I get so tired I either can't sleep, or my body shuts down but my mind stays up.

Consequently, I sometimes wake up tired...like I did today.

I admit to whining to God about it. After all, I'm trying to do what He's asked. I'm leaning on His strength, because I know the task is beyond my own strength. If I'm following Him, why can't I at least get a good night's sleep?

He wasn't long in answering me. When I opened my devotional booklet from Our Daily Bread, this is what He told me. (https://odb.org/2017/03/20/running-and-rest/)

"If our lives are defined by work, then what we do becomes less and less effective. Jesus invites us to regularly join Him in a quiet place to pray and get some rest.

Lord Jesus, thank You for Your example of prayer alone with Your Father. Give us wisdom and determination to make rest a priority as we follow You. In our life of faith and service, rest is as important as work." [45]

A week from today, my workplace is closing for the day for further maintenance. When this happened before, I felt God leading me to spend the day at church in prayer. His perfect timing allowed me to be strengthened for the difficult days that followed, when three ladies I know lost their adult children. This time, perhaps He's calling me to a day of rest in His presence.

Are you tired? Or tired of being tired?

Put down your To-Do List.

Pick up your Bible.

And find rest in His arms.

step 8

Planting His Seeds

Plant the good seeds of righteousness, and
you will harvest a crop of My love.

Hosea 10:12a NLT

March 23

Seven months and counting, and there are still feather moments that come from out of nowhere and lay me out flat.

This past weekend, I was encouraged to take a CPR class because I volunteer in our church ministries. I didn't want to take it, but I knew in my heart that I should. I signed up, and God showed up. I am blessed beyond measure by His constant presence in my life. He is so awesome.

I'll admit to a few tears on the way to church to take the class. I thought perhaps releasing them beforehand would give me some relief as well as reduce the possibility of breaking down in the class itself.

Right.

It started well. I felt a little weepy when the instructor was talking about his family, but it passed relatively quickly. Once I was over it, I thought I'd do okay.

Then he started speaking about what happens when you stop breathing. Without conscious thought, images of Mom and William slammed through my brain. I had to actually leave the room.

I can't tell you how much I dislike being at the mercy of my emotions, but now that this feather moment is behind me, I've had time to look at it more clearly. I don't think it was "emotions" that had me fleeing the room. I believe it was love.

Love is what drove me out. Love is what had me in the bathroom pleading with God to release me from this class and let me go home and lick my wounds. And love is what my Father showed me when He listened, He dried my tears, and He sent me back into the fray.

For Round 2.

I was okay through the rest of the instruction. I was even okay through the CPR demonstration. It was the tiniest thing that tripped me up. I guess you could say I choked on one of those feather moments.

It was the preamble to CPR - all the calling out and asking if the person is okay, can they hear you, trying to get a response, the assessing the person to see if they're breathing. I just could not get the picture of William out of my head. I got so choked up, I had to back away. Twice. Finally, the instructor (who I had learned, after my first exit, had been informed about my situation) had mercy on me and had me go straight to chest compressions.

Those I did with no trouble.

I doubt there will ever be a time in our lives when we're completely free from feather moments. The only way they could end is if our love for William were to end, and that's never going to happen. It's just that feather moments are so incredibly hard to endure. There's no warning, no chance to steel myself, or avoid them. Anything I try to do in my own strength only ends up multiplying or prolonging my pain. God is my only source of comfort in these moments. When I reach out to Him in faith, He always answers.

So, I passed the class. I'm certified in CPR.

Are you?

If so, thank you. I hope you never have to use it, but I praise God you know how if you do.

If you've never taken a class in CPR, I encourage you to do so. If it's cost-prohibitive at this point, I'm sure there are probably internet videos that at least show you how it's done. There are even books at the library, though hands-on training might be more helpful. If it's availability, call your local fire department, hospital, community college, or day care. Someone is bound to know where you can take a class. If it's embarrassment or shyness, well be embarrassed or be shy, but learn CPR anyway. Embarrassment or shyness or cost or availability won't help you if someone you know and love falls unconscious at your feet and all breath leaves their body. CPR might.

And I think William would be pleased to know that you stepped outside your comfort zone in honor of his memory.

God bless you all. Thank you for continuing to post your stories. They provide me with a great deal of comfort, and I appreciate you all so very much.

It's been seven months today. It sounds like a long time. At least it used to sound like a long time.

When you've lost a child, the way you measure time changes. Length seems to lose meaning. There's just before...

And after.

I've seen God do some amazing things in the last seven months. On good days, I rise with a sense of expectation, waiting to see what God will do. On tough days, and admittedly there are more than a few, He will send one of His little miracles to show me that He is not unaware of my struggles. And, yes, I do see them as little miracles.

While looking for the ASL sign for "miracle", I found one interpretation of it as a "holy work". That's really what miracles are: holy works of a holy God - who loves you....wholly.

Last week I was approached about speaking with a young lady who's lost a beloved relative and is struggling to cope. I was trying to explain to this sweet, grieving soul the small, everyday miracles God has done in my life these past months. God even orchestrated our meeting when we did, because, just the day before, I discovered that my coworker not only had a passing acquaintance with this young lady, but my coworker's grandmother was good friends with the young lady's relative who had passed away.

While I was speaking with her, trying to encourage her with the comfort God has given me, I suggested she keep a journal and write down the things that God does for her, the small things that show He loves her. As an example, I said she might write down, "Today I saw a bird and it reminded me of my grandmother." She got the smallest of smiles on her face and then told me that birds, do indeed, remind her of her grandmother. I didn't know that.

But God did.

And that's what I told her. I was blessed to be able to share that moment with her. It's just one in a long line of small miracles my Father has given me to comfort and sustain me on this journey through the valley.

He's blessed me with two - so far - this morning.

First, when I awoke too early, I turned on a podcast of a woman's testimony. It concluded with a reminder that the present is the only thing that's guaranteed. There's no promise that we will still be here tomorrow. I needed that gentle reminder to keep me from sliding off this path onto a detour filled with resentment that leads to bitterness and despair. That is not my destination in this journey.

The second miracle today was my devotional in Our Daily Bread (https://odb.org/2017/03/23/cradled-in-comfort/) this morning, the first thing I read when I get up. The whole devotional was relevant to me this morning, but the prayer especially so: *"Lord, help me to look to You for my comfort in times of distress."*[16]

Perhaps you're on a journey of your own. Perhaps you, too, are struggling to keep afloat in a sea of grief. Or strife. Or disappointment.

Keep your eyes open for God's little miracles in your life. They are His way of encouraging you, of showing you He sees you, He hears you, and He loves you.

Blessings from the valley,

Me

This evening at worship team practice, the set included "Expect the Great."[47]

Do we? Do we expect the Great?

While practicing, one of the wireless microphones stopped working. Adjustments and changes had to be made. One team member went in search of a substitute. Talk began about requisitioning a new one, or possibly two for a backup.

And all the time, the words to "Expect the Great" [48] were projected on the wall.

I admit I had a fleeting thought that God could fix the microphone, that nothing is beyond His ability. I also admit that I didn't voice the thought or pray.

Shame on me.

About twenty minutes later, the sound tech's voice came through the p.a. system. He said, "I was just working with this mike, and I don't know what happened, but it's working now."

I don't know what happened, either. But I know Who.

How about you? Do you expect the Great?

You should. He'll never disappoint.

March 26

You're being watched. I don't mean all the surveillance and social media that bombards us day by day, minute by minute.

No. You're being *watched*. Ears are listening. Eyes are watching. There are people in your life that hear what you say about your relationship with God. And they are watching how you act in that relationship.

They know when you're real and when you're faking. They may not be able to put a name to it, but they can tell when you don't say what you mean and mean what you say.

There was a praise and worship service at our church tonight. I love to praise and worship God. It's taken God a long time to rid me of the "we-don't-do-that-in-church" mentality that I developed at a young age. Praise and worship was my solace during the first pain-filled days after William died, and in the months since, I have felt the Lord continuing to remove the shackles of my own making and to free me to worship Him in spirit and in truth. I often sing with my hands as well, and it's for this reason that I almost always sit in the front.

That's where I was tonight, worshipping and praising, eyes closed, hands moving. That's when it happened. I stretched out my hands in a sign. My right hand felt nothing but air, but my left hand contacted with...something.

I had been sitting alone when the service started. The contact caused me to jump, startled, and I opened my eyes.

There, on either side of me, were two precious little girls. Each one was trying to copy the signs I was using to worship my Father. They were excited. They were joyful.

And their eyes were on me, while my eyes were on God.

My child may have left this earth, there are others that are watching, and God is best served when what I say and what I do both point to who He is.

March 27

My workplace was closed today for maintenance. The last time this happened, I spent the day in prayer at the church. God knew I needed His strength for what was around the corner. Within 15 days of that time of prayer, three women I know joined me in this valley; two lost sons (age 25 and 33) and one lost a daughter (age 33).

I had been on the fence about what to do with this day off. Oh, there were some administrative things I *had* to do, but I didn't feel the urgency to fast and pray that I did last time. The temptation was to roll over and go back to sleep. I have been called to several tasks recently, and I'm tired. I really wanted to justify taking the day off as a reward for all the hard work.

But I headed out to run errands. The first one was to drop off our taxes to the CPA. Right in front of the accountant's office is a church. Right in front of the church is their sign. Right on the sign.....

"Pray the hardest when it is the hardest to pray."

Doesn't it seem like the hardest time to pray is when everything is going fine?

So I went to the church today, and I spent the day resting in the arms of my Father. He led me to read verses about resting and pray them back to Him. He allowed me to pray with a dear friend.

He restored my soul.

I will be busy for the next several weeks. This day may be the only respite I get until after Easter. There's really no other way I would rather have spent it.

"Come to me, all of you who are weary and carry heavy burdens, and I will give
you rest. Take my yoke upon you. Let me teach you, because I am humble and gentle
at heart, and you will find rest for your souls."
Matthew 11:28b-29 NLT

March 28

Today I had an eye appointment for a regular checkup. It was years overdue. I thought sure I'd have to have my prescription strengthened.

My eyes are exactly the same.

Funny, that. Because these days, I see things a lot differently than I used to. Loss will do that, I think. Bring important things into focus. Shift the mundane into the background where it should have been all along.

My loss has also coated my lenses with grace, I hope, imparting to me the sight of my Father, allowing me to look beyond the outward appearance, the outward actions of others, and see the broken soul beneath.

It's unfortunate that I sometimes remove those particular glasses, and thus lose sight of what's most important in my relationships to others.

I am no better than others. They are no better than me. We are all leaky vessels on the sea of life. Some of us are rowing eagerly toward the shores of heaven. Some of us are desperately bailing trying to keep ourselves afloat.

God loves us all.

How's your eyesight?

April 2

Today someone inflicted pain on me. It's been coming for a long time. I even knew it was coming. I also knew there wasn't anything I could do to stop it happening.

I'll not shrink from the truth. I had a choice in how I responded. Just because my own wound was deliberately poked, I didn't have to retaliate with a wound of my own making.

I meant for it to hurt.

To shock.

To silence.

And it did. But it reverberated through my spirit and wounded me as well, because I knew I had disappointed my Father. He called us to live a different kind of life.

I have apologized and I've confessed to God my shortcomings. Even though that is what I'm called to do, I can't undo the damage done by my cruel, selfish words.

Your wound does not entitle you to a free pass on your words and actions to others. If you find yourself falling prey to thoughts of condemnation for those around you who carelessly or ignorantly wound you in word or deed, STOP.

Take a breath.

Inhale the grace God has given you, time without measure.

And exhale His mercy to those He's brought into your orbit.

They need it just as badly as you do.

"Lord, how often should I forgive someone who sins against me? Seven times?"
"No, not seven times," Jesus replied, "but seventy times seven!"
Matthew 18:21b-22 NLT

April 3

Seven months ago yesterday, I buried my son. With him, I buried a lot of other things, too.

My expectations of years spent with him, living, laughing, loving.

My hopes of seeing him find true love.

My taking for granted that my children will outlive me.

If I pause to think about it, there are subtle changes in me. When the phone rings these days, I don't have the slightest inclination to pick it up. I may not know who it is, but I know who it's not.

I don't anticipate holidays like I used to. Instead of marking the time until they come, I mark it until they go.

I don't look at our photos very often. Remembering what has been often brings on thoughts of what will now never be.

I don't enjoy superfluous activities anymore. Time seems more precious. I don't want to waste it on things that don't matter. I don't even want to waste it on things better done by someone else. (Tax season is in full swing. Thank You, God, for CPA's.)

My sleep habits have changed. I used to lie awake at night, trying to get my mind to follow my body in sleep. Now I keep going all out during the day, so that, at night, my eyes are shut before my head has hardly indented the pillow.

I seem to be more sensitive to the pain of others, perhaps because I look through different eyes now. I don't just *see* people now, I *look* at them. My own experience has taught me there is often more than meets the eye.

My worship has changed. I'm less concerned with what others think about how I worship and more concerned with being genuine in my relationship with God.

My prayer life has changed. I've seen God do amazing things over the last seven months. I don't doubt He'll do even more. I pray not only in hope, but in expectation. I watch and wait to see how He's going to accomplish His will.

Looking back, God has used everything that's happened these last seven months for my good. That's not easy to say. Many of the changes I can see now, I couldn't see when they were taking place. They were lost to me in the day to day struggle to regain my equilibrium in this life I didn't choose.

Are you learning to survive a loss? As the months pass and the tsunami of grief recedes and becomes more manageable, start a new tradition on the milestones.

Look back, and see how far God has brought you. Thank Him for all the times He saw you through a rough spot. Praise Him for all the friends and relatives that have held you and cried with you and prayed for you. Thank Him for His comfort and presence each and every day of the journey.

Take stock and check yourself. Make sure your wounds are clean and healthy. Don't neglect yourself or allow your wound to fester. If you're not healing well, seek the counsel of others.

After looking back and taking stock, look ahead. Thank God for all the things He is doing or going to do. Thank Him for giving you comfort that you can share with others. Thank Him that nothing coming your way will get to you without going through His hands first.

Don't let your milestones become millstones. Use them as stepping stones into closer fellowship with our Father.

April 7

My Bible reading today was the book of Ruth. The Bible I'm using prefaces each chapter with an introduction. These are some of the comments in today's introduction:

"What do you do when life caves in?" [49]

When my mother died, I was surprised, but not shocked. She had a heart condition. She was 84. She'd been sick. Granted, we thought she was getting better, but each time she became ill it took her a little longer to bounce back. When she died, I was sad, but I felt able to handle all that would come in the wake of her passing.

"I."

> *"Then, as you're still reeling, life suddenly deals you another harsh blow, another tragedy. Now what do you do? Do you run away, crawl inside yourself, lock out the world?"* [50]

When my son died, I knew I could not handle it. There was nowhere to run. I couldn't hide inside myself, because that's where the wound ran deepest. Locking out the world would have only hurt me, because it would have isolated me from the hands and feet of Christ - my spiritual brothers and sisters that came along side me and protected and loved and prayed for me when I was beaten down by life and robbed of my joy, like the man found by the Good Samaritan.

> *"The next time your life caves in, remember Ruth's faithfulness. Remember her commitment to family and to God. Self was last. God and others came first."* [51]

We don't often think of Ruth in terms of all the tragedy she suffered. She lost her husband. She didn't have the consolation of children. Her mother-in-law was leaving the only home Ruth had ever known. No one, not even Naomi, would have faulted Ruth for returning to the bosom of her family for comfort and the hope of a future family.

Ruth decides not to think of herself first. She focuses on the needs of her mother-in-law, and she willingly gives up all that's familiar to her in order to follow Naomi to care for her.

In the midst of your own hurt and anguish, is there a lost soul that needs your help? Are you willing to lay down your own pain to help someone else deal with theirs?

Whenever I have time on my hands, it sits heavy on me. I feel the enemy whispering despair at the door to my heart, so I make a conscious effort to stay busy. Tonight, time slowed as I hit a pocket of inactivity.

Before I slid too far down the slope of despair, I received a message from my sister's friend (and now my friend, as well) who lost her daughter two months ago. She'd received a letter concerning a gift I made in memory of her daughter. In thanking me, she also blessed me for sharing my journey with her. Her words encouraged me, just as my Father meant for them to do.

Later, while I was working on an entry for this chronicle, William's father called with questions about the myriad of details still in flux from our son's death. Dealing with these details pulled on memories that, tonight, I had no wish to revisit. In my heart I cried out for help.

This time God told me to put feet to my prayer. I texted my friend who's going through radiation for throat cancer. She texted me back with the good news that she's doing well. She, too, blessed me by telling me she had been praying for a request I had mentioned to her a week ago.

God is aware of all your ups and downs in the valley. If you cry out to Him, He will respond. Sometimes He sends help to you. Sometimes He sends you to the help. Keep your eyes and ears open for His answer.

April 8

Like everyone else, I have good days and bad days. Sometimes the bad days come at times that make sense. At other times, they just fall on me. I don't give in to them, but their weight can press against me until I feel like I'm constantly walking through dry, shifting sand wearing a lead apron.

The last couple of days have been some of those inexplicably bad ones. It's just a matter of time before the enemy realizes that I won't give in, but that doesn't mean I don't get weary in the battle.

Last night my Father sent the encouraging words of two friends to help me. This morning another friend contacted me with even more encouragement.

Then, this afternoon, God did this:

At Christmas, my mother always gave us each a card with her "present" inside. Since she'd already set aside her gifts before she died last August, my sister and I agreed to honor her by delivering the gifts in her absence. My sister actually wrote out the cards and put in the "presents".

It's a recurring joke in my family about me and this type of "gift". At any point in the year, I'm likely to have a portion of it sitting in its envelope at the bottom of my purse. I believe my mom secretly got a kick out of periodically asking me if I had any left and shaking her head when I reached into the depths of my purse and produced the card with a portion of its "present" still tucked inside.

Today, while completing some chores, I reached into my purse for something, but came out with something else. In exasperation, I hauled out more contents of one compartment.

I came across the proverbial envelope with the card and "present" from this past December 2016, the one my sister had given me. Then, I pulled out the second card in the picture. Apparently, in 2015, my mom gave me the same card as my sister chose for me this year. And I know for certain that my sister didn't know that, because, until I pulled the two out, even I didn't know it.

But God knew it. And He knew I needed a spiritual hug today to encourage me to keep on keeping on until the enemy retreats once more.

You are not alone in the valley. Your Father is with you. Don't be afraid to tell Him anything. You won't surprise Him, because He knows your thoughts before you do.

He is more than able to handle your discouragement and your pain, even your anger.

Let Him.

April 9

I am still fighting a heavy heart. I am not giving up, though. This, too, shall pass.

At church today, I ran into a friend from Bible study a few years back. She attends another church, but occasionally comes to ours. I know a bit of her story. She lost one son to an accident, I believe. She lost another to suicide. Her husband was injured many years ago, and has suffered many health problems since.

My friend and I haven't seen each other since before my own son died. We spent a few minutes catching up and becoming reacquainted. She shared a hug and "the look". Mothers with children in heaven know the look that I mean. It's the one that says, without words, that we understand. Then she shared some of the current leg of her journey.

Her husband's nerves are beginning to deteriorate. The pain that radiates through his body has found an outlet in words. Harsh words. Cruel words. Accusing words. Words that tear and slash and wound. In the midst of sharing her burden with me, my friend said something profound.

"I've discovered that there are worse things than death."

You know, I think she put paid to my doldrums. I really think she did. And I told her that her presence today was no accident. God knew I needed to hear from her. He knew I needed a reality check, a reminder to be thankful for all He's done for me.

So, you have problems?

You're not alone. If you look long enough and hard enough, you'll discover that nearly everyone you know is harboring a struggle in their heart.

Is your problem weighing you down? Taking more time and attention than it should?

Turn your eyes upon Jesus,
Look full in His wonderful face,

And the things of earth will grow strangely dim,
In the light of His glory and grace. [52]

April 11

I watched a documentary this past weekend where the host was visiting extremely remote islands. On one leg of his journey, he had to charter a boat to travel over 2800 miles of sea. A couple of days into the journey, the winds and the sea flattened out. The sailboat had no wind to propel it, and only enough diesel for a few days. When the diesel ran out, they did the only thing they could do.

They waited.

I think that's where I am right now. I'm waiting. I'm not even sure what it is I'm waiting for, but I'm keeping busy while I wait. I'm also keeping my eyes open, watching for God's messages to me, the little things He does to tell me He's with me, He loves me.

He's done it several times today.

The first instance was this morning. In the course of my job, I came across the book *Every Day Deserves a Chance* by Max Lucado. Once I was finished with it for the purpose of my work, I checked it out for myself. It sounded like a good source for a Bible study group, but before I recommended it to our pastor, I wanted to read through it to see how it would work.

This morning I read chapter six, "Hope for Catastrophic Days".

Been there. Done that.

Max Lucado is a gifted writer, and the chapter was filled with encouragement for those of us who've had an experience that knocked us over and broke our stride in the race of life. The whole chapter was a soul lifter.

But it was in the very last paragraph that I felt the breath of my Father across my cheek as He whispered in my ear.

"Follow the resolve of Paul: 'We don't look at the troubles we can see now; rather, we fix our gaze on things that cannot be seen' (2 Corinthians 4:18 NLT). Christ can turn your toughest days into an Easter weekend." [53]

Today is Tuesday. Easter weekend is three days away.

The first of my Father's hugs.

The second instance was on my way to work. I had to pick up a donation from a local florist shop for an event at work. When I walked through the door of the establishment, my first impression was color. The arrangements were beautiful. My second impression wasn't long in coming. It was the scented air. The perfume of dozens of flowers. But they didn't smell like flowers to me.

They smelled like two funerals.

While waiting for the owner, I began to pace, trying not to breathe too deep. I examined plants, trying to keep my eyes off the flower arrangements. I really didn't want to have to explain tears today, so I gulped them back and tried to focus on anything but flowers. The Easter lily almost did me in. My mother bought them from her church each year and always sent me home with one.

There won't be one this year.

The owner was finally free. She handed me the donated item, and she mentioned it had a good message, too. I looked down, and felt my Father kiss the top of my head.

The day continued in the same vein. My sister called to say that she'd found a piece of mail at my mother's house. The writer expressed sympathy for the death of William but asserted that, until his death was "verified", the interest and late charges on his student loan would continue to accrue. Wonderful.

But God sent another hug - this time a real one. Remember the lady that made me the scarf? She came by work today. While she was in, she asked for me. She asked me how I was doing, gave me a hug, shared some of her story of how she's coping. God knew I needed that hug from her today. I told her so.

My work day ended with an opportunity to share some of the comfort God sent me all day. It was a lady who lost her mother last October to a vicious battle with cancer. I asked her how she was doing. That's when she told me that her grandmother had also passed away recently, and they would be burying her over the Easter weekend. I told her how sorry I was. She shared some of the things she's been going through. I empathized where I could and sympathized where I couldn't. I also shared with her that I spend a lot of time praying, and that I live, walk, and breathe these days by the grace of God. May the seeds of hope I sowed be watered by the peace of God.

God gave me comfort and encouragement all day. It wasn't for me to hoard, like the servant with one talent. It was for me to share. Has God helped you in your journey? Good. Now, take a look around. Someone needs to hear what He's done for you to give them hope and faith that He will hear and help them, too.

Go plant a seed of hope. Then, watch God water it.

April 13

I'm beginning to see, in the distance, one of the destinations to which God may be sending me. Today I received a letter from a friend in Oklahoma. Many years ago I served as administrative assistant to her husband, our pastor at the time. When I wrote her in November, I asked her to pray with me about the seed of an idea my author friend had planted about publishing my journey.

My friend in Oklahoma doesn't know that, within the past week, I have contacted my author friend and asked her assistance in taking the next (baby) step toward publishing. The prospect still overwhelms me, but I feel led to pursue it, even though I am timid and hesitant about each step.

This is what my friend wrote:

"I have been thinking about what your friend suggested about publishing your grief journey. Leslie, a lot of people do not even know how to grieve or even allow themselves to do so. One of my prayers for people who have lost a loved one is that they grieve. It

is biblical and it is essential. There are even books written on how to grieve the loss of a pet. Learning how to grieve the loss of a son can be powerful. Your writing is very vivid and intimate – you should consider it."

Keep your eyes open as you walk through the valley in your life. At any point, God may call you to share what He has done and what you have learned so that others will be equipped for their own journey through the valley.

April 14

Today is my sister's birthday. I actually stayed up past midnight so I could be the first person to post birthday wishes on her social media site.

MAY 20 2017 Never Forgotten Floating Lantern Release

Saturday, May 20 at 7:45 PM

Later this morning I was scanning my own social media site and came across this invitation.

This event is sponsored by a local support group for those who have lost loved ones. I've been invited to many of their functions, activities, and meetings, but I just haven't felt called to attend. I nearly responded "Can't Go" to this one as well. Then I looked at the date a little closer.

I mentioned today is my sister's birthday, right?

Would you believe that May 20 is MY birthday?

Tears welled in my eyes when I realized what God was asking me to do. Even now, I can't say for certain I will be able to do it. But I'm going to try.

Sometimes in your journey, God calls you to a difficult place. Be assured He wouldn't ask it of you if it wasn't going to bring blessing into your life. Step out in faith. Show yourself willing. God will never let you down.

On May 20, I'm going to step out in faith and wait to see what gift God has waiting for my birthday.

April 15

We are all vessels. The Holy Spirit finds us most useful when we are empty of ourselves so we can be filled with Him.

It's no secret that I've been struggling with Easter coming up tomorrow. I've worked diligently to keep my eyes on Jesus. I'm still trying. But, last October, as William's first birthday in heaven neared, I learned the depth of love my Christian brothers and sisters had for me. I knew this holiday would be best spent by using my time to serve in the church.

Today there was a family Easter event there. I worked with one woman yesterday to do some last-minute preparations. While we worked, we talked. My work hours make it a challenge to serve at the church in this way, so this was a special time for me. It was a blessing to share it with someone who's also a sojourner in this valley. She lost her child ten years ago, but time is measured by a different ruler in the heart of a grieving mother. We didn't talk much about our loss, but just knowing she understands brings me comfort.

At today's event, I had an opportunity to speak with two other women who have been in this valley. One lost a daughter and then a son, both shortly after they were born. Many years have passed, and she was sharing with me how she has reached a place of reconciliation with her grief. A recognizing of her loss without succumbing to the sorrow. I welcome the idea of being at peace with my pain.

The second lost a son, perhaps five years ago, maybe a little more. The scar on her heart is more tender. She intimated that she still has times of sorrow. Tears were shed. Hugs were shared. I believe we were both blessed.

So, sharing my journey with others seems to be the direction in which God is sending me.

Late this afternoon, I got home and checked the mail. There was a card in it from my friend who lost her daughter in February. I have regularly shared with her the installments on my journey.

This is what she said:

"Dear Leslie,

I so can not express my thanks to you! This rollercoaster is brutal. Just reading your journal has made so much sense to me."

If you had told me in August that God would find a way to use my loss for His gain, I would have believed you because it is biblical. But, I would have had no conceivable notion of how on earth He was going to go about it.

Are you so deep in the sea of despair that you're beginning to sink? Take a deep breath, reach out your hand, and let Jesus raise you above the waves.

April 16

Today is Easter Sunday. Last Easter season was one of the last holidays we celebrated with my mother and my son. Today, my family celebrated by serving in our church. My husband served communion. My son played guitar on the worship team. I led the children in a sign choir for worship.

Getting ready on Sunday mornings is usually no challenge. We eat. We dress. We go. Today, however, we were all going to be more visible than usual, so we dressed with a little more care.

When I'm signing for others, I dress in a dark, long-sleeved shirt. Of course, today the temperature was supposed to top out at 85 degrees. I managed to find a black, long-sleeved shirt in a lighter material that would do.

But it's Easter. Everyone would be in bright colors - everyone except me. I took the scarf my library friend had made for me to dress up the shirt. If the air conditioning was high enough, I might be able to put it on after I finished with the kids. I looked for something that would hold the neckline a little higher. A necklace would do it. I pulled out the only necklace near at hand. It was a small gold cross.

It was too short.

I started checking small boxes packed in a dresser drawer, gifts from a dear friend in Texas. I found a silver cross with blue stones in one.

It was too long.

Now, I had an aunt that was an Avon representative. I have jewelry. Lots of jewelry. But if you asked my friends, they'd probably be surprised to know it. Further down in the dresser drawer, under a laptop case, some clothes, a book, and two boxes, I unearthed my jewelry box.

Amid all the pieces in there, I found a rather ornate pendant with the look of a cross in clear stones on the front. I didn't recognize the piece. (Not surprising, since I've hardly opened this box in 15+ years.) The pendant was larger than I usually wear. It looked almost like a locket.

It was a locket. I didn't remember receiving it. Still don't, for that matter. Out of curiosity, I opened it...

and felt God hug me as I looked straight into the faces of both my boys.

So I put it on and carried my babies near

my heart and thanked God for the blessings that they have been in my life.

Once at church, I began to pace before first service. I knew the children would do fine. They aced their practice yesterday. I was concerned that *I* would choke. One of the mothers that had volunteered to help saw my distress. She stopped me, spoke encouragingly to me, and gave me a hug. It took me a minute to figure out that God had hugged me again.

Her name is Elizabeth. Not Beth. Not Liz. Not Betsy.

Elizabeth. My mother's name.

God's gifts to us didn't end at the cross or the empty tomb. They began there. When you feel the weight of life press in on you, call out to Him - but not in desperation - in *expectation*.

God is waiting for you to call out to Him in faith. He wants to give you good things.

Let Him.

Dear William,

I hope you and Grammy are enjoying your first Easter in heaven. If I had known that last year would be our last Easter season together, I would have hugged you both more and told you both how much I loved you and how much you both blessed me.

The days leading up to this holiday have been fraught with battles. The enemy has tried to steal the joy I have in knowing where you are by constantly reminding of where you are not. God has sent reinforcements in the shape of friends who have listened, prayed, and encouraged me. He's even used strangers. I have learned to cry out to Him now, and then wait expectantly for an answer. It's never long in coming.

Like most of our holidays since you and Mom left, we're stepping outside our traditional celebration. All three of us are serving in all three church services today. Sherman will be involved behind the scenes. Your brother will be playing guitar on the worship team. Then, there's me.

Do you remember when you played on the worship team in Texas? I once made a comment about raising my hands during worship so you would see me. You remarked,

"If you do, Momma, it'll be just for show, because I know you won't mean it." You were right - at the time.

But that was a whole lifetime ago. I have learned to overcome my hesitancy to worship God with joyful abandon. These days, it's more unusual if I DON'T have my hands in the air during worship.

But that's not all. Today, I'll be leading our children's elementary class in signing a song during the worship services. The song is "I'm Free."[54] It's all about the freedom we experience when we ask Jesus to be our Savior. For me, it's also about you and Mom, and Dad, too, actually. You're the truly free ones.

Free from sickness.

Free from sorrow.

Free from death.

It's because of the resurrection of our Savior that we celebrate today that you are both free. Jesus' sacrifice made that possible. His death made your death a doorway. His resurrection redeemed your eternity.

When He sets you free, you are free indeed.

I love you, son. I miss you and Mom and Dad, but I take comfort in knowing where you are and Whom you're with.

Easter Blessings, William. Kiss Mom and Dad for me.

Love,
Momma

April 18

Two days ago God invited me to a holy moment, and I am still in awe of it. If you go to church where I do and were in the 10:00am service, you were a witness, though you might not know it. I want to invite you, and those of you who couldn't make it, to that holy moment.

For the Easter service, the children were slated to perform a song in sign language. God allowed me the privilege of being a part of that. The children were singing/signing the last song in the set, and they were cued to walk on stage just after the last line of the previous song.

The 8:30am service went just as planned. The children did the great job that I knew they would. We set up for the 10:00am service, got the cue, and the kids walked on stage.

That's really when the Holy Spirit began to move. One of the worship singers that day felt Him move on her. She and the whole worship team yielded to the Holy Spirit, and He swept in and amazed us all. I am shaking, just writing about it. After the singer spoke the words God laid on her heart, she invited us all to sing the last verse of the previous song one more time.

Now, in the natural world, the singer is speaking and I am facing a dozen or so children with perplexed looks on their faces, because this is NOT what was supposed to happen. I am aware that the Spirit is moving, because, instead of panic, I feel immeasurable peace, and if you know anything about the last few months of my life or the way I feel standing up in front of people, you know that was a gift straight from God. I did what I could to attract the attention of the kids, and motioned them to watch me.

Then the people began to sing.

And the kids began to sign.

And we were all swept away into the presence of God.

What a powerful Name it is, the Name of Jesus.

Those kids had never learned that song, never practiced that song, may have never heard it before the 8:30am service - I really don't know. But, God in His infinite wisdom chose a song that had some signs they *did* know, and they picked up more as we sang and they blew my socks off.

It's a moment I will never, ever forget. My thanks to the worship leader for giving me the opportunity to be a part of it. My thanks to a good friend for actually capturing the moment on film. The picture itself is part of the miracle because the man who took it was at the back of the church and didn't realize what was happening. (I enlarged the picture just to make sure, and I believe he really did catch the kids signing the unpracticed song, because the kids are on stage and the song on the projector is the one they didn't know.)

As I write this, it occurred to me that there was a turning point in that moment that I hadn't considered.

What if the singer hadn't followed the leading of the Holy Spirit?

What a wonderful blessing we would have missed if the singer hadn't stepped out of her comfort zone and yielded to the move of the Spirit in her life.

By the same token, what if I had said "no" when I was asked to teach the children? What would have happened if I decided my pain was more important than His purpose?

> Remember, it is sin to know what you ought to do and then not do it.
> James 4:17 NLT

Where is the Spirit leading you? Are you outside your comfort zone?

Good, because that's where you know that anything you accomplish is God's doing, not your own.

April 21

I am struggling with how to deal with the things William left behind. Having them around is still painful. Getting rid of them seems heartless and obscene. I know they're just things, but they're HIS things. Things he touched. Things that held meaning to him. Things that might hold meaning to others, but I just don't feel ready to willingly expose myself to the pain of sorting through them yet.

Because of my inability to do this, my grief style has been rubbing against someone else's. The friction has been uncomfortable at best and painful at its worst. I have prayed and prayed and asked others to pray. And yes, I have whined, too. I was praying again this morning, and I think it was the first time I did so about this challenge without trying to dictate to God like a child on Santa's knee. Instead of "Help me get this person to see MY point of view," I prayed "Show me how to cope with this. Show me what to do."

And He did. This morning in my time with God, He used the devotion in Our Daily Bread (https://odb.org/2017/04/21/the-gift-of-giving/) [55] to lead me to a verse that spoke to me about this tug of war going on in my heart and in my relationship.

> *John replied, "If you have two shirts, give one to the poor. If you have food, share it*
> *with those who are hungry."*
> *Luke 3:11 NLT*

What the verse doesn't say spoke to me as much as what it does say. It does not say, "Take everything you own and share it with others." It does say, "If you have two shirts, give one."

I don't have to deal with all of William's things at once.

Just one at a time.

God hasn't yet revealed how He will help me show respect to the other person's grief style while being true to my own.

But He will.

April 22

I have learned to expect the enemy to attack after an extraordinary move of the Holy Spirit. After the children's moving worship at church Sunday, I was surprised when the enemy remained silent.

I just didn't realize he had already fired his opening volley. It came in the mail, which all week I had repeatedly set aside. Until this morning. There, amidst all the bills and circulars was more paperwork concerning William's death and estate.

I'm ashamed to say that, not only did I still not recognize the enemy's trap, I fell right in it. I began to fret and stew and work myself up into a fine state.

Then God used a social media notification - of all things - to get me to take my eyes off of me and put them back where they belong. On Him.

Each morning after my quiet time with God, I post three Bible verses on social media to encourage friends and family. The notification I received was someone "liking" one of the Bible verses that I had posted three hours earlier - before I had opened the mail.

So be very careful to love the Lord your God.
Joshua 23:11 NLT

If I had been careful this morning, focusing more on loving God and less on the enemy's attempts to distract me, I wouldn't have fallen prey to his scheme. I repented, prayed, and worked at letting go of all the fretting and fussing, and focus on loving and trusting God instead. God's answer was to encourage me to reach out to someone who had offered to help before. I did. They just "happened" to be online when I sent them a message. They answered with an offer to take care of the issues.

Thank You, God.

Then, in the awesome way my Father has, He reminded me why I received the answer to my plea for help with a *second* social media notification. This one was a "like" on another of the Bible verses I had posted this morning.

I will always trust in God's unfailing love.
Psalm 52:8b NLT

Trust. That's what life with Jesus boils down to.

How about you? We all say we trust God, but what's the first thing you do when you run up against a problem?

Worry?

Whine?

Or pray?

Heavenly Father, forgive me for failing to trust You and turn to You right away when I came up against the enemy. Forgive me for forgetting that I am a child of the King. Forgive me for dropping the armor You have given me for such moments. Help me to surrender every moment and every situation and every breath to You, and to trust You to use them all for my good. In Jesus' name I pray. Amen.

step 9

Seeing Him Work

And we know that God causes everything to work together for the good of those who love God and are called according to His purpose for them.

Romans 8:28 NLT

April 23

It's been eight months today. I somehow had it in my head that it was nine months. I've tried to figure out how that happened. I guess it's just because it feels like it's been forever since I heard his voice. Saw his face. Told him I loved him.

It feels like forever, and yet it feels like five minutes. How can that be? Is it because we have an eternal soul trapped in a finite body?

We live in a wondrous age. I can call up an image of William with the punch of a few buttons, or the turning of a page in a photo album or the slipping of a video into the cassette player. On one hand, that's a marvelous comfort.

On the other, it can be very, very painful.

———————————

This morning, my Bible reading began in 1 Chronicles. The introduction mentioned the movie series, "Back to the Future." [56]

It was one of William's favorite movies.

The introduction said some things that I felt God calling me to consider.

"Are you facing a new day, a new chapter in your life?" [57]

Every day since William died is a new day and a new chapter. In each one I'm learning to redefine who I am. Not who I am in Christ. That will never change. I'm having to learn how to live as a mother who's survived her child. It's not an easy road. Who I am in Christ is what makes it bearable.

"Are you now ready to move ahead to the future?
Stop! Remember! Reflect! Look back before you look ahead." [58]

In essence, that's what this season in my life is all about. I had begun to wonder if I was walking in faith or wallowing in futility. This is confirmation that I am on the right path. I didn't learn how to be a mom overnight. I won't learn how to be a bereaved mom quickly, either.

"Remember your heritage and how God led you to this point." [59]

I've shared before that God had planted in my heart the assurance that by the time William was 33, he would be reconciled to his Father. I accepted that in the spiritual sense long before I knew the form it would take in the natural.

"Reflect on God's wonderful way of working in your life." [60]

There are so many places where God's hand was at work in this situation. In speaking to my heart about William's return to his spiritual roots, God led me to a place of acceptance before William died. God used that acceptance to comfort me when the enemy struck. He also used the Bible studies I'd taken with the ladies in our church to strengthen me for the battle, and to give me comrades-in-arms to hold me up when I fell. His whole plan is a marvelous tapestry that He has masterfully woven. It is glorious and precious, because He is glorious and precious.

"Look back so you can look forward,
and then the future won't seem so uncertain." [61]

Before August 23, there were many things I fretted over or was hesitant to do. However, I see things from a different perspective now. After all, God has pulled me through the death of my firstborn. Those other things seem insignificant in light of that.

Sign a song in church? On stage? Sure, why not. Nothing that could occur in that scenario even comes close to what I'm learning to live out each day.

Teach and lead a children's sign choir in church? On Easter Sunday? Of course. It's certainly better than sitting in the church crying at my loss instead of praising God for what, through His Son Jesus, I've gained.

Share all the parts of my journey - the good, the bad, the ugly - laying bare my heart in printed word for all the world to see?

Well, if you're reading this, then you know the answer to that one.

With William and my mom's milestones so close together, the loss of my mother is often eclipsed. I was feeling her loss keenly the last week or so. This morning in church, I was hugged by a woman sitting in the row behind me. I had never met her before, had not even been introduced. She was the mother of one of my friends. Her hug was a mother's hug, and it felt so good. It was a gift straight from God.

No matter where you are, no matter what you're facing, pray. Give God the opportunity to work on your behalf. Be willing to follow Him, not just in faith, but in expectation of the amazing things He has in store for you.

Dear William,

It's been eight months since I heard your voice or saw your smile. I could have sworn it was nine.

Sometimes it feels like it's been forever.

Then in the next breath, it feels like it's been five minutes.

Does a broken heart transcend linear time?

If you were here, I bet you could explain it to me.

I miss you.

April 24

A patron called in to work today to conduct some business. She recently lost her husband, and our office had sent her a card. She thanked me for the card, and told me a little of the story of what her journey has been like. I explained why I understood and expressed my sympathies. Then she shared something from a Christian grief support group that she's attending. She told me how the group leader explained that, due to the upheaval and disorientation caused by grief, you should put off major decisions for a time: no selling possessions, no getting rid of things, no major decisions until you've had time to process your loss.

That makes a lot of sense, at least to me. The difficulty comes when someone else's "for a time" is not equivalent to yours. Still, she also shared that the leader said not to allow yourself to be forced into doing something you're not ready to do. I understand the premise, but how does one do that without appearing uncaring of someone else's grief needs?

Lord, please show me the path between these two mountainous struggles, and help me to walk in it.

Before she hung up, this patron blessed me by expressing how much I had inspired her and encouraged her. While I know this patron by name and have conversed with her, my treatment of her - in my eyes - has not been different from my interactions with others.

Do you interact daily with dozens of people? Or just one or two? Be sure you treat them the way God commands us.

For the whole law can be summed up in this one command:
"Love your neighbor as yourself."
Galatians 5:14 NLT

You never know who is watching. You never know who is being blessed (or cursed) by your words and actions. Live as if Jesus is standing right by your side.

Because He is.

The local pregnancy center has an annual "Walk For Life" to raise funds for operations. I have participated in it every year since we moved here. Below is the sponsor letter that I sent out to raise funds for the Walk For Life this year.

For as long as I've lived in Roanoke Rapids, I've participated in the Pregnancy

Center's annual Walk For Life. It's one of the two major fund-raising events that the Center uses to support the many services and outreach programs it provides to area residents. Some of those services include free sonograms, a fatherhood class, abstinence classes in the local high school - and just recently one at the local community college as well - and, of course, pregnancy counseling services and parenting classes.

I have always set $1000 as my target goal in sponsorship. I've never made it, but I am hopeful to do so this year.

Because this year, I am walking in honor of my son, William, who died last August.

I was twenty-one when I got pregnant with William. He was an unexpected gift from God. I was months from graduating from college. My husband and I had no savings and no insurance and were barely making ends meet. But, the one thing I did have in abundance was a loving, supportive family.

But, what about women who find themselves carrying new life that don't have the support of family or friends? What do they do? Where do they go? Who encourages them, explains the choices they have, and counsels them?

That's why I walk. That's why I write this letter. I am standing in the gap for the babies who've yet to be born and their mothers who need love and support for the decisions they have to make.

I had thirty-two wonderful, infuriating, exciting, exasperating, exhilarating years with William. I would not trade a single heart-wrenching, heartwarming minute of them.

I want to give other women the same chance that I had.

While sorting through William's things, we came across two boxes of his business cards from when he was a Navy recruiter. I had no idea what I was going to do with them, but I felt God whisper to me to set them aside.

There are two enclosed with this letter. One is for you to keep, to remind you to pray for me and for the Walk for Life and for the families the Pregnancy Support Center is helping. I'm asking that you take the other and return it to me with your donation or your prayer card. Somewhere on it, write an encouraging scripture reference for a Bible verse. If you can't think of one, look me up on social media and write down one from my page.

Whether or not you can, or feel led to, donate, please pray for the Walk For Life and return the card with the Bible verse on it. It will mean a lot to me. I hope to carry them when I walk that day. I'd like to have one from each and every one of you.

Blessings to you and your family,

Me

April 25

Today was the second time I met with the person who initially saw a book in this story. Her heart for people is as big as her vision for their purpose in life. For timid little me, meeting with her can be overwhelming - but in a good, "stretching beyond my comfort zone" way.

As I pulled up in front of her home, knowing we would be discussing the next steps for transforming her vision into a reality, I was apprehensive. Am I really ready for this? What about the obstacles I face? How on earth will I overcome them, when their resolution doesn't lie within my power? When the enemy gets a volley past my armor, I can work myself up into a right fine stew. That's where I was headed, when a song came on the radio called "Giants

Fall" [62] sung by Francesca Battistelli. It's all about putting the giants in our life into perspective. After all, in light of who our Father is, the giants just don't measure up. It's only takes a little faith to make them come tumbling to the ground at God's feet. You just have to pray and believe what God says is true.

Now, I was almost exactly on time for the meeting, but I was familiar with this song, and I knew that God allowed me to hear it at that precise point to encourage me. So I sat there, eyes closed, and listened to every word. When it finished, I opened my eyes and looked at the clock, already making plans on how to explain why I was late.

The car's clock showed exactly 8:30am.

The time I had set for the appointment.

I knew God was at work. I knew we would be operating within His presence during that meeting. And I knew that God was working on something besides the reason for the meeting. I didn't know what it was at first, but it slowly became clearer.

My friend's vision extends far for those to whom she feels called, but it falters when she looks on her own purpose.

Isn't that true for all of us? Isn't it much easier to see what's obvious in someone else's life than to look into your own? Perhaps it's because when we look from the outside in, we are, to a degree, insulated from the situation. After all, it's far easier to encourage someone walking a four inch beam across a chasm of uncertainty than it is to crawl up there and walk on it yourself.

We're very alike, my friend and I. Before I left, I was led to play "Giants Fall" [63] for her on my computer. She'd never heard it before. She was moved to pull up the lyrics for herself.

Are there giants in your life? Naysayers that are wet blankets on the flicker of faith God has kindled in your heart?

Ask God for the faith to believe Him.

Trust that He will do what He says.

And then, watch the giants in your life begin to fall.

April 27

William, today is your brother's 21st birthday. You weren't big on remembering birthdays, but social media wouldn't have let you forget this one. I shudder to think what hare-brained scheme you would've come up with to celebrate it, or how many more gray hairs it would have given me.

Love you.

Miss you.

Love and miss you.

April 30

It's been four years today since my father passed away. He was the first of our nuclear family to leave here for his eternal home.

He was hardly ever sick. I'm grateful for that. And, while I've learned to live with not seeing him, my memories of him have not faded. I am grateful for that as well.

I remember his glee at telling the story of when I became ill at Murry's while we were shopping, and the employee told my dad, "Just take him in the bathroom and wash his face and hands."

I remember traveling to North Carolina to visit Daddy's relatives. On the way home he'd stop and get us a moon pie and a coke. Driving home we would sit quiet as mice in the car, so we could count the number of "splats" from the juicy bugs that floated into the path of the car. The louder they were, the more we laughed.

I remember how Daddy spoke to everyone he met. If we went somewhere together and got separated, we might find him deep in conversation with someone. When they were done, I can recall my mom once asking him, "Charlie, who was that?" I can still remember the uptilt of his head and the tiny smile that played on his lips when he quietly answered, "I have no idea."

Man, that drove Mom wild.

I remember going to the Robo-Wash car wash Sundays after church. I remember the old blanket he'd give us as we scrambled into the back of the station wagon to "plug" the corners of the tailgate window as the robot sprayed the car, because they leaked.

I remember how he'd start to tell a joke, then get all tangled up in the details. The end result was sometimes funnier than the original joke would have been.

He called paying the bills "crying."

He called me "Lollipop" and my sister - well - she had a nickname, too. I'll leave it up to her if she wants to share it.

I don't know if he was color blind, but he certainly loved putting together "unique" combinations. One of his favorites was a red and blue checked shirt and a pair of yellow and green plaid shorts.

Which he wore with football tube socks.

To the roller rink.

Where he proceeded to skate. In front of God and everybody, including at least one angst-ridden teen daughter.

My dad was raised in a different age, where men were stoic. He wasn't often emotional, so when he was, it was more profound for me to witness it.

Once when I was a teenager, sometime on a weekend, when I was sitting up watching television - probably a Saturday night - I remember he was sitting in the dining room. I got up for one reason or another, and out of the blue he said, "I just want you to know I love you." I don't know where it came from or why he felt compelled to say it, but I know it was important to both of us.

Because it was the first time I can remember him saying it. (Usually when we said "I love you", he would smile and say "Me, too.")

I'm blessed to say that as he got older, it got easier for him to say. And easier for me, too

I remember the respect he paid to my mother's parents. As kids we regularly visited their graves as well as his mother's.

I remember the only two times I saw him cry. The first was when his mother died. The second was when a family pet died.

I'm so grateful he went to heaven before William.

Daddy, I don't know how much traveling you did in heaven before Mom and William got there, but think I see some more "hysterical" tours in your future.

I love you, Daddy.

I've already written why today's date is significant in my family's life. Writing about them releases some of the sorrow as I pour out my heart, but putting that sorrow into words sometimes presses on the tender spots in my heart.

That's where I am today. I'm doing all the right things, saying all the right words, smiling, talking, but it's as if there's a ten pound weight tied around my neck - but nobody sees it.

I don't want them to see it. I don't want to see it. I don't want to feel it, either.

But there it is. God doesn't promise to give you what you want...

but He does promise to provide for all your needs.

Today I needed a hug from God. He gave me three.

Between the first and second worship service this morning, I saw a young girl headed my way. I recognized her as part of the signing choir from Easter. After we chatted a bit, she shyly handed me a picture she'd made in children's church. I recognized it as one they'd done on Easter, but she made a point of telling me, "I made another one. This one's for you."

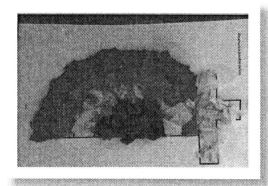

The significance of the rainbow didn't even connect with me until I began typing this. I was just blessed by the gift and the fact that she'd made it for me.

But she made a rainbow.

And the subtitle I'm currently set on for this journey is "Viewing the Rainbow from the Vale of Tears".

But there's more.

During the second service, one of the worship leaders spoke a word that God laid on her heart about the song we were getting ready to sing. Her words are lost to me, but the presence of God in her voice and her spirit touched that sore place in my heart. She pulled my attention off of myself and back to God, where it should have been. Then we sang the song "Oceans," [64] and my heart was laid bare before my Father. I remember one of the first times I heard this song, it was sung by a young mother in our church, just months after she and her husband had buried their firstborn daughter, who lived only hours here on earth.

The song is all about following God, no matter if where He leads is fraught with danger and heartache. It's all about how it is in these deepest parts of the valley of the shadow that our sense of His presence is heightened and out faith begins to grow. I had signed it in the first service by rote, I'm ashamed to say, more focused on getting it right *before* God than getting right *with* God. But this time, it landed straight on my heart and wrung it fiercely.

I needed the reminder that I am no longer defined by my circumstances, but by my Creator. Yes, He called me to walk a hard path, but He hasn't made me do it alone. He'll never make me do it alone.

That was my second hug. My Dad really does like doing things in threes.

Between service two and three, I was speaking with a young friend of mine. She was asking about the upcoming Walk For Life that supports the Pregnancy Center here in town. She knows I participate every year. I generally walk it alone, and I don't have a problem with that. This year, however, I'm walking in memory of William, and I know that all that time walking will probably be filled with memories. My young friend wasn't asking about the Walk For Life just to make conversation.

She was checking to see if she could walk with me.

Hug number three.

Usually, when I feel the weight of my losses, I keep an eye out for God's blessings because I know that He knows when I need a word or a friend.

Or a rainbow.

When the weight of your own life story weighs heavy on you, look up. Some of the most beautiful rainbows come after the biggest storms.

May 1

My work schedule had to be rearranged, and today I was off. I didn't feel the urgency to spend the day in prayer like I have in the past, but I felt a desire to be at the church. I planned on getting there around nine, but God kept putting obstacles in my way. One of them was my hunt for a shirt for the Walk For Life. Because I'm walking in memory of William, I wanted to do something to represent him. I found a bag of his t-shirts and went through them, looking for one that would: (a) not fall off if I tried to wear it, and (b) make me think of William. I found two and I set them aside to look over again later.

As I was preparing part 8 of this journey to be saved, I came across my April 23 entry with its picture.

One of the two shirts I set aside looks very much like the one William is wearing in that photo.

Now I know why God made me set them both aside.

I made it to the church just before 10:00am, but only the preschool was open at that point. I sat down in the cafe and began to work on something God had laid on my heart.

Almost three weeks ago, I came across a highly discounted daily planner at the local Christian bookstore. I stood there for a minute, trying to justify spending $3 on a four-months-gone daily planner. What would I do with it?

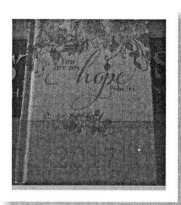

It was the word on the cover that God used to prompt me. Hope. In a Bible verse. How many verses in the Bible contained some form of the word hope?

Well, it was a Christian bookstore, so I picked up a Strong's and checked.

A lot. There are *a lot* of verses with hope in them. Perhaps enough to write them out in this book? That sounded like a decent reason to spend $3.00.

So, I've been writing out the verses in the journal. I don't yet know what God's plan for it is, but He will reveal it in His time. For now, I'm content to write them down, ponder some of them, rest in the promise of others.

Sitting in the church's cafe, I continued on with writing down hope verses. I don't know how many I had done when I came across one that quickened my spirit.

> *May all who fear You find in me a cause for joy,*
> *for I have put my hope in Your Word.*
> *Psalm 119:74 NLT*

That's me. That's what I'm doing. All my hope is in God's Word. John 1:1-2 NLT tells us, *"In the beginning the Word already existed. The Word was with God, and the Word was God. He existed in the beginning with God."*

Jesus. My hope is in Jesus. And I do want others to find in me a cause for joy. When they look at me, I want them to see Jesus.

This wasn't my purpose in stopping by the church, but it was God's purpose. I did some other things while there, prayer included, but I think His sole purpose for me today was to show me my sole purpose for Him:

> *May all who fear You find in me a cause for joy,*
> *for I have put my hope in Your Word.*
> *Psalm 119:74 NLT*

When God calls you to a plan that differs from yours, don't let the enemy knock you out of sorts. God's plan is better. *It is!* Try to rest in Him and trust in Him, and watch what happens when you do. You may well be surprised, but I don't believe you'll be disappointed.

May 2

A few weeks ago, my mind wandered to the words to the song "Taps". I was thinking about William's service held eight months ago today and the bugler playing taps while my sister clasped my shoulder from behind me. I really think, at that moment, God allowed her to hold me in one piece. It was the closest I had felt to coming unglued since it had all started.

I don't know why the words to "Taps" suddenly became important to me. I went on an internet search, and this is the information in found at www.tapsbugler. com.

> **"There are no official words to the music, but below are some of the more popular verses."* [65]

> **© copyright 2010 tapsbugler.com*

> *"Day is done, Gone the sun,*
> *From the lake, From the hill,*

From the sky.
All is well, Safely rest,
God is nigh." [66]

When the sun set on August 23, life as I had known it ended. When August 24 dawned, I started a whole new life. And while I didn't have a choice about starting down this new path, I did have a choice on how I would do it. I could do it in faith, trusting God that all would be well, or could do it in my own strength. I could safely rest in God's presence, or I could shake my fist at Him and wail about my circumstances. I chose God then, and I choose Him now.

And though my heart was cracking while the bugler was playing, I knew God was near. I felt Him in my sister's hands when she reached from behind me, clasped my shoulder, and spoke words of comfort to me.

"Thanks and praise, For our days,
'Neath the sun, 'Neath the stars,
'Neath the sky,
As we go, This we know,
God is nigh." [67]

It's difficult to thank and praise God while you bury your child, but there were things I was grateful for. I was thankful for all the days we did have William. I was thankful that he lived all his life to the fullest. I could praise God that William accepted Jesus as his Savior.

Focusing on all the good things that William brought into our lives helped me feel the nearness of God.

"Fades the light; And afar
Goeth day, And the stars
Shineth bright,
Fare thee well; Day has gone,
Night is on." [68]

Even though the sun has set on life as I knew it, there are bright points of light that shine through the darkness like stars in the night sky. The loss that those of us who knew and loved William have experienced has drawn us all closer together. It's loosened our hold on the unimportant things in this life, and made us appreciate the things that truly do matter. It's drawn us closer to the only

One who can comfort us.

And we have learned just how close the night is to the day, and that has given us the courage to use our time more wisely, to love and live more fully.

> *"Go to sleep, Peaceful sleep,*
> *May the Soldier or Sailor,*
> *God keep.*
> *On the land or the deep,*
> *Safe in sleep."* [69]

One of the most tender moments in a young mother's life is watching her newborn in sweet slumber. I will never - not EVER - forget my last look at my firstborn, whose mortal frame lay in repose but whose spirit was resting in the bosom of my Father.

He is safe, now and forever.

> *"Love, good night, Must thou go,*
> *When the day, And the night*
> *Need thee so?*
> *All is well. Speedeth all*
> *To their rest."* [70]

No matter how much we thought we needed William, we need God more. As long as He is on the throne in our lives, all is well. Storms will come, but the Rock of our salvation will remain, steadfast and immovable.

And one day we, too, will speed to our rest in Him.

May 7

Today is International Bereaved Mother's Day. I had never heard of it before this week. From what I've read, it began as a memorial day for mothers whose children left this earth very early, sometimes in utero. It seems to have grown to encompass those of us who've lost an adult child. In truth (and I don't share this often), I've lost one both ways. My youngest would be sixteen now, and though there was no way to tell, I've always imagined her as my daughter.

Among the posts for this day were stories about pictures taken with your hand over your heart. I'm not photogenic, and I don't like being photographed, but I did want to do something to celebrate William today. I didn't want to make a big fuss or have anyone notice. I just wanted one of those mother-son moments. I decided to wear a necklace, one that had a heart on it, if I could find one.

I've explained what it's like to try to get to my jewelry box. And it was Sunday morning. I was going to be pressed for time if I was going to try to dig it out

again. Then I remembered that, nestled around the jewelry box, are smaller individual boxes, gifts to me from a dear friend out west where we used to live. I can't remember if it was the first box I pulled out or the second, but when I opened it, I knew it was right.

The heart being pierced by the cross spoke to me of both pain and love. That's where a grieving mother's heart sits - on the threshold between pain and love. The absence of your child means the two are intertwined, just like the heart and the cross on the necklace.

I didn't tell anyone the significance of the necklace. I touched it often and thought of my firstborn and celebrated in my heart all the years that God gave me with him.

When I got to church, the worship leader greeted me. She spoke with regret that she hadn't contacted me sooner to ask me to sign the song "Fierce" [7][1] in worship today. I took a few seconds to think and then told her I would do it if she wanted me to. She said yes. So I did. It wasn't perfect and I stumbled in places, but it came straight from my heart. If you look up the words, you'll understand why.

When you are God's child, He won't let you hide - not from Him and not from life. It may hurt. You may cry. But you will never be alone in your sorrow and tears. Never. Sometimes, that's the only comfort you have. Always, it is enough.

Today at church I also had a chance to share a kindness with a young boy - the worship leader's son, actually. A Legos book he enjoys borrowing from the library was nearly worn out and had to be removed from the library collection. I bought it and obtained permission from the worship leader to give it to him. I explained to him that it was quite beat up, but the light in his eyes wasn't dimmed at all, and with great enthusiasm he thanked me and said, "I don't care if it's worn!" Sharing that book unleashed memories of William and his enthusiasm for everything Legos. William and I would play with them for long stretches of time. (Okay, I mostly organized and he played, but we both had fun.) The memories didn't sting, as they have in the past. Instead, they warmed my heart.

Lord, thank You for the opportunity to celebrate William in my heart today. Thank You for the gift of memories of good times. May each bereaved mother have the joy of a memory today. In the name of your Son Jesus I pray. Amen.

May 10

Today was the start of a new ladies' Bible study. It's based on Shawna Niequest's book *Present Over Perfect* [72], and it's about learning to live our lives with the balance God has always intended. For the most part, I have learned this lesson. That's why I was puzzled about why God put me in this class.

Then, one by one, the ladies began to share their stories. In at least two, I heard the voice of loss and heartache. Their stories aren't mine to tell, but in those stories I heard God whisper part of my purpose in being in the class. Certainly, I will gain valuable wisdom from the curriculum, but I will also have an opportunity to share what God has taught me on this journey.

It will be challenging and stretching. I don't doubt it will be painful, too, but I am willing to bare my pain if it will help someone else avoid it.

May 11

I saw an online popup advertising low cost airline tickets for Mother's Day, which is May 14. I never thought about airlines taking advantage of this holiday to boost sales. One ad says "Go visit Mom or bring her to you."

Oh, if only it were that simple.

God is not unaware of the sorrow that settles in my heart at the mention of Mothers' Day. If I turn from the pain of my son reaching heaven before me, then I come face to face with the ache of missing my mother. Added into the mix is my effort to appreciate the living while cherishing the memories of the dead.

I honestly don't know how I'm going to do it.

Today I received flowers and chocolate from my stepdaughter and her fiance'. They wrung my heart, not because William had ever made such a noble gesture, but because now he never could.

Included was a note from them encouraging me that they were praying for me at this milestone. Those flowers were on their way, probably, before I saw that ad that plucked my heartstrings. God knew I would need them. He knew I would need prayers and encouragement.

My Father always knows what I need. And what you need. Trust Him. He will provide.

> Happy Mother's Day Leslie!
>
> I will be thinking of and praying for you as you pass this next milestone. Blessings!!! I love you!
>
> Sherrie & Bryan

May 12

Today, my friends and family helped me reach the $1000 goal I set for the Walk For Life. I know many of them sacrificed to make this possible. One is recovering from cancer. Several know the heartache of child loss. There is a story behind each of the thirty-eight people who responded to my letter. Because I know a portion of their stories, their sacrifice is all the more precious to me, especially since this year I'm walking in memory of William.

Mothers' Day is around the corner. It's followed closely by my birthday and my anniversary. Even though these are my milestones, not William's, it still hurts that he's not here to share them.

God knew I would need encouragement for these days. He sent it in the shape of friends and family who, once again, stepped up and became His hands and feet.

Are you facing an uphill climb? Are you out of breath? Exhausted? Discouraged? Call out to God. Be totally honest with Him. You won't be telling Him anything that He doesn't already know.

May 13

Many of you have expressed your encouragement and prayers for me for Mothers' Day tomorrow. I want to say thank you. You're all such a blessing to me. I wanted to share with you how God answered your prayers yesterday.

In the morning, I often pick up a crossword puzzle from my "Mom" stack after my quiet time with God. Something about focusing on the words and filling in the blocks helps me organize my thoughts. Yesterday finished a Crytoquip (a word puzzle where each letter has been replaced with another letter so that the message is coded), then moved to a crossword puzzle that I had begun previously. I found the next blank answer, 34 across, and looked for the clue.

"34. Carpe _____: seize the day"

William's phrase from high school.

In a crossword puzzle my mom gave me.

Happy Mothers' Day to me.

God has always been aware of how difficult Mothers' Day would be for me. As the day draws nearer, I feel the weight of my sorrow press hard on me, and the enemy has issued more than one invitation to a "poor pitiful me" party thrown in my honor.

He will attend that celebration alone.

Because, even on days when the fog of grief is so thick that I can't see God's answers, they are still there. He is still at work on my behalf, using the ugliness of this sin-broken world to point me to the beauty of the spiritual one.

The same holds true for you. No matter what your circumstances, God has not forgotten you. Yes, it's tough to hold on. Yes, you might get frustrated, angry, tired. You might even cry a flood. But just remember this.

God hasn't given up on you.

Don't you give up on Him.

His timeline is not our timeline, but His is supremely superior to any plan we might attempt to make. He is working. You may not see it at first, perhaps because it doesn't look the way you thought it would.

Perhaps it will come in a bouquet of flowers.

Or a social media post.

Or a clue in a crossword puzzle.

But it will come. Don't let the enemy distract you so that you miss it.

May 14 - Mothers' Day

For the first time I can remember since I asked Jesus to be my Savior 29 years ago, I got out of bed, glanced longingly at my pillow, and entertained the thought of deliberately skipping church.

Just being honest here.

Because today, when I walk into church, I know I'll see a lot of smiles. There will be laughter and joy and thankful mothers with their children everywhere I look.

But I also know that behind some of those smiles are people who can only celebrate their mother in their heart. Her memory will be treasured as much as her presence will be missed.

I know there will be mothers hiding broken hearts, too. They will work hard to keep the pain from showing. What mother would bare her brokenness in the sight of her surviving children whose sole purpose today is to celebrate her? It wouldn't be right and it wouldn't be fair.

Losing your mother is hard.

Losing your child, doubly so.

Losing both really sucks.

And yes, I just said that.

And God knows my feelings on the subject. He's strong enough to handle them. I'm weak enough to let Him.

If at times today I look like I'm walking on eggshells, I probably am. I'm tiptoeing around my grief because I want it to lie dormant for this one day so I can celebrate with my family. If it means skirting issues and topics and stepping outside for a moment here or there, then that's what I'll be doing. If you're tempted to follow, be forewarned. The state in which you find me probably won't be pretty. I won't mind, but if you will, then just pray for me. I'll understand.

Happy Mothers' Day, Momma. I love you.

———————————————————————

Church was hard for me today, but then, it would have been a hard day no matter where I was. A few people wished me a Happy Mother's Day, and each time it was like being jabbed with a very sharp pin. I hope that doesn't sound condemning or judgmental. I don't feel either, because I know they meant well. They didn't mean to cause me pain. They loved me enough to acknowledge the day, and I am blessed that they care.

There was one dear friend whose love truly touched my heart, though. After second service, she came up to me, hugged me long and hard, and kissed my cheek. She didn't say a word, and she didn't have to. She knew. I knew. And it was enough. It changed my perspective on the day. Instead of remembering those that unintentionally caused me pain, I remember the love that helped me bear it.

There are places in this journey that are fraught with pain and heartache. You can't avoid them, and some you just can't share. Walk through them in faith. God will not let you down.

May 17

Tonight was the second meeting of our ladies Bible study. I signed up for the class primarily because it fit into my schedule. The study is on learning to strike a godly balance in your life. God has repeatedly taught me this lesson so that I'm in a good place right now, but it doesn't hurt to examine your heart regularly and make sure your priorities align with God's.

Last week I had an inkling that God was using me in a way He hadn't in the past. It was brought home to me even more clearly today.

The leader shared with us that one of the ladies was going to be absent. Her husband's twin brother, at only 40, had passed away unexpectedly.

His name was Will.

I couldn't make this up. I wouldn't make this up.

Does God have you in a place that puzzles you? Be assured that it is not a mystery to Him. Ask Him to prepare you for what He's got planned for you.

God delights in concealing things;
Psalm 25:2a MSG

May 18

It's been nine months since my mother died, but today I want to talk about some other mothers.

For as long as I've lived here, I've participated in the local pregnancy center's annual Walk For Life. It's one of the two major fundraising events that the center uses to support the many services and outreach programs it provides to area residents. Some of those services include free sonograms, a fatherhood class, abstinence classes in the local high school - and just recently one at the local community college as well - and, of course, pregnancy counseling services and parenting classes.

I have always set $1000 as my target goal in sponsorship. I've never made it to my goal before.

This year I did. Well, actually, YOU did. I put out the call, asking you to help me honor William's memory by sponsoring me in this year's walk.

You have responded and blessed me beyond measure. So far (and I say so far, because I know you're not done yet), you have donated or pledged a total of $1,515.

I was twenty-one when I got pregnant with William. He was an unexpected gift from God. I was months from graduating from college. My husband and I had no savings and no insurance and were barely making ends meet. But, the one thing I did have in abundance was a loving, supportive family.

But there are other mothers out there that don't have that support system. They scared. They're confused. And vulnerable. Very, very vulnerable.

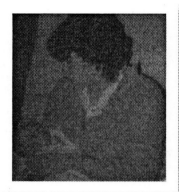

That's why I'm walking tomorrow. I am standing in the gap for the babies who've yet to be born and their mothers who need love and support for the decisions they have to make.

I had thirty-two wonderful, infuriating, exciting, exasperating, exhilarating years with William. I wouldn't trade a single heart-wrenching, heartwarming minute of them.

I want to give other women the same chance that I had.

To those of you who have donated, thank you so much! It is a privilege to present your offerings to the support center on your behalf. Thank you for your encouraging words and verses. I will carry the cards and notes with me as I walk, and I have looked up and written out all the verses. They have been a blessing to me, not only for their content, but also because you all took the time to look them up and send them to me. Thank you, again.

For those of you who are interested in donating, it's never too late. Contact me and I'll send you the info, or, if you received my letter, you can use the info in it to donate. In fact, if you want to pledge $10 or more, the pregnancy center will bill you for your convenience. Just let me know.

Thank you for praying for me and helping me honor William's memory in this special way.

And, if you're in my area, consider coming out to show your support for the pregnancy center and for Fridays in the Park. The Walk For Life will be sharing the park with a band and a number of activities that your family will enjoy. I would love to see you there.

May 19

Tonight is the pregnancy support center's Walk for Life. I took the day off so I would be ready for the event. While at home, I was helping my husband do some "housekeeping" in his social media account. In the process, I came across an old group message that I had started back when my mom first fell ill in early August. I remember the group message, but I don't remember William's response. The message is long gone from my account, but I am grateful to God that my husband is not as vigilant about his messages.

Note the date. My mother died August 18, and my son on August 23.

I know God allowed me to see this to encourage me that I'm in His hands. He is aware of the sorrow and pain that I carry. I often try to keep it tucked out of sight of friends and family, but it is always in full view of my Father.

I am not ignorant of the fact that the enemy also knows of my pain. I can see his taunt evident in William's ironic reply. However, God has given us the gift of free will. I can't always choose my circumstance, but I *can* choose how I respond to it.

I choose to be grateful for the reminder that William loves me. And I used present tense because I know he still does.

A week ago I pointed out the tough moments coming. I knew this would be one of them. God did, too, so He sent me a hug from William.

I won't let the enemy steal my joy in that. Don't you let him steal yours, either.

In about an hour, I'll be headed to the pregnancy support center's annual Walk For Life. I am honored to be able to deliver the pledges and donations of all my family and friends.

ALL $1,760 OF THEM!

So far, I have received 38 letters with donations, pledges, encouraging words and Bible verses. My heart is full and I very much suspect that my eyes will soon overflow. God knows how much it means to me that William, even after leaving this earth, has been able to be a part of giving life to others. It cannot heal my broken heart, but it does soothe the ache.

Ordinarily, we wear a specially designed t-shirt for the walk. This year I have chosen to wear one of William's shirts. I thought it was the one he's wearing in this photo. It isn't, but it's very close and it's his. I don't think he'd mind that it will be sweaty and tear-stained by the time this night is over.

I am so grateful to God for all of my friends and family that have supported me in the Walk for Life. In addition to the thirty-eight who responded beforehand, the pregnancy center director, who is aware of my journey, shared a special scripture with me just before the walk began. I carried everyone's notes and prayers and scriptures with me. I wrote out the scriptures in a small notebook, and when I felt the weight of my grief, I pulled it out and read from it the precious words that my dear ones shared with me to encourage me and give me hope.

Because of their generosity and prayers, I turned in the highest amount of donations for adult walkers at the Walk for Life tonight. In addition to the special t-shirt for surpassing $100 and a gift basket for surpassing the $250 mark, I also received a trophy for turning in the most donations for an adult. I believe I will add the trophy to the shelf with William's memorial candles and vase.

After all, it's really HIS trophy.

———————————————

I'm friends with the pregnancy center director. When she was announcing the top walkers, she told the story of why I was walking this year, why I was wearing William's shirt. Usually, I don't like being singled out like that, but it felt right to share William tonight.

Of course, the director also stood up there and said my story was being published. Perhaps God has convinced everyone but me.

Oh me of little faith...

May 20

I don't usually announce this, but today is my birthday. When I say I don't announce it, I mean I keep so quiet about it that, many years, my own immediate family has forgotten it.

I really don't mind.

Lucky for them.

Even though it's likely William would have forgotten, hope springs eternal in a mother's heart. He *might* have remembered. Maybe.

Probably not.

But I love all my boys the same, either way.

As I mentioned a month ago, I received an invitation to a local event for those

239

who have lost loved ones. I've been invited to many of their functions, activities, and meetings, but I just haven't felt called to attend. I nearly responded "Can't Go" to this one as well. But God made it very clear that He wanted me to be at this one.

I received the invitation on April 14......my sister's birthday.

The event is today........my birthday.

The event is a floating lantern ceremony. The lanterns are decorated for each lost child, a battery-operated tea light is put inside, and they are floated on a pond in a local cemetery. I picked up the lantern a week ago. I decided that I wanted to share the event with William's family members that have also lost children. There were four sides to the lantern, so William's image is on one, and memorials for his uncle

Wes, his brother DJ, and his cousin's son Ryder are on the other three sides.

I've never done this before. I might never do it again. But I know I'm supposed to do it tonight. You and I are not alone on this journey. There are others in this valley before and behind us. Tonight I'm asking that you pray for them, especially those that don't know Jesus as their Savior.

Getting ready for floating lantern ceremony, I remembered that there were two shirts that I had waffled between wearing for the Walk for Life yesterday. I suppose God had me pick two, so I could wear the alternate tonight.

Public recognitions of my loss are very hard for me, but I'm not doing this just for me. I'm doing this for all of us who lost William and DJ and Wes and Ryder. I don't enjoy the thought of my loved ones enduring the same kind of loss as I have. I know I am as helpless to relieve their sorrow as they are to relieve mine. However, I can honor the memories of their loved ones in this one gesture, however small it seems in the face of such huge loss. Knowing that I am there representing them as well as myself brings me a measure of peace, too.

We just returned from the Never Forgotten Floating Lantern Release. It was beautiful. I can't explain the strength it brings to stand with a group of people  whose names you don't know, but whose pain is all too familiar. There is an invisible thread that connects people who have experienced this kind of loss. I can't explain it, but if you're "one of us", then you'll understand. If you're not one of us, then I thank the good Lord.

The ceremony was planned by a local group called Trinity Outreach Ministries. One of the ministry's leaders led out in prayer. Then one of the bereaved mothers spoke a few heartfelt words. Then, each child's name was spoken aloud. There were six pages that held 140 names. I was asked to read the last page of names. God was merciful, because I don't think I could have read William's name. It was crushing just to hear it

After all the names were spoken, we moved down to the pond and released the lanterns.

The weather was cool and breezy, and it was beautiful. While I watched the lanterns glow and float, I opened my music and played "Amazing Grace (My Chains are Gone)." [73] As the sun set and the light faded, I snapped a few pictures to share with loved ones. The one here was the final one that I took.

I've looked at this picture several times. To be honest, I don't actually recall lining this one up. In the top left corner, you can barely see the plumes of the fountain that sits near the middle of the pond. When I studied the picture, the three plumes reminded me of the Trinity. That's when I felt the Spirit move on my heart.

This branch of the ministry is called Trinity's Angels. Yes, I'm aware of the theological inconsistencies of calling our loved ones angels, but bear with me here.

It's amazing how God can take one picture and speak so many things to your heart. When I first looked at this picture, what I saw in my heart was the Trinity lighting the way for our children who have been called home. Some of our children are farther ahead on the path than others, but they are all in our Father's hands.

As I contemplated this thought, I realized it also represents the families they've left behind, because we're also in different places in our journeys of learning to live with loss.

While I was still adding that second thought here, I realized there is a third perspective, too. (Our Trinity God does love showing me things in threes). Those lanterns headed toward the fountain are a picture of our overall lives, our journey here on earth. Our ultimate goal is still ahead of us, and while we are here, it is our privilege to let God's light in our hearts shine through our lives so that others can see that He is the reason we have survived the tragedy of child loss. His light is what gets us through the dark places. The winds of change blow may across our lives in hurricane force, but they cannot extinguish the Light of the world that resides in God's children. And the thinner the paper gets as we are buffeted by the storms of life, the brighter God's light can shine.

I wish I were better with words. Perhaps it's true that a picture is worth a thousand words, because even if I used that many, I don't think I could describe all that God showed me in that one picture - one I don't even recall framing and shooting.

I know for a fact that some of these children have been gone a long time. I found it very comforting to know that their loved ones still felt the tug to memorialize their absence. Society often seems uncomfortable with our grief and would prefer we "get over it". It's comforting to know that there is a group of people who understand that that is never going to happen on this side of heaven.

If you are in this valley, I encourage you to at least consider looking into a support group such as this one. You may not need it for yourself, but someone there may need to hear your story. Ask God to show you how and where His purpose would be best served.

May 21

I received a message from one of the Trinity's Angels ministry leaders today. William's memorial lantern survived the overnight swim. Once it dries out, I will pick it up. I think I'll add it to William's memorial shelf. When I feel the solitude that often accompanies sorrow, I can look at that lantern and know that I am not alone. I can pray for those before and behind me in this journey.

This afternoon I saw a post on William's memorial page. One of his friends was at the cemetery trying to find his grave. They didn't have directions or a map. If you've ever been to a military cemetery, you know the difficulty they were having.

God made sure I saw their post within minutes of their sending out the SOS. I've only been to the site once. I have no desire to return, at least not right now. However, I can close my eyes and I can see in my heart exactly where William's grave is. So I did, and I gave them directions.

Me.

The one who is so geographically challenged, I often visit a place before I have to be there. The one who once, years ago, got lost between home and church, a roughly two mile trip. The one who, more recently, spent an hour riding up and down a country road looking for the driveway of a friend, which I passed by more than once.

But this destination, I knew only too well. And, with God's help, I led them right to it.

If you've weathered a storm in your life, you have a responsibility to those coming behind you to share what you've learned. You should prepare yourself to help them navigate unknown territory. So take note of your journey. Record it. Photograph it. Scrapbook it. Post it. Do whatever it takes to take what the enemy meant for your harm and use it for the good of others. It won't remove the pain in your heart - nothing will - but it will bring you a measure of comfort to know that your pain is helping others manage their own.

step 10

Accepting His Change

...let God transform you into a new person by changing the way you think.

Romans 12:2b NLT

May 23

I have been mourning the loss of my son for the same length of time it took for God to knit him together beneath my heart.

Nine months.

We as a culture have a great deal of patience with expectant mothers and their talk of the impending birth. We even have a great deal of patience for new mothers when they, rightly so, enthuse about their newborns, toddlers, and even their young children.

We "ooh" when Johnny gets a new tooth.

We "aww" when Sally says her first word.

We "wow" when they take their first steps.

Does our culture show the same patience for a mother going through the "firsts" of child loss?

The first birthday.

The first Christmas.

The first Mother's Day.

Are we as careful of the new *grieving* mother's feelings as we are of the new mother's?

I am blessed to be able to say that almost everyone I know has been. God has gifted me with amazing family and friends who've walked with me through this valley with patience, love and compassion.

However, I have to admit to some misconceptions on my own part. Before last August, I thought grief had a beginning and an end. I thought there was an established time frame. The "pre-loss" me thought that grief and mourning were straightforward, natural processes: step 1, then step 2, then step 3.

Ignorance, in this case, truly was bliss.

Because my grief is not a process. Processes end. They come to a conclusion. Task completed. Line item checked. Done and done.

But I will never be done. How do you "finish" grieving the loss of your child?

As a young mother's child grows and leans less on her and stands more on his own, her conversation will reflect that time and distance. As I grow farther from my son's death, I suspect mine will reflect that time and distance, too.

But a young mother will ALWAYS be ready with a word or a story about the blessing that is her child.

So will I.

> *...but Mary kept all these things in her heart*
> *and thought about them often.*
> *Luke 2:19 NLT*

Dear William,

I've been mourning you now for the same amount of time that I carried you.

Nine months seemed a long time when we waited expectantly for your arrival.

It's not long enough to recover from a blow like this.

Life is not the same without you.

Now I wait expectantly for the day we're reunited in heaven.

Until then, there will never be a day I don't miss you.

You will always live in my heart.

I will forever be...

Your Loving Momma

May 24

A good friend at work announced her retirement today. I knew it was imminent. The signs were there, but like we all sometimes do, I walked around the elephant in the room.

But the elephant just stepped on my heart.

I've known this woman of God for ten years, and we've weathered quite a few crises - work and personal. The one thing I knew through all the madness that is life is that she had my back. She even had my back when I didn't. In those times when I couldn't or wouldn't speak for myself, she did. She is an incredible witness for Christ.

Who's leaving.

I know it sounds whiny and self-pitying, but this is another blow to my already wounded soul. In essence, it's the death of my job as I know it, at least for the foreseeable future as we try to fill the shoes of someone who's job might be taken but whose place never will be. My relationship with my friend will necessarily change, because we will no longer share 40 hours a week.

Don't get me wrong. I'm ecstatic for my friend. She's worked long and hard, and she deserves this. She's earned it ten times over. I can only see good things ahead for her as she steps out in faith to follow God's leading for the next part of her life's journey.

But I am feeling awful sorry for me right now. Awful sorry.

Change. Change. And more change. That seems to be what this season in my life is all about.

That's what I feel in my earthly, sinful self, but in reality, we are changing from the moment we are conceived until the day we return to God's presence. I think I am just more sensitive to it at this point because so much of it came to me in such a short span of time. Now I find my first reaction to change is dread, and that's downright ungrateful of me. After all that God has seen me through and shown me in the process, how dare I whine because I've been given more

248

opportunities to see Him work?

Perhaps you're in a season of changing, too. Won't you join me in looking for the good God has promised us in all things?

And we know that God causes everything to work together for the good of those who love God and are called according to His purpose for them.
Romans 8:28 NLT

May 25

Dear Friends and Family,

Thank you all for your outpouring of love for the Walk for Life. Your donations tallied up to $1760 when I turned them in. Since then I've received a few more donations and the total has risen to $1830. The

encouraging words and verses you shared filled my heart. I wrote out all the verses in a notebook, and I read some of them before the walk started. I carried your messages and cards with the scriptures on them with me as I walked. They gave me strength, because they were shared in love.

You all raised so much money that I was the top adult walker. In the grand scheme of things, that means very little. However, as an expression of your love and respect for William, it blessed me beyond measure to know that, even after he left this earth, he was able to save lives through your generosity.

From the bottom of my full but aching heart, I thank you.

Sincerely,

Me

May 28

I had a feather/hammer moment today. I don't know which to call it, because it may have been a feather, but it landed on an already heavy heart, so it felt like a hammer.

They played a Memorial Day video at church today. In the video were scenes of military cemeteries. If you've been to one, you know how similarly they are laid out. It reminded me of the one where William is buried.

But it was the photos of flag-draped coffins that did me in.

So many milestones this month. So many days fraught with emotion and sorrow that I've begun to suppress because I unconsciously assume it's as hard for people to understand this kind of grief as it is for me to experience it.

But I'm weary. So very weary.

Not tired. Tired implies that a little rest will eliminate the problem. Sleep won't fix this. My weariness is a condition of my heart. And I've brought it on myself, for the most part. It comes from carrying all the milestones of this month as if they were just that - stones. It's not that I could avoid them. I couldn't. What I could have done, however, was lay each one at the feet of Jesus. Instead, I think I've emotionally held on to them, dragging each one into the next and the next and the next until I'm barely able to move forward.

Weary.

Tired goes away with sleep. Weary rises with you each morning and follows you throughout the day. It's that feeling that you get when you wake up knowing that you're facing another day of uphill climbing. With a full pack. Loaded with all the emotional baggage you added to that already-full pack.

Weary is in your every step. It's in your every breath. And, if you're not careful, you can become so accustomed to its presence, you find yourself uneasy in its absence.

Stop often on this journey. Examine yourself. Do you feel like you're out of gas all the time? Are you spreading yourself too thin, perhaps in an effort to dull the ache in your own heart? Do you wake up in the morning in expectation of what the Lord has for you, or in dread of what He hasn't?

Weariness is not working for me. It won't work for you, either. Only one thing will cure it.

> Then Jesus said, "Come to me, all of you who are weary and carry heavy burdens, and I will give you rest."
> Matthew 11:28 NLT

Give the milestones to Jesus. Find something in them to thank God for, even if it's only because you survived them and they're over. Pray, and be honest in your prayers - with God and yourself. It's not as if God doesn't already know the truth. And giving voice to it might just set you free from it.

May 29

I've gotten the (possibly mistaken) impression that there are those within my circle of acquaintances that think it's time I "move on" from my grief. I can understand where they'd think that nine months might be enough time to "get over" my loss. I've read a couple of articles written by wounded people who have been further injured, unintentionally I'm sure, by well-meaning friends and relatives who think they know better.

Please understand I am not speaking of unhealthy grief, and I acknowledge that it does exist. However, I suggest that, if you suspect such a thing, you seek the assistance of a pastor or a trained counselor. Unless you are one yourself, please refrain from offering your loved one help or advice. It will not be well received and it will most likely cause a fresh wound to their souls that they don't deserve.

Having your child precede you in death is like being pushed down a deep, dry well. It's dark. It's scary. And you feel so isolated, because the circle of people you know that have walked through this is small to non-existent. In the bottom of the well, you find a table spoon. After you conquer the shock and fear of being thrust down a dark shaft with no way out, you turn to the practical issue of trying to make a way out.

So, you take the spoon, you feel around, and you decide to dig out steps in the side of the shaft. It's hard work. You sweat. You blister. You cry. But you keep digging. Every once in a while a step crumbles and you get discouraged, but eventually, you pick up the spoon and try again.

Your friends and family stand at the lip of the well and shout encouragement - for a while. Then one by one, they fall silent. As you continue to dig and slip, dig and slip, dig and slip, the murmurs start.

"Maybe you're not trying hard enough."

"Maybe you really don't want to get out."

"You'd be out by now if you just did 'a' or 'b' or 'c'."

Then, one by one, they drift back to their own lives and leave you to get to it.

And still you dig. Still you slip. But the only person who hears you now is God.

Unless you have been in the bottom of that well of grief, unless you yourself have clawed your way out of that deep dark pit, you have no point of reference for the monumental task before those of us down here. You can try to imagine, but we all know that imagination is not reality. If you have true concerns for the mental health and physical safety of your loved one, seek professional help. You wouldn't attempt physical heart surgery if you weren't a doctor and you should attempt spiritual heart surgery unless you are a counselor.

June 1

There was worship team practice tonight. Afterward, the leader encouraged us to gather and share what God has been showing us in our lives.

At first I drew a blank. So much of what God is showing me is tied up with my loss. As time passes I become more reticent to speak of it. It's as if there's an invisible "expiration date" stamped on my mourning that I feel has passed.

At any rate, I was racking my brain, trying to think of something that wouldn't sound like I was camped out on my grief.

Then one woman shared a verse that God had used to show her a truth about worship within our church. While she was speaking, I remembered the verse that God showed me about hope. In fact, it had been in my chronological Bible reading just two days ago. (Another of God's "incidences".)

May all who fear You find in me a cause for joy, for I have put my hope in Your Word.
Psalm 119:74 NLT

I retrieved my device and brought it up and shared it when it was my turn. I didn't expound on it (much); I just told how I found it, read it, and explained that I wanted to live out that verse - for everyone to be able to see that any strength or faith or hope they see in me comes straight from My Father.

It wasn't until I got home and was thinking about it, that I realized I *have* been living out that verse without being conscious of it. Nine months ago tomorrow was William's funeral. I remember after the service, I stopped to speak with some high school friends that had come to pay their respects. They remarked about me signing a song at the service, and one commented that she didn't know how I did it. I responded almost without thinking, "That wasn't me. That was the grace of God." They may have thought it was a figure of speech, but it wasn't. Any serenity and peace they saw that day was all God, because inside I wanted to wrap my arms around that casket and scream long and hard about the insanity of outliving my own child.

In thinking about it, I realize there have been others that have commented on how encouraged they've been by the strength God has given me for this journey. It's a comfort to know that God is bringing good out of my grief.

There will be times in your journey where you are sorely tempted to ask the Holy Spirit to step aside so you can "let 'er rip." If you surrender to the temptation, you'll hurt not only yourself, but all those who are looking to see if you will really live what you believe.

Don't forsake your faith for the temporary relief brought about by an emotional explosion. You don't know what kind of collateral damage the shrapnel will cause.

June 2

Today in my quiet time, I read the following quote in Our Daily Bread (https:// odb.org/2017/06/02/table-rock/):

"A temptation when hearing Jesus' words is to be moved and inspired without wrestling with the ways His words demand change in our lives. . . Building our lives on Him means a daily transformation, of daily following Him." [74]

The subject of the devotion wasn't change, but the quote caught my eye, because this season in my life is characterized by change, both drastic and gradual.

A second coworker from another department confided in me he's considering retiring this December. We have known each other several years, and again, I'm happy for him, but feeling even more sorry for myself.

God, I know You're listening. Can You please slow down this merry-go-round of change? I'm getting dizzy and a little nauseous.

I've never been good with change, or spontaneity, or going with the flow. I have learned how to adapt - to a point - but even as old as I am, I know I still have a way to go.

God is in the business of change. His desire for us is to be transformed into the image of His Son. If I dig in my heels because I don't like the discomfort that, for me, comes with change, He sometimes sends a change from the outside so that He can expose my stubbornness inside.

God is not a finger-pointing, fault-finding Father. He's gentle. He's compassionate. He loved us enough to sacrifice His Son for us. I believe today's quote is His gentle reminder to me that digging in my heels will not keep change from happening. It will only tire me as I fight against it - as I fight against Him. I don't want to fight.

I surrender.

I could try to articulate some of the struggles I'm discovering that I didn't suspect I would have. It would only breathe life into the strife. Suffice it to say that I am a work in progress.

So are you.

June 3

Yesterday I was reading a book that mentioned an old English village that had been swallowed by encroaching seas, and though the village churches were all underwater, their church bells could still be heard to ring.

I was curious, so I did a little research. There is, indeed, a town called Dunwich, and local legend claims that you can hear the church bells toll around midnight at certain tides.

At first, I was just curious if it was true. Then I realized that those churches buried underwater remind me of William. People who walk in and out of my life from here on out aren't going to know him, or know me as his mother, because they will never witness our interaction. Even though he is still a part of me, he's hidden from view. But like the underwater bells, William's memory resonates across my life as well as the lives of all who knew him. And if those church bells actually do ring, then I suppose their sound is a great deal like our memories.

Resonating.

Mournful.

Memorable.

June 4

This morning I was the lone member of the prayer team during our first worship service. It doesn't happen often, but I was determined to make the most of the hour. I prayed through my mental list of needs, requests, and people that the Lord brought to mind. It was a precious, intimate hour with my Father, free of distractions and interruptions. I don't know if I've ever heard the term or if I'm making it up, but it felt like an hour of power prayer (sort of like power walking).

At one point I was praying for someone who is struggling with a burden they are not meant to carry. As I was praying for this person to be able to let go of whatever is hindering their ability to receive God's grace and healing, this phrase came to mind.

Park your loss at the cross.

I thought the message must be about the person for whom I was praying, because I had already laid my burden at the foot of the cross.

Hadn't I?

The more I think about loss, the less I realize I know about it. I didn't lose William once on a day last August.

I lose him all over again every day that he's not here.

No wonder I've been fighting weariness. I laid the burden of my loss at the feet of Jesus last August, but what about all the grief and sorrow since then? At first I regularly laid it down, giving God my sorrow in exchange for His strength. But, just lately, I've hesitated.

It started with a well-meaning friend. When this person checked in with me, I shared with them one of these entries. This was not a passing acquaintance, but a true heart-friend. Sharing this journey is like baring my soul. It's not easy, and it leaves me feeling exposed and vulnerable. And my friend, who does not share my experience and therefore has no frame of reference, lovingly suggested that I shouldn't spend so much time thinking about the past.

It would have stung less if they had slapped me.

That's when it started - the withdrawing, the holding it in. I just assumed there was some truth in what this person said. After all, they knew me well. Because I was now sensitive to outside opinions, I saw confirmation everywhere I looked. When I walked in memory of William at a local event, I asked friends and family to send me notes and verses. One sent a passage in Ecclesiastes. In it I saw condemnation and an admonishment that the time for mourning was over and I needed to move on. Each time I interpreted a message like this, I withdrew a little more. I have even gone to my social network site and privatized my entire journey on my personal page, and I've cut back posting to William's memorial page - not for my benefit, but because of what I perceived to be the opinion of others.

Really? Peer pressure? At MY age?

And not even peer pressure per se, because neither person intended their remarks to be anything but helpful. But somewhere, somehow, I bit the apple. I bought into the lie that there is a right way and a wrong way to grieve healthily.

Not so. We are individuals. Our loss is individual. Our grief is individual. It will share some characteristics with the grief of others like sisters that share hair color or blood type, but grief will look different on everyone.

So, I withdrew my grief from the public. Then, I made an even bigger mistake,

I withdrew it from God. After all, if my friends, who only heard and saw my grief occasionally, were tired of it, how much more exasperated must God be?

Lord, forgive me for such convoluted thinking. Forgive me for not being totally honest with You for the last few weeks. I still miss him, Lord. Tears still fall. Memories still shatter me. But no matter what, I trust You, Lord. You knew what I was doing before I knew it myself. Thank You for revealing it to me.

Help me, Lord, to continue to park my loss at Your cross.

June 7

Laughter can conceal a heavy heart, but when the laughter ends, the grief remains.
Proverbs 14:13 NLT

This is what, I think, is the hardest for those outside the valley to understand. Yes, we smile. We laugh. We enjoy good company and good times.

But it takes a lot more energy than it used to.

Because "when the laughter ends, the grief remains."

There are those who think it shouldn't. I've read where some have called them grief bullies. I think that's unfair. Misunderstanding, yes. Well-meaning, most of the time. Clueless, absolutely. But, do we really want them to know what this feels like? How much energy it takes? How lonely it feels?

I recently read a post from www.thelifeididntchoose.com about the energy it takes to hold the grief at bay, to keep from succumbing to its onslaught. The author explained with perfect clarity the reality of why many of us hold back from overtaxing ourselves.

Because we are already overtaxed. Living with loss takes the strength of God, because we're not strong enough to carry this. Just living with it is hard enough.

The tears will come and go.

The sorrow will ebb and flow.

But the grief remains.

I don't think I could lose my son and have the grief disappear. To me, it would be as if all he was and all he did here were to disappear. That can't happen for me. Even if I could see the grief of his passing disappear, the grief of all he's missing (and I'm missing because of his absence) will remain. Every day there's going to be a word or thought or memory I want to share with him, but I can't. That's the part it's so hard to explain to someone who hasn't experienced it. Yes, we can shelve the grief and set it aside - but it remains, waiting for us and sometimes ambushing us when we least expect it.

Do you know someone going through loss? Don't discount what they say...
and what they don't say. A smile on their face does not necessarily mean there's
a song in their heart. They're just doing the best they can. There's no instruction
manual or detailed map for this difficult journey. Sometimes they need your
encouragement. Sometimes they need your shoulder. Always they need your
prayer.

June 8

Today I saw a question posted on a page for a local support group. In short,
it was addressed to mothers who've lost children in the past, and it asked their
advice for mothers on how to get through the first year of child loss.

I haven't actually hit the one-year mark yet, but from what I've experienced,
I've come to recognize that grief and loss are as individual as we are. Oh, they
share some common traits, but they don't look the same on any two people.

First and foremost, I depend fully on God and His strength and mercy for
each breath, and there are days when each breath takes His strength.

That being said, what has worked for me is admitting that I can't do things. In
a society where we are bombarded with the self-sufficient, suck-it-up-buttercup
mindset, I've chosen to lay down the ask-Mom-she'll-know role and have become
more genuine. For instance, if someone asks me how I am, they're going to get
the truth - and sometimes it won't be pretty. I try not to apologize for the tears,
because I'm not sorry I miss my son. I do try to look at those "outside the valley"
with compassion when they speak a misconception aloud, because they don't
have a frame of reference - and I don't want them to.

God has also given me many friends who've traveled through this valley, and
I sometimes seek their advice or just their company, because they *know*. They
just know.

Tonight I went to worship team practice. The leader allows me to attend so that I can practice the signs in the songs. The leader starts each practice with prayer, and ends with a time of sharing and another prayer. Tonight was no exception, but while the leader spoke to us about God using us as instruments to lead His church into worship, I was contemplating my own journey through the lens of worship.

My son died on a Tuesday night. My mother's visitation was two days later (Thursday). Her funeral was the day after that (Friday).

But Sunday morning, I was in my Father's house. I didn't want to be anywhere else.

But it wasn't easy.

I remember one of the songs we sang was "Good Good Father." [75] It's all about the goodness of God, and how He always provides, always loves, and always walks with us. Singing that song in light of what had happened was truly a sacrifice of praise. And that's what I was reminded of tonight.

Worship is more than a ritual or an attitude or a performance. Worship is acknowledging who God is, praising Him for what He's done, and letting go of the burdens of this world so we can raise our hands in surrender and praise to the only One who deserves it. It's an emptying of self so we can be filled with His Spirit. It is powerful. It is awe-inspiring. It is intimate. It is love.

And it is hard to do when the burden you're carrying is the loss of your child - a piece of your heart, which, though it will heal, will never be the same again.

I went to church that first Sunday, I thought, for ME. During the time of worship, I realized it was for HIM. Because, while I wanted to sit and sob and soak up sympathy, God had a different plan. His question whispers across my heart now, months later, when at the time my soul was crying too loud for me to hear it.

"I know you're broken. I know you're bleeding. Can you still worship me?"

That, for me, was the crux of the matter. I went to church for comfort. God sent me the Comforter. I went to church that first Sunday for me, but the minute we began to sing "Good Good Father," [76] it became all about Him. I had to lay down on His altar all the chaos of pain and sorrow and mourning and surrender everything - including myself - to God. I signed and cried my way through that song, and it was in the surrendering of my heart to His that I was able to accept the beginnings of a healing that will continue for the rest of my life.

You have pain? Sorrow? A burden too great for your back? Take your loss to the cross. Jesus is waiting there for you.

June 9

The Walk for Life donations in William's memory reached $2025 today - more than twice what I had set as my goal.

When the donations surpassed the $1500 mark, in my heart I whispered a hope that God would double what I had asked for. I don't know why I never voiced the desire aloud or shared it with anyone, but I know God heard even that doubt-filled whisper, and He gave me the desire of my heart.

God has given me incredible friends and family. They have helped me honor William's memory in an incredible way. They have helped save babies' lives. Knowing how much William loved his own son and loved to help others, I think this is a good way to honor his memory.

Delight yourself in the Lord, and He will give you
the desires and petitions of your heart.
Psalm 37:4 AMP

June 11

Today our church had a Coffee Connect time for the ladies. I signed up to go, but I really wasn't feeling it. However, a good friend asked me if I planned to go, and I said yes. She reminded me as we left after morning services that she'd see me later. I know she probably wouldn't even recall the exchange, but it encouraged me to make an effort to attend.

I'm so glad I did.

It was a great time of food and fellowship and faith-sharing. The food was awesome. A couple of ladies even shared recipes for the dishes that were presented. The fun was hilarious. It was a Purse Scavenger Hunt. Who knew I could win a prize for carrying a "Mary Poppins" purse? The friend that encouraged me to come? She was my partner in the game. We won with 161 points! We laughed so hard, because I don't think we missed too many items, perhaps with the exception of a pen that wrote with purple ink!

It was the faith-sharing portion that pierced my heart, because the speaker, who I've known for some time, is also a grieving mother. She lost both her children pre-term due to a chronic illness. Until that moment, I never knew.

My friend's testimony was filled with faith. Even as she spoke, she was suffering a condition for which doctors are still performing tests and seeking treatments. And still, my friend spoke with the confidence and joy that comes from placing all her trust and hope in her Lord. Some of God's children get stuck at the cross and never reach the altar, but it's obvious that she has fully surrendered her burdens to the Lord.

I have a lot to learn from her.

Some of her final words to us were, "I have learned to listen and look for God. He never leaves me alone."

It's true. Look back and see all that He's done for me since I was pushed into this valley. Look at all the people whom He encouraged to reach out to me to show me love, encouragement, and comfort. To pray for me. To text me in the *exact right moment*, when I needed to be reminded that I am never alone. Look at all the everyday miracles He has performed on my journey.

As a child of God, you are never alone. Let that truly sink in. *You. Are. Never. Alone.* Your Father will never leave you. He will never give up on you. He will believe in you even when you don't believe in yourself. The minute the enemy begins to whisper in your ear, silence him with the truth of who you are and Whose you are. Then, look for the evidence of those truths in your life.

It might be a timely text.

It might be a friendly phone call.

It might be a silent sunrise.

It might be a "See you later" from a friend.

June 12

Today at work, I had an opportunity to speak with the leader of a local writer's group. I shared with him that I had been encouraged to consider publishing my journey. He mentioned I would probably need an editor, and he shared with me some of the challenges he has faced with his upcoming book.

All at once, I was overwhelmed at the amount of work this endeavor will take. I began to doubt my ability to do it, to look back on the totality of this journey and tackle the desperately needed editing and polishing and permission seeking for all the materials cited. I really floundered at the thought of whether I could do it.

When I arrived home, there was a card in the mail from William's 3rd-through-8th grade teacher and his wife, both of whom became good friends when William attended their church's small Christian school. They had donated to the Walk for Life, and in my thank-you note, I mentioned the encouragement to publish the story God is writing through my journey. This was their response:

"I wanted to share Ps 56:8 (KJV) with you. 'Thou tellest my wanderings: put thou my tears into thy bottle: are they not in thy book?' Your journal is like a bottle of tears - precious to our Lord & He bore those griefs & sorrows already at the cross. He shares them."

"I'm hoping you do continue with your journey's journal of the story of God's love & faithfulness through this fire."

"When you do consider self-publishing let us know. We'd like to help out with the cost."

I'm so moved. These are mighty people of God. They walk closely with Him. They don't speak thoughtlessly or without great consideration. Did God send this message through them? You bet. Did He work to make sure this note landed in my mailbox today? Absolutely.

Remember my friend's words yesterday?

"I have learned to listen and look for God. He never leaves me alone."

Amen.

June 18 - Father's Day

Dear Oliver,

From the time your dad was little, I always included him in my Fathers' Day celebrations. When he would ask why I got him a gift, I would explain that, while he wasn't a father yet, someday he could be.

One of the greatest moments in your dad's life was the day you were born. Oliver, YOU were the greatest gift your father ever received. God blessed your dad with you, and your dad loves you so very much.

I know you are glad that you and your dad had such an awesome life together while he was here. I hope today is filled with beautiful memories of all the terrific times you had and all the great adventures you shared.

I know your dad taught you the important things, too: love, respect, honor, responsibility. I know you have stored them up in your heart, because they are reflected in the way you love and respect your mom, work hard in school, and show kindness to others. Your dad would be very pleased with how you are living out everything he taught you.

Someday, God willing, it will be your turn to be a father. I know that when that time comes, you will be fully prepared, and you will do as good a job as your dad has done. You are one terrific son, and you will be one amazing father.

I love you very much, Oliver. God bless you.

Love,

Grammy

Dear Sherman,

The minute you married me, you gained an instant family. Along with a new bride, you received a four-year-old stepson filled-to-bursting with exuberance, joy, laughter, and yes, a fair amount of trouble, too. You were very brave to accept the task of raising such an active little boy...or perhaps it was a case of ignorance is bliss.

Through the years, your instant fatherhood has gifted you with a great deal of experience as a leader, an encourager, a taskmaster...an EMT. You fixed toys, rode bikes, played basketball, cut hair, ferried kids to gym meets and Awana club. As the years rolled by you celebrated a lot of firsts: first day of school, first pet, driver license, first car...first speeding ticket. You were also there with advice and a helping hand when needed. It may not have always been fun (for them or us), but it has never been boring.

I am sorry that you're hurting today. Even if you don't say so, I know you are, because I am. But you know what? I think the pain of losing William is the flip side of the coin. If we hadn't loved him so much, then it wouldn't hurt so much that he ran ahead of us to heaven.

You are a true man of God. Your first goal for each of your children was that they accept Christ as their Savior. Thank you for being diligent in that. It's a comfort to know that, no matter what happens on this side of heaven, we will see them all again.

Thank you for being such a good father to William. Thank you for the gift of our son Anthony. Thank you for sharing your daughter Sherrie. And thank you for the little one whose name we won't know until we reach heaven. She (or he) would have been 16 this year.

Happy Fathers' Day, Sherman. I love you.

I felt a burden in my heart today for all those fathers that have lost children.

Dear Bereaved Fathers,

I want to express my sorrow for your loss. I wonder how you manage to deal with this heartache on a regular day. How much more painful is it on a day like this?

As a bereaved mother, I've found comfort in the company of other bereaved mothers.

We share an unwanted bond that makes it easier for us to open our hearts to each other and share the good and the bad, seek advice, console, exhort, and empathize.

Do you have that, I wonder? Do you have a safety net of friends that are open to your pain? Do they check with you to see how you're doing? If you try to blow them off with "I'm fine", do they grip your hand a little tighter and say, "No, I mean how are you really doing?"

Do you feel conflicted in your heart, like us mothers, when you celebrate with your living children today? Are you smiling at all the right people in all the right places, when part of your heart is on a hill in a quiet cemetery somewhere, gazing down at a headstone you never expected to see, much less purchase?

A familiar refrain in many homes is, "Daddy will fix it." Many of today's gifts will reflect that role. Is today a reminder that this was one thing you couldn't "fix", even though there was nothing you could have done that would change what happened? Do you carry the burden of thinking that if you'd said (or not said) something, done (or not done) something, that you could have changed the outcome? Are you haunted by thoughts that, if you had just done things differently, you could have prevented your tragedy?

You are a father, yes, but you are not THE Father. Your role is challenging enough without trying to take on responsibilities not meant for your albeit strong shoulders. God knew the number of our children's days from the minute they were conceived. I hope you can take some comfort in knowing He was not surprised when your child walked through the gates of eternity.

Heavenly Father,

Please bless all the bereaved fathers today. Comfort them with Your peace. Fill them with joyful memories of all of their children. Give them opportunities to share these memories today. Encourage their friends and family to share their own memories. Lord, help bereaved fathers feel Your presence, especially in the hard places of this day. Help them laugh about the good times, even if their laughter is laced with tears. Help them love their living family, knowing each moment and every breath is a gift from You. In the mighty name of Your Son Jesus I pray. AMEN

On behalf of your children who forged ahead of you into heaven,

Happy Fathers' Day

From the time they were old enough to know what Fathers' Day was, I celebrated my sons as well. When they asked me why I got them a gift for Fathers' Day, I explained that, while they weren't fathers at the time, God willing they would be in the future.

I don't even have words for today. I miss William. My heart weeps for his son, Oliver. I hurt for his father, Doug. I hurt for my husband, Sherman. At the same time, I'm grateful for the fathers of my boys and excited about what the future holds for my son Anthony and my grandson Oliver.

So many emotions swirling in a volatile cocktail of grief and gratefulness and anticipation...I can't even begin to articulate them. Add into the mix the loss of my own father a little over four years ago and the loss of my mother ten months ago today, and the whole concoction begins to bubble over.

I'm a mess, God. I just want to curl up, hold my breath, and wait for the pain to stop. But it doesn't stop. Oh, it ebbs and flows, but it is a constant companion. All the sayings about time healing all wounds promised that it would happen. Why hasn't it happened?

Because this is not just a wound. This is a permanent disfigurement, an amputation of a part of my heart, one that I am discovering has left me with limitations.

I don't have the same tolerance for drama that I once did. Life is too short to indulge in such things. I'm nearly compulsive in completing tasks ahead of schedule "just in case something happens". I'm uncomfortable just relaxing, doing nothing productive - it feels wasteful when I think of all the things my son is missing now. The stark reality of the brevity, the very fragility of life has left a lasting mark on me.

Regardless of my grief today, I will chose gratefulness. It is Fathers' Day, and my son is spending it with his eternal Father.

Thank You, Lord.

step 11

Spreading His Love

Don't just pretend to love others. Really love them.

Romans 12:9a NLT

June 23

Dear William,

It's been ten months since I heard your voice, saw your smile, got exasperated with your antics, or sprouted a gray hair over your shenanigans.

Ten months, and there are still moments when the sledgehammer blow of your death seems so fresh and so severe, it takes my breath away.

Ten months of reaching for the phone because I have a question only you can answer. Ten months of tripping over words in prayer when I ask God to bless my boy"s". Ten months of learning to text only one son good night. Ten months of stumbling over verb tenses when I speak about you. Ten months of tears and sighs and pain and sorrow.

Ten months.

304 days.

And it doesn't feel one single bit easier than it did on August 23. Just more familiar.

I will never stop missing you.

I will never stop loving you.

I will never stop speaking your name or sharing your memory.

Love,
Mom

As each month's milestone passes, I wait expectantly. Is this the month that I turn the corner, take a step beyond the loss, "move on"? I sometimes wonder if friends and family get tired of hearing me natter on about this journey. At times I've held back from sharing - not because I didn't want to, but because the whisper of the enemy has planted seeds of doubt in my heart about whether they want to hear it.

Ten months.

I've been ten months without seeing my son's face, hearing his voice, or feeling his bear hug.

The "experts" that say the pain lessens with time?

They LIE.

If the pain has lessened, why can't I view videos of him? Why can't I visit his social media page? Click through his pictures? Why do I still suffer tidal waves of grief, some triggered by a thought or a word, some by nothing at all?

The writer of www.thelifeididntchoose.com recently posted the infamous "stages of grief". I won't argue with the experts, but I would like to know which of them has lost a child. I would like to know if their journey through child loss followed the "stages" they set up as a standard - one that any grieving parent will tell you is not that simple, regardless of how much they might wish it to be so.

I've tried several metaphors in an attempt to explain the devastation that follows the death of your child. I can't do it. None of the metaphors hold up in the long run, because this just isn't like anything else you will ever encounter. Unless you experience it, you just can't comprehend it.

If you are on the outside of this experience looking in, I prayerfully ask that you keep that in mind: you can't know what it's like. If you're walking alongside someone who's trying to survive child loss, there will be a point at which you run out of words. That's okay. They don't always need words.

But they do need compassion. This is a heavy burden to bear. Sometimes they don't have the strength to live up to your expectations of what this journey should look like. Some days, it takes all the strength God gives them to bear up under the weight of their sorrow.

If you're struggling to understand your grieving friend, there's a good reason for that. Your friend is not the person you knew before. They are FOREVER changed by what they've experienced. They will never be the same. If you're waiting for your "old" friend to return, you're doomed to disappointment. And if you can't live with the changes, then you have some praying to do, some soul-searching about what exactly your friendship was based upon.

Your grieving friend understands your frustration, because they feel it, too. They are tired of grieving, too. They wish they could go back to "before," too.

Keep in mind, that, while you have the option to walk away from the pain and grief, they don't. There's no place to run from it, no place to hide. It eats with them, sleeps with them, laughs with them, works with them. There is no escape for your grieving friend. Is it any wonder that they're different?

It goes without saying that there are exceptions to the rule: grieving parents whose wound is not just tender, but festering. If you don't know the difference, I suggest consulting someone who does, preferably a Christian counselor who can advise you on how to approach your friend in love. If you think they need help, don't just suggest they go get it. Offer to go with them.

Being the friend of a grieving parent is not for the faint of heart. If God has called you to that role, seek His wisdom in fulfilling it.

You will need it. You will need HIM.

June 27

I was recently thrust into a position of responsibility for which I have no inclination. Circumstances made it impossible to refuse it, no matter how much I really wanted to. The duty itself is not onerous nor one for which I have no experience, but it entails a more than likely chance for criticism and conflict. I don't feel up to facing either of those fellows at this point in my life.

So I made a request of God. I didn't ask for deliverance from the duty, because that action would bring an added burden to others. I asked only for deliverance from the criticism and conflict. I was willing to shoulder the responsibility, but I didn't feel strong enough to carry the added weight of criticism and conflict for doing so. I had no ulterior motives, save from sparing myself additional pain. Still, it felt selfish to voice such a request.

But God granted it, at least temporarily. That's the essence of grace: getting a gift you don't deserve.

June 28

My husband spent last week visiting his daughter out of state. She was ill the entire time he was in town. He convinced her to make a doctor's appointment. The appointment was two days ago, after my husband had returned home. Shortly after her appointment, she called to tell my husband that the doctor had sent her to the emergency room. After that, he heard nothing for several hours.

You can imagine my husband's first thoughts. By the time I got home from work, he and I were both in quite a state. I was able to contact the hospital, and through a series of extremely helpful people, my husband was able to speak to his daughter. She was diagnosed with pancreatitis. How sad is it that we were relieved to hear that?

Before last August, no phone calls meant all was well, no news was good news. Now, when a friend or relative "drops off the grid," I feel compelled to check on them.

Today our younger son went hiking with some of his friends. His car has been acting up, so he rode with one them.

Before last August, my biggest concern when Anthony traveled was the car breaking down, or him getting a speeding ticket. Now, I understand how quickly it could all change: a deer in the road, a thick fog, a bad storm.

Funny, the ways that you change when you've lost a child. Where you once expected a good outcome from the mishaps of everyday life, now your first thought is often dire. You no longer assume the best; instead, you steel yourself for the worst. Sometimes it's a deliberate thought process. Sometimes you just feel inexplicably uneasy. That is, until you stop and examine why you feel that way. Then you realize...

You are not in control of anything.

You cannot change anything.

You are not guaranteed anything.

Living with the personal experience of the truth of these statements brings you to a fork in the road of your faith. Will you trust? Or will you tremble?

Can all your worries add a single moment to your life?
Matthew 6:27 NLT

Don't worry about anything; instead, pray about everything. Tell God what you need, and thank Him for all He has done. Then you will experience God's peace, which exceeds anything we can understand. His peace will guard your hearts and minds as you live in Christ Jesus.
Philippians 4:6-7 NLT

June 29

My husband passed the test for his motorcycle license today. He rode for many years in his 20's and has longed to do so again. Today he passed the final test to get his full license. I am happy, because I know he so very much wanted this...happy for him, that is.

I'm not so sure about me.

About a month ago, I received an invitation to a bike rally and prayer vigil being sponsored by the same local support group, Trinity's Angels, that conducted the Never Forgotten Floating Lantern Ceremony on May 20. The Bike Rally is one of their principle fundraisers. From what I've read, each lost child is represented by a motorcycle rider. The ride begins at the ministry office and ends at a gathering place where food, fellowship and prayer are shared. I knew when I received this invitation, God might be asking me to once more step outside my comfort zone. At the time I felt a certain amount of relief in knowing that, since my husband only carried a motorcycle learner's permit, I wouldn't have to ride with him, should he feel led to ride.

That relief was nipped in the bud today, because there is no longer a restriction on passengers on his license. I get the distinct impression that Sherman believes he'd like to have me on that back of that bike. (He wouldn't, but he thinks so. If I don't crack his ribs holding on, I'll probably leave hand-shaped bruises). He sends me subtle messages by raving about all the ways he enjoys being on the bike and experiencing the world from a more intimate perspective than from a car.

So far, I've only mentioned the rally in vague terms. I don't even know if it would be something in which my husband would feel called to participate. What I *do* know is that God has called me to be open to the possibility of crawling on the back of that monster and riding with him (and more importantly, with Him) if Sherman chooses to attend.

Like the floating lantern ceremony, I don't know if I'll ever do it again. But just this once, God has asked me to be available, to step out in faith, and allow Him to move through me.

God has walked me through the death of my child. If God puts me on the back of that bike, He will see me through that, too.

Has God called you to make a step of faith? One that makes your heart pound and your palms sweat and leaves you feeling nothing but panic? Take a moment to examine what you're afraid of, what your true reasons are for hesitating. Then invite God in to your doubts, your fears, your anxieties -- all the things that are holding you back. Ask Him to shine His light on what needs to change in order for you to grow.

Then close your eyes, let go of your fear, and step out in faith. God is worth it.

More than worth it.

June 30

Today in my Bible reading I came across the following verse:

Jehoram was thirty-two years old when he became king, and he reigned in Jerusalem eight years. No one was sorry when he died. They buried him in the City of David, but not in the royal cemetery.
2 Chronicles 21:20 NLT

274

Second Chronicles is not always the most exciting or uplifting book to read. This king was bad. That king was bad. This king killed that king.

But the middle of this verse struck me. *"No one was sorry when he died."* Nothing could have been further from the truth when William died, but because of the distance of the funeral from the cemetery (45 minutes), and the cemetery from the reception (another 45 minutes) - not to mention that none of these services were held where William lived - I truly didn't expect many people to be able to attend them. The suddenness of his passing and the fact that his friends are scattered across the country made it almost impossible for many to attend.

At least that's what I thought.

When my son's funeral procession reached the military cemetery, we drove a circuitous route around the perimeter in order to reach the pavilion where we would hold William's service.

The lane that encircled the pavilion was bumper to bumper. There was barely room for us to park.

My heart broke a little more as I walked up to the pavilion and looked on a sea of faces, most of which I didn't know but all of whom made the sacrifice of time and energy to bid my son farewell. They filled the seats that I could see, and were standing around the perimeter.

Military cemetery services must, of necessity, be brief, so time didn't permit me to speak to many of these beautiful people, these precious ones who hold memories of my precious one in their hearts. While I wish I'd had the chance to speak (and listen) to each one, I didn't. But each and every one will hold a small place in my heart for what they did.

They showed up.

Do you have someone who's going through a time of grief or suffering? Are you avoiding them because you don't know what to do or how to help?

Just show up.

Sometimes just the fact that you made an effort to be there for them is the best you can do. Don't quantify it. You can't. It means more than you can know. It's as if you've stepped alongside them, helping them carry the burden that's buckling their knees and breaking their hearts. For a brief moment they can focus on the comfort of your presence instead of the crushing weight of their loved one's absence. Whether you knew their child or not, your presence helps.

Just show up. If there's more for you to do than that, God will show it to you.

July 1

Today I received an email from a good friend. She recently read the previous installment of this journey, and she had a question about my spiritual condition. It was a valid one, and it was asked out of love and concern for me. God has, indeed, blessed me with friends that love me enough to ask the hard, uncomfortable questions. My friend was concerned about the weight I spoke of back in April. Her question prompted me to reread what I had written, and I was able to clarify what I had meant and what I had learned. In the process I came to realize something.

I almost think there is a distinction to be made between a weight and a burden. Losing a child definitely carries with it a weight that's nearly impossible to explain. I believe that weight is in proportion to the part of your heart that was exclusively theirs. It is no more a burden than being their mother was. However, trying to live exclusively in the role of grieving mother is not any healthier than being a "s"mother to your living children, and *that* is when it becomes a burden - one that we are not called to bear.

I believe my friend's concern was that I might be clinging to a burden that God never meant me to carry. I'm grateful for her friendship. It took courage to ask me about that, and it took wisdom from God on how to do it in love. Being a pastor's wife, she's blessed with both.

When you suffer a tragedy of this magnitude, it doesn't hurt to have a spiritual checkup periodically, just to make sure you're moving in the right direction. My friend doesn't know that about two weeks before I got her email, I had done just that. God arranged it so that these things would fall in this order so that I could, with confidence, speak about where I am in this journey.

Are you in this valley, too? There is strength in seeking spiritual guidance for this journey. Even if you are comfortable with how you're coping, it doesn't hurt to have someone ask you the challenging questions that encourage you to step out of your comfort zone and into God's purpose for your journey.

He may call you to step alongside someone who's just entered this valley.

He may call you to float a lantern or ride a motorcycle.

He may even call you to write a book.

July 2

Last night, as I lay down to go to sleep, I reached for my device to listen to a podcast. When I opened the app, I was unable to retrieve my saved episodes. Suspecting some type of glitch, I tried to power down and reboot my device. When it didn't respond, I asked the device for help. He (yes mine is a "he") gave me the digital version of "Sorry, can't help." Then the screen went dark. Thinking it had finally powered down, I waited, and then tried to restart it.

Nothing. And it's been unresponsive ever since.

The thought of being "unplugged" does not send me into a frenzy as it might some of my younger friends. Indeed, I have sometimes "fasted" from electronics. I admit I'll miss the convenience of being "in the loop" with friends and church events that are communicated via email and social media, but, I am not unfamiliar with the telephone and snail mail.

What did send me into a panic last night was the fact that there is a month of this journey chronicled on my device that was due to be backed up.

Today.

On the ten-month milestone of my son's burial.

Some of the entries can be pulled from my social media page. A larger portion cannot. And I am humanly incapable of reproducing them.

That my device would crash the night before I would back it up is no "coincidence". This is not the first attack of the enemy. Unfortunately, recognizing the enemy's tactics didn't keep me from succumbing to them. It was a long time before I fell asleep last night...well, actually, this morning. Like a hamster on an exercise wheel, my mind went round and round on how to recreate the entries. And just like that hamster, I didn't get anywhere. I would confess to worry, repent, and lay it down at Jesus' feet, only to circle back around in prayer to pick it up once more.

Now, you would think that with all that I've experienced in the past ten months, I would have enough faith to believe that God can handle this. I don't struggle to believe He *could*. But the chasm between *could* and *would* is one I find difficult to bridge in the still of the night when everyone (but me) is asleep and I am helpless to fix the problem.

So, I confessed some more and repented some more and prayed some more, and, much later (or earlier this morning) than I anticipated when I went to bed, I finally fell asleep.

Responding to my 5:00am alarm was...a challenge. Continuing to leave my electronic dilemma in God's hand after discovering no change in the "patient's" condition even more so.

More confessing, more repenting, more prayer...

I pulled out my devotional and read the verses and the entry (https://odb. org/2017/07/02/all-the-work/). Each devotional ends with a summary thought, a one-liner, if you will: a nugget you can carry with you for the day to meditate on. Today's final thought:

"Most things worth doing are difficult." [77]

Baring your soul in written form is difficult. Entertaining the idea that God wants it to be published, even more difficult.

But my God is greater than "difficult".

At the juncture of each installment's completion, I have faced some form of attack from the enemy. Up until now, they were aimed at me. This one felt like it was aimed at William's memory, and *that* struck the "mother" chord in me.

It's one thing to try to discourage *me* and distract *me* by honing in on my insecurities. It's a whole other ball game to try to wipe out a portion of William's story as if it doesn't matter, that *he* doesn't matter. Instead of throwing up my hands in despair, I have decided that, in God's strength and according to His will, I will continue to record what the Lord has done for me.

So, I began to seek God's solutions for the battle at hand. No keyboard? Back to pen and paper, which, in the house of a former homeschooler, is easily found. With the myriad of choices on hand, I chose one that would encourage me to keep on keeping on. William had numerous pads of paper he used in his work. They ended up here.

Another God "incidence".

So this installment of William's story is being recorded on his own note pad. While that hurts to know and to say, it seems very fitting to me.

So, pen and paper in hand, notes made of the morning's story, I continued my quiet time, pulling out my Bible to read my portion for the day: 2 Kings 1-4. Past readings through this section caused me to expect today would be a chronicling of more kings, good and bad, and the results of their reigns.

You would think I'd know better by now.

In the introduction to the book, before I even read a word of the Scripture, was a line summarizing the theme of 2 Kings. *"It is a story about stewardship - what we do with what we have."* [78] That sums up the life of all of God's children. We have been given the gift of salvation. We have been given the gift of our testimony. What are we going to do with it? Are we going to hide the light we've been given under a basket? Or set it on a hill like a beacon for shipwrecked souls? Even a candle can be seen in the darkness from over a mile and a half away. Who knows whose darkness God might use your light to dispel?

As I read 2 Kings 3, verse 16b spoke to me.

"This is what the Lord says:
This dry valley will be filled with pools of water!" NLT

The God that can fill the dry valley with pools of water can certainly handle a few pages of notes. Then verse 18a says:

"But this is only a simple thing for the Lord..." NLT

My God created the earth in six days. He parted the seas so His children could pass through on dry ground. He provided daily food for His thousands of children for 40 years as they trekked around the desert. Am I really going to fret over a few journal entries?

The last chapter of today's reading was 2 Kings 4. It opens with the story of the widow and the oil: another reminder that God is not unaware of our needs and will meet them - not a minute too soon or too late. The widow's story is followed by the Shunamite woman's son. Born as a result of Elijah's obedience to God in prayer and prophecy, the son dies quite suddenly and with little warning. Convinced that Elisha has God's ear, the Shunamite woman determines to do whatever it takes bring Elisha to pray over her son.

When You are following God's leading, don't be overcome by the setbacks you may face. When you know you are in His will, take your problems straight to the God of all comfort. Pray in expectation of seeing Him work, because He *will* work.

After my Bible reading, I concentrated on my Bible study work. In it, I came across the statement about how saying "yes" often makes your heart pound and your palms sweat, and it ultimately doesn't guarantee a perfect outcome. [79]

And that's okay. God didn't ask for perfect, He asked for willingness.

I moved on to the workbook, where the next exercise called for setting aside a 20-minute time slot to pull away and "unplug" from the world and concentrate on God. [80] I'm already halfway there, because for all intents and purposes, I *am* "unplugged". So, for today I will stay that way. No more testing, but much more praying in anticipation of a 20-minute visit solely with my Dad tomorrow.

And all this happened *before* I went to church.

I am human. I am weak. I fall prey to the enemy's schemes. In the past, a problem like this would send me into a spiral of worry and anxiety that would distract me to the point that corporate praise and worship became mechanical - all the physical aspects would be there, but my spirit would be constantly chewing on my problem. To prevent falling into old habits, I focused solely on praising God during worship. In our prayer group, I (once again) handed the issue to God and moved on to the needs of others, trusting that no matter what happens, it will bring God glory.

Between the first and second service, I sought out a friend who needed to know I would be offline for a while. When I told her of my dilemma, she asked me to speak to her husband, who happened to be nearby and joined us. In the way He has so many times before, God orchestrated a conversation with the one person in church that morning that might have a solution to my problem. Her husband used to work in IT, and he told me a couple of things I can try to "revive" my device. He even said that if it still didn't respond, he would look at it for me.

God was already answering my prayer. He was showing me that He was aware of the problem, and He was also aware of my efforts to trust. Am I guaranteed that these solutions will work? No. But you know what?

I still trust Him.

During the second service, the pastor made the statement, "You have a story to tell." I heard my Father's voice in those words. Whether I can reconstruct last month or not, I still have a story to tell. After second service, I ran into several ladies from those prayer Bible studies I've mentioned before. Sharing my prayer need with them necessitated sharing the possibility of this testimony being published. The number of people who know is increasing, like the concentric circles that proceed outward from a rock that is thrown in a pond. The enemy may have meant for those circles from the tragedy he threw into the waters of my life to be waves of shock and grief, but God has made them waves of comfort and encouragement as I watch Him trade the ashes of mourning for the beauty of His joy.

I was also able to share my need with a dear friend who is reading this as I finish each installment. She prayed with me right then and there in the church hallway that God would use this to bring Him glory.

The next time someone approaches you with a need, instead of saying you'll pray for them, go ahead and do it. It doesn't always have to be long and detailed - that can come later - but stopping long enough to lay their need before God will bring a measure of comfort to them that nothing else will.

After church, I once again picked up my Bible study book and started on the next chapter. It was all about the author's search for a new motivation for her writing to replace the motivations of anxiety and fear that used to fuel her goals, of how God's love has changed her life. [81]

That's what this story is. It's the story of how God's love has changed my life. It's the story of how He has loved me through a valley of immense pain and indescribable heartache. It's really *His* story, and if last month's words are needed to complete that story, He will make a way for them to be included.

As I (painstakingly) handwrite these words, I still don't know if I can access last month's files. I am laying the problem aside today, and instead, concentrating on praising and worshipping God. After devotions tomorrow morning, after that 20-minute "unplugged" assignment, I will try again. I know My Father. I know I can trust Him.

I *will* trust Him.

> *Trust in the Lord with all your heart;*
> *do not depend on your own understanding.*
> *Seek His will in all you do,*
> *and He will show you which path to take.*
> *Proverbs 3:5-6 NLT*

July 3

"When the computer screen went black, my reflection scowled." [82]

That was one of the lines in my devotional reading in Our Daily Bread this morning (https://odb.org/2017/07/03/destroying-the-divides/). God's gentle reminder that He's heard my prayer and He will answer in His time.

I found a quiet spot, set the alarm on my phone (I knew it would come in handy for something) for twenty minutes, and sat down to empty myself of all the cares and concerns of this world and concentrate solely on God and on His love for me. I let go of words and feelings and thoughts and concentrated on what my relationship with God looks like right now. In my mind, I had a picture of a strong but gentle hand holding on to a much smaller, much more frail hand stretching up to reach it.

That's where I am. When I was pushed into the valley of the shadow, I chose to reach up for God's hand instead of trying to stand up on my own. I've never been sorry. I never will be sorry. His hand is what has steadied me and supported me as I learned to walk the path of my new identity.

It was a new experience for me. Words flow through me like a never ending river. Damming the flow to concentrate on their Source was not as difficult as I supposed it would be. It felt good to sit in my Father's presence and just be His daughter.

Afterward, I picked up my Bible to read. In 2 Kings 6:1-7, I read the story of the floating ax head. While chopping trees, a man's borrowed axe loses its head and the head falls in the river. The man appeals to Elisha for help. Elisha cuts a stick and throws it in the river, and God makes the axe head float to the surface.

Imagine that. Something hopelessly lost by human standards, but found by God.

Is it any wonder I trust my Father so?

Once I had finished my quiet time with God, I retrieved my device, prayed, and followed the instructions God provided through my friend's husband.

And like the axe head that floated to the surface, my device powered right up.

And that, my friend, is why you were able to read June's entries.

July 4 - Independence Day

This past Sunday in church, there was a short video about Independence Day. There was a line in it that stuck out to me.

"This is my country, but it is not my home."

That's very comforting to me, especially today, when memories abound.

My husband and I decided to ride over to a nearby city today to window shop. We stopped at a local car wash before we left town. It's the kind that you drive onto a track, then you're pulled through the unit. When we actually drove onto the plates, I thought about the Robo-Wash trips my sister and I used to make with my dad after church on Sundays (only back then there was no blow dryer - just a man, two girls, and a lot of hand towels).

Later, we passed a business that specializes in garden sculptures. We have made past trips to this place, because my mom had sheep sculptures in her yard and was always on the lookout for a shepherd to go with them. I nearly asked my husband to stop so we could check again. Then I remembered that Mom has now met the Good Shepherd. She no longer needs a statue.

Later, when we got home, there was a dragonfly resting on the sidewalk outside our house. When I approached it, it flew a little further off and landed on the porch. When my father died, William saw a dragonfly at the hospital, and then several times afterward. It became a "thing" in our family, a reminder of my dad. When my mom was in the hospital last year, shortly before she (and then William) died, William saw one in the parking lot at the hospital. According to what he said, he chased it down in an attempt to squash it, and then had to explain to his son his strange behavior. The dragonfly today made me think of how comical he must have looked, running across that parking lot like a madman, chasing a bug.

It also reminded me that at the funeral home when we were saying goodbye to William, a dragonfly landed on his ex-wife's purse in the parking lot. It stayed long enough for several of us to see it and comment on it.

So many memories. I miss all three of them: my dad, my mom, my son.

That's why I'm comforted by that line from the video. Yes, this is my country. I am thankful to be an American, for the freedom to worship openly without fear of prosecution.

But this is not my home.

For this world is not our permanent home; we are looking forward to a home yet to

come. Therefore, let us offer through Jesus a continual sacrifice of praise to God,
proclaiming our allegiance to His name.
Hebrews 13:14-15 NLT

July 5

Yesterday was full of memories. They were good, but they were bittersweet, too, knowing that I won't be able to add to them now that Dad, Mom, and William have gone home.

I had to work today. Remember the lady that made me the lovely scarf? She came in this afternoon. She asked me how I was doing (and she really meant it). She shared a precious memory of her mother with me, and I shared with her how God had allowed me a precious memory of each of my loved ones yesterday.

Just before she left she told me she loved me.

She was a gift straight from God.

When you give God your sorrow and your pain, He will not leave you empty-handed.

To all who mourn in Israel, He will give beauty for ashes,
joy instead of mourning, praise instead of despair.
Isaiah 61:3a NLT

July 10

Some days are inexplicably filled with the presence of William's absence. It's not that I'm sad, exactly. I'm not fighting tears or memories. I'm just feeling the void in the place where William should be. It's not missing his presence so much as it is experiencing his absence.

Remember, as a child, when you lost a tooth? How you would repeatedly put your tongue in the space it left? It was as if your brain kept expecting the tooth to be there, couldn't accept the fact that it was gone.

Multiply that by a million. It's like that.

I don't often tell others about these type of days. Few outside the grieving parent community can understand. They can sympathize on the days where milestones fall or memories flow. Those make sense to them. These kind don't, and that's understandable, because they hardly make sense to me. I can't even explain it well. All I know is I feel it today, like the void that used to hold your baby tooth.

For as long as I remain here, I will feel William's absence. It's not because William and I were extraordinarily close; it's just that he's *not here*. Even when we had little contact, I still knew he was here.

Now he's not.

And some days it takes all God's strength to make that bearable.

Don't be dejected and sad, for the joy of the Lord is your strength!
Nehemiah 8:10b NLT

July 11

During my quiet time this morning, I looked out the window and watched the bird feeder for a minute. I saw a female cardinal, and I got up to look at her with the binoculars. It wasn't just random bird watching. I was looking to see if this was a particular female cardinal that has often visited our feeders. She's distinctive, because she is smaller than most adult cardinals and one of her legs hangs useless. Given the fact that she made it to adulthood, I suspect she has suffered some kind of wound. I grabbed the binoculars this morning, because we haven't seen her lately.

My husband keeps the two bird feeders in our back yard full in the winter, but often in late spring he will begin to wean the birds so they will seek their natural foods. This spring, however, he decided to keep them full.

For one small, wounded, feathered reason.

We were in the kitchen one day when he pointed out how she often came to eat at the feeders. Something he said stuck with me. I remembered it today, though I'm sure it's not word for word.

"As long as she keeps coming, I'm going to keep food out for her."

In essence, that's what God does for you and me. We all carry wounds, some of which can never heal to complete restoration. Do we choose to sit in the ashes of what used to be? Or do we seek sustenance from our Father, the Bread of life?

Just like that cardinal knows where to find nourishment for her body, so we know where to find strength for our souls. My husband doesn't force feed the cardinal; he just makes food available for her. Our Father does the same thing for us. He is always available to equip you for the trials you face in this life. You need only to come to Him.

So let us come boldly to the throne of our gracious God. There we will receive His mercy, and we will find grace to help us when we need it most.
Hebrews 4:16 NLT

I had a dental cleaning appointment today. My hygienist asked an innocent question. "Do you have just the one son?" (She's only met my younger one.)

How to answer? Especially with a mouth full of grit?

I told her I had two sons, but my older one had died last August. It may have made her uncomfortable, and I'm sorry for that, but any other answer would have made me uncomfortable. I still waffle on verb tense: I *had* two sons? I *have* two sons? The first seems more socially acceptable, but the second is more spiritually correct. My response often depends on the audience and on how much energy I wish to expend explaining myself. Some might wonder why I mentioned my son's death. I assumed saying I had two sons would lead my hygienist to ask questions about the one she didn't know. It seemed more compassionate to tell her outright, than for her to stumble into an awkward situation by asking about my older son, only to be told that he's gone.

If you're on this path, you will encounter similar questions. I wish there was an easy answer to the dilemma. Not much about this journey is easy. Just pray for guidance and follow your heart.

July 12

I began my quiet time this morning with my devotional booklet (https://odb.org/2017/07/12/approaching-god-with-confidence/) [83], and the scripture reading was Hebrews 4:14-16.

Look back at yesterday. See what God did?

He's there.

He's listening.

Come to Him.

I was assisting a patron today in locating a particular series of books. In the process, she told me she'd lost her husband recently.

I checked. (It's a small town, so this is easy to do.). She lost him less than a month ago.

God doesn't put people suffering loss in my path by accident. He has given me comfort so that I can share it with others, even if it's only to tell them I'm sorry. I know how hard it is to open your mouth and drop the bomb on others that exploded in your own face days, weeks, or months earlier. I just did it yesterday.

But the sharing goes both ways. This precious lady said she'd come in to find a book because she needed a laugh. First of all, I understand her need to feel something besides sorrow. Second of all, she reminded me that my life may be completely different now, but it consists of more than grief.

And that's good.

*I will turn their mourning into joy. I will comfort them and exchange their sorrow
for rejoicing.*
Jeremiah 31:13b NLT

July 15

"*When you reflect on experiences in your life, can you identify any that God used to
minister to others or to further His kingdom? Are you in a difficult situation right now?
Ask God to help you learn from it and to trust Him for your future.*" [84]

These were the questions in my *Our Daily Bread* devotional booklet this
morning (https://odb.org/2017/07/15/prepared/).

Before I even read that, I woke up thinking that this story wouldn't be complete
without my story as a background, because a lot of what you've read thus far
seems improbable if you don't know who my Father is.

I've often said that I can't imagine walking this path without Jesus by my
side. I really mean that. I don't even want to try to imagine it. If you're trying
to do that, I'm here to tell you that you don't have to. You can become my Father's
child, too. It's so easy it will also seem improbable, but I promise you it's true.

I was 26 years old when I figured out that everything in my life, regardless of
how full or busy it was, was meaningless. There was no purpose, no goal, except
to work and raise my son (I was divorced) and keep my financial head above
water. When I thought about what my life would look like in the long term, I
just saw more work, more financial water-treading, and a son who'd grow up
and go off to lead his own life. I felt a strange unsettledness in my heart that I
couldn't satisfy and I couldn't ignore.

Have you felt that? Have you done all the right things, followed the world's
prescription for happiness, and still feel that it's just out of reach?

Not long after I admitted to myself that I felt this void I couldn't fill, I met someone who obviously didn't feel this way. I couldn't put my finger on what was different about him, but he had a sense about him of comfort within his own skin. He wasn't perfect or anything like that, but he was content.

Do you know someone like that? Someone whose life, no matter what they may face, exudes a peace that is just as undeniable as it is inexplicable?

I had several long talks with this person. Most of them were the superficial, social kind, but a few were deeper. In one, my friend asked me flat out, "Are you going to heaven when you die?"

At this moment, how would you answer that question?

My first thought was, *I hope so.* Before I could get the words out of my mouth, my friend said that lots of people hoped so, but few could actually say yes. Then he went on to explain that he himself could say yes, but not because of anything he had done. My friend had asked Jesus to be his Savior.

I went to church as long as I lived at home with my parents. I knew who Jesus was and what He had done, but somehow I had missed out on the why.

Do you know why?

We do bad things, say bad things, think bad things. There is nothing we can do to fix ourselves. We are broken. Many think - hope - that the good they've done outweighs the bad, and on that basis they "hope" they'll go to heaven when they die.

They won't. Only a perfect sacrifice could outweigh all the bad we've done, thought, or said. And we're not perfect. But there is One who *is* Perfect. And He loved us enough to make the sacrifice that was needed so that it would be possible for us to enter heaven. Possible, but not automatic. The sacrifice was made for us, but we have to claim it as our own. We have to admit it was necessary because we're unable to make it ourselves.

My friend's job required a transfer. He was leaving in a few months. I remembered how lonely and unsettled I'd felt before we met. I dreaded facing it again when he left. Eventually, I figured out that it wasn't my friend that was filling that lonely place inside me. It was *his* Friend, Jesus. I dusted off my Bible and started reading it for myself. Everything my friend had told me about heaven and Jesus had come straight from the Bible.

Do you wonder about the things people have told you about the Bible? Check it out for yourself. God has blessed you with a plethora of ways to find out: Bible apps, audios, and eBibles in a myriad of translations. If you have trouble choosing, ask the advice of your friend with the peace that you don't understand.

A few months before my friend was transferred, I came to the realization that I could have what he had; I could experience the same peace and contentment that he did. So one night, I knelt beside my bed and prayed. I told God that I understood that no matter how good I was or how many kind things I did, I could never earn my way into heaven. I told God that I believed that Jesus had died on the cross to pay my penalty, and He rose again to make a way for me to go to heaven. I asked Jesus to be my Savior.

And He said, "Yes."

If you ask Jesus to be Your Savior, He'll say "Yes" to you, too.

No bells or whistles went off when I trusted Jesus to be my Savior, but I knew something had changed. Though I would miss my friend when he transferred, I knew I'd never be alone again. Jesus had filled the void in my heart, and He promised to never leave me or forsake me. I hadn't been missing some"thing" in my life, I'd been missing some"One": Jesus. And He has given me a purpose; I live to praise Him and tell others what He's done for me. But the greatest thing of all is knowing for certain that I have eternal life, and I'll be spending it in heaven with Him.

And my friend? He later became my husband.

After we married, my son William accepted Jesus as his Savior.

This afternoon, while going through some things, I came across this biography assignment that William wrote for school...

"I was born in Virginia Beach, Virginia. I've lived in Virginia Beach and I'm living in Arlington, Texas. I'm nine years old. Lots of important things have happened in my life, but the most important thing was accepting Jesus Christ to

be my savior when I was four years old."

Amen.

I saw her today, the cardinal with the wounded leg. Her presence is an encouragement to me to keep going, in spite of my own wound, my inability to function as I once did. I know as long as I go to my Father for comfort and strength, He will continue to provide. Just look above at what He did for me today.

I have a good, good Father. You can have Him, too. Do you?

July 16

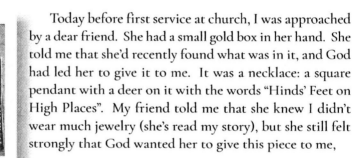

Today before first service at church, I was approached by a dear friend. She had a small gold box in her hand. She told me that she'd recently found what was in it, and God had led her to give it to me. It was a necklace: a square pendant with a deer on it with the words "Hinds' Feet on High Places". My friend told me that she knew I didn't wear much jewelry (she's read my story), but she still felt strongly that God wanted her to give this piece to me,

I recognized the words on the pendant. My friend mentioned they referenced a Bible verse, and I recalled there was also a book by the same title. [85] In fact, shortly after William died, another friend had recommended I read the book by Hannah Hurnard. As first service began, I tucked the box inside my pocket and concentrated on worshipping my Father.

Today's message was entitled, "It Takes a Thief". It was about the character of our enemy and how he's been trying to rob God of His rightful place in our hearts since the dawn of time. Part of the enemy's thieving character is stealthiness. (After all, if you *see* a thief coming, you prepare yourself.). His desire is to catch you unaware, when you least expect an attack.

Like while you're planning your mother's funeral, and your son dies before you can bury her.

The summary of the message included these thoughts:

"Bad things do happen to God's people."

Oh, yes, they do.

"We must trust God through them."

Oh, yes, we must.

Some days life flows along and the pain of my loss is familiar, but manageable. Other days, life bumps along through a string of "potholes" that weary my soul and make the pain of my loss difficult to endure. On the milestone days where I anticipate it, I pray for strength. On the days I don't expect it, I don't know to pray against it. When my guard is down, the enemy can use grief to rob me of my joy, to distance me from God, and to isolate me from the very brothers and sisters in Christ whom God put in my life to encourage me. On those days when the grief dogs my every step, I must turn my heart away from its insistent call and toward the gentle whisper of my Father's invitation to walk in His ways and rejoice in His presence. It takes discipline and commitment to turn from the cacophony created by a grieving heart and to listen for the still, small voice of God calling you away from the pain and into His peace.

After we got home from church, I pulled out the necklace. I looked up all three scriptures (more "threes") containing the phrases "hinds' feet" and "high places" (2 Samuel 2:34, Psalm 18:33, Habakkuk 3:19) and read through them, asking God for clarity and direction. I studied the individual words. I read several different translations. Nothing clicked.

I took a break, then picked up the necklace and examined it. I turned it over and was intrigued to find inscriptions on the back. Among them was "Hab 3". I went back and read that whole chapter to get the context of verse 19. It is a prayer which speaks of all Habakkuk has seen God do. Near the end, Habakkuk acknowledges the fact that life will contain trials and tribulations, and how we respond to them will determine our outlook.

It's not so much where your feet are in your journey as where your heart is. Can you look at the struggles you face and still rejoice in the God who saves? Can you trust that, whatever your path on this earth, God will give you the sure-footedness to walk it in His strength?

When we got home from church, there was a present for us. Someone (it turned out to be our neighbor's son) had put a sign in our yard, one whose message reinforced what God had shown me in today's message and in my dear friend's gift.

Although the fig tree shall not blossom, neither shall fruit be in the vines; the labour of the olive shall fail, and the fields shall yield no meat; the flock shall be cut off from the fold, and there shall be no herd in the stalls: Yet I will rejoice in the Lord, I will joy in the God of my salvation. The Lord God is my strength, and He will make my feet like hinds' feet, and He will make me to walk upon mine high places. To the chief singer on my stringed instruments.
Habakkuk 3:17-19 KJV

step 12

Counting His Blessings

When they walk through the Valley of Weeping,
it will become a place of refreshing springs.
The autumn rains will clothe it with blessings.

Psalm 84:6 NLT

July 23

It's been eleven months since my older son William died. Eleven months ago tonight I got a phone call no parent should ever have to take. I, in turn, made phone calls no mother should have to make. In the blink of an eye, my whole world changed.

God has been the only constant in my ever-changing world these last few months, the one Person I could count on to be the same yesterday, today and forever. He has never left my side. He has promised He never will. He has held me as I cried in grief and confusion and frustration. He has listened to me whine and moan and gripe. He has comforted. He has exhorted. He has admonished. There is not one instance where I have called out to Him that He has not answered.

Often, His answer comes in the form of His children: brothers and sisters in Christ who are His hands and feet to me. They hug. They pray. They cry. They talk. They listen. They encourage. They counsel. They love.

His answer also comes in His Word. The fact is, I would have missed a great deal of comfort and peace if I had chosen to shake my fist at the heavens and turn my back on God. Instead, I choose to dive headfirst into my Father's presence and immerse myself in His Word. I've never been sorry.

Sometimes, His answer to my cries comes in a tiny, timely miracle, one whose significance is unique to me. A candle from a loved one. A scarf from a new friend. A vase from family. An ornament that was lost, but now is found. A necklace from a friend.

I have truly learned the meaning of "faithful". No matter when I've called, no matter where, God has answered. I don't question *if* He will answer, only *how*.

Many times I've awakened with a heavy heart. Instead of holding on to it, I've learned to lay it bare before the Lord, and then wait expectantly to see how He will answer. He never disappoints and often His answers go far beyond what I expected or imagined.

I'm in my infancy of being a bereaved mother - only eleven months old. I've learned a lot in a short time, but there is so much more before me. One of the greatest blessings in this journey is knowing that my Father will always be there to teach, guide, and comfort.

If you haven't met Him, I'd love to introduce you.

Blessings from the valley,
Leslie

I posted the above on my social media page just after midnight, and then spent a very restless night for no obvious reason. I woke up after a perfectly miserable few hours of sleep, just before my radio alarm went off. I literally was praying (well, whining, really) about being tired of being so grief stricken and asking God would He please just take this burden from me.

When my radio went off, the first thing I heard was the last three (again with the threes) lines of "What Faith Can Do" [86] sung by Kutless, reminding me that falling is what allows God to give you the strength to get back up.

The very next song? Without even an announcement or ad beforehand?

"I Will Trust in You" [87] by Lauren Daigle.

God did just what He's been doing for eleven months, and He's going to do it for the rest of my life.

And I'm going to have faith and trust Him.

How about you?

Dear William,

Another month has passed. I still have days when I wonder why you don't call. I still sometimes wake up wondering if I've had a terrible nightmare. While everyone around me picks up the pieces of their lives and moves on, there's a piece of mine missing.

It has your name on it.

There's never going to be a day where I won't feel the ache of your absence. Sometimes it's just a whisper of pain, a sigh. Sometimes it feels unbearable, shouting so loud it drowns out nearly everything. I'm learning to keep it mostly to myself these days. It's becoming a private thing between God and me. A select few know when I'm struggling to bear up under it. God stays very close on those days, and I am very grateful. When the desire to see your face or hear your voice or give you a hug is overwhelming, I cry out to Him. He always answers. I'm never surprised that He answers, but I am often amazed at how.

There have been changes in me since you left. Some are good changes. I've stepped outside my comfort zone several times to honor your memory. Some are not. Just recently, I've noticed that my social greetings have changed. I don't ever answer "I'm fine" in answer to "How are you" anymore. I usually say "So far so good", and then change the subject.

Because I'm not fine. I stopped being fine eleven months ago.

But I'm choosing to focus on the good and give the bad to God so He can redeem it. Even in death you continue to reach out to those in need like you did in life. Some have donated to your cousin's animal rescue organization in your honor. Others donated over $2100 to the local pregnancy center here in your name. It brings a measure of comfort to know that so many think so highly of you, and love and miss you as I do.

There aren't words to adequately express the pain of outliving your firstborn. I'm grateful you'll never know it.

I wish I didn't.

I love you.

I miss you.
Mom

July 24

Yesterday was a hard milestone for me. I don't know why. I wish I did, because then I could have prepared in advance for the onslaught of sorrow. From the outside it probably looks like wallowing in self pity. Not so, my friend. It's like the lead apron you have to wear at the dentist office: heavy, but unavoidable. I strive to keep my mind on God, but it takes a lot of energy when these attacks of the enemy (and that's essentially what they are) come. My energy reserves are being taxed right now because of two large projects at work that both reach their final culmination this week.

I got home late from work, and I couldn't settle to anything. I decided to look up some quotes I had set aside a few months ago that spoke to me. I found the quotes in my computer notes file and opened them. The top one on the list looked familiar. I thought I might have written about it, so I arbitrarily selected an entry about six lines down from the quote file and opened it up.

It's the entry for April 3. I read the whole thing. While I was reading, I could almost feel God's breath against my ear as He whispered to me through my own words - words He gave me for such a time as this.

Go ahead and flip back. You know you want to.

He surprised me again.

And again with a three...

July 25

God got my attention today through a friend I've only known for a few months. Earlier in our relationship, she had told me that she lost an eight-year-old daughter many years ago, but at the time I didn't know her well enough to do anything more than offer my sympathies.

Today I shared with her how this past weekend was a struggle for me, because I knew she would understand. During our conversation, she shared more details of her loss. It happened the day after Christmas. Her daughter was hit by a car while crossing the road. My friend was seven months pregnant at the time.

I have so much to be thankful for.

So do you.

July 28

Today was the last of a series of work projects that I had to complete. While waiting for one of the events to begin, I was talking with one of my volunteers. She's a school librarian who graciously volunteered her time and talents to the project I was heading up. I've worked with her for about four weeks.

In the course of conversation today, I was telling her about something William had done or said. I've learned to qualify my conversation about him ("my late son" or "my older son who died last August") to ward off questions that ultimately pinch my heart and embarrass the one who asked them. After I shared my thought about him, she paused and said, "You know, we lost a son too. He was fourteen. Cancer."

My heart lurched. I had no idea. I only had a few minutes to share with her how sorry I was and how much God has done for me on my journey. However, I am praying and listening for God's leading on whether I should say more.

I know some of you reading this are in the valley, too. I know it's dark in places. I know it's lonely. I know it's difficult and exhausting. But you are not alone, not really. God is walking with you, and He's just waiting for you to ask for His help. When you do, He will help you, comfort you, strengthen you for tasks you never thought you'd have to perform. Reach up. He's there for you.

And there are more people in the valley than you can see. You can meet them in a local group or a social media group, or, like me, God will draw you together in unexpected and surprising ways. On the days where the sorrow lies heavy on your heart, reach out - before and behind you. Grasp the hand of someone who knows your pain and can empathize with your loss. Those ahead will have a word of encouragement for you. Those behind could use a word of hope from you.

Let everything you say be good and helpful,
so that your words will be an encouragement to those who hear them.
Ephesians 4:29b NLT

July 29

This week has been hard. My coworker of ten years retired yesterday (Friday). I finished a major work project that very same day. I am fairly spent, but God has given me His strength to see me through.

Thursday night I was asked to sign "Ever Be" [88] for our worship services on Sunday (tomorrow). In spite of the fact that I haven't learned the song yet and have never signed it, I said yes.

Some might wonder why I'd tax myself after such a monstrous week. I can't think of a better way to thank my Father for the strength He's bestowed upon me at every point where I needed it than to sign praises to His name.

I sent a scripture verse to a friend today, one that reminded me of the mission she feels God has called her to. In her response she included the remark:

"You have been heavy on my heart. August."

Yes. August.

God will get me through August. Instead of dreading the days, I'm going to anticipate all the ways and people He will use to encourage me and help me through.

July 30

Yesterday I said I would watch to see how God would reach out to me next month with comfort and encouragement. I don't doubt He'll do it.

He's already started.

A couple of weeks ago, I asked for August 23-27 off from work. I explained why, and my boss was very understanding. He granted my request, but then I found myself in a quandary. What on earth would I do for those five days? Wasting them sitting around stewing in my grief wouldn't honor God or William's memory.

But God already had it in hand.

He started by arranging a back-to-school event at our church. On August 26. Working to help other children would be a good way to show thankfulness for my own.

And then I received a message today from one of the servants in the local bereaved parent ministry. They are doing the memorial bike rally in September. Part of the message read:

"Leslie, we are decorating bandanas for the bike riders to wear in honor of our angels in the rally. We are doing that August 24."

God is on the move.

Hallelujah.

July 31

The following verses came up in my chronological Bible reading today.

"No longer will you need the sun or moon to give you light, for the Lord your God will be your everlasting light, and He will be Your glory. The sun will never set, the

moon will not go down. For the Lord will be your everlasting light.
Your days of mourning will come to an end."
Isaiah 60:19-20 NLT

Of course, it was the last part of the verse that caught my eye. It actually reaffirms what I and so many other bereaved parents know from experience. There *will* be a day when our mourning comes to an end, but it will *not* be on this earth. It will be when our family is reunited in heaven. Expecting us to "get over" our loss will only discourage us and frustrate you. Even God doesn't expect that of us.

I've mentioned before that the same organization that did the floating lantern ceremony is doing a memorial bike rally in September. I've also mentioned that my husband recently got his motorcycle license, and I have felt God prodding me to ride in that bike rally. Today, for the first time in my entire life I climbed on the back of my husband's bike for a test run. My son, William, would get a kick out of knowing he got me on a motorcycle. I'm sure I'll be able to laugh about it - after my stomach climbs down out of my throat and my head stops spinning.

August 1

"Dear August, I hate you with every ounce of my being. That is all!!!"

This was posted to social media this morning by my cousin, who lost her mother (my mother's younger sister) exactly eleven years to the day William died. She later shared that she had almost become reconciled to the loss of her mother (she was barely eighteen when her mother died) when she lost my mom and then my son.

What she didn't know is what God had done for me this morning, the first day of a month that most certainly weighs heavy on my heart as well.

I start most mornings with half an apple. This morning I cut into the apple and cored it. When I removed the core, two of the seeds stuck together in the shape of a heart. I've never seen that happen before. When two more came out stuck in the shape of a heart, I thought to myself, "wouldn't it be something if God gave me a third pair in a heart shape".

And then, He did. I was so excited to be able to share on social media what He'd done, but alas, the third pair slipped apart. I decided that this must have been a "hug" just for me, one of those little gifts God gives me to comfort me when I'm feeling the weight of my grief.

Then I saw my cousin's post and realized that I'm not the only one feeling the weight of this month. I went back and checked and, sure enough, the other two "gifts" were still intact. I think perhaps they weren't meant just for me, but for my cousin *and* me. God loves us. He sees our pain. He's with us. And my aunt and my mom and my son are with Him. We can have joy, even in our mourning.

I picked up a book this weekend for a light read. In it, I came across the following lines:

> *"Even if you're having a hard time loving Him, He's not having a hard time loving you."* [89]
> from *The Red Door Inn* by Liz Johnson

I have never had an issue with loving God, but for a time after William died, I had a hard time verbalizing it. I can't explain why I couldn't. It just felt... uncomfortable. I confessed this shortcoming in a small group of prayer warriors at the time that I was struggling with it, and they prayed for and with me. God used them to help me through that rough spot.

Maybe you're going through a rough spot. Perhaps you need to be reminded that God's love for you is not dependent on your love for Him. He loved you first. He'll love you always.

We love Him, because He first loved us.
1 John 4:19 KJV

Give thanks to the Lord, for He is good! His faithful love endures forever.
1 Chronicles 16:34 NLT

August 2

Do you remember the last time you saw your firstborn?

This is a picture of the last day I saw mine.

Eleven months ago today we buried him.

Nothing will change that. Nothing will make it better or easier. Pretending that it will would be a vile act of hypocrisy on my part. A portion of my heart's been amputated. I won't get that back on this earth.

You will continue to post about your children.

So will I.

If you get tired of hearing me repeat the same stories, keep in mind that I can't make new ones. I have to celebrate the ones I have until I get to heaven.

Please share your memories of my son on his memorial page. What may seem ordinary to you is precious to me, because memories are what I have for now.

If you never met my son, drop by the page and see him through the eyes of those of us who did know and love him.

And the next time you hug your child, say a prayer for me and those like me who no longer have that precious privilege.

We buried him eleven months ago today.

When I woke up yesterday, it was with a heaviness of heart that I suspect I will carry right through September 2. I believe some of you might, as well.

I have a cousin who lost her mother on August 23, eleven years before we lost William. She posted her opinion of August yesterday, and I could hear the pain in her words.

Because it echoed mine.

I shared with her an incident from earlier in the morning. When I cut and cored an apple, three pairs of the seeds inside it came out stuck together. They looked like hearts. I had thought I would post about them, but then one of them came apart and I forgot about them until I saw her post.

This morning, when my radio alarm went off and my brain finally engaged, the song playing was "Count Them All" [90] sung by the JJ Weeks Band. The whole song is about being able to count your blessings in the good times and the bad, the easy times and the hard, the painful places and the pleasant.

So, I got the message. This month my goal is to count my blessings. It won't be easy, but God didn't promise us easy.

I got up, went in the kitchen and got out my morning apple, and got to work.

I cut it.

I cored it.

And out popped another pair of seeds in the shape of a heart.

Blessing #1.

August 3

Blessing #2 popped up in my social media news feed first thing this morning. It was an article from www.thelifeididntchose.com (http://wp.me/p6Kfmo-aUu) about the various ways bereaved parents have learned to cope with grief anniversaries.

In twenty days, I will reach the one year mark since my son died.

It was encouraging to hear some ideas about how others have coped. I haven't been able to think beyond taking days off and waiting to see what God would have me do with them. However, the post gave me helpful ideas for those days when I fall prey to the enemy's attacks and need to make a deliberate decision to use that attack to glorify God, not my grief.

If you're a bereaved parent, I recommend the website listed above. The author is a bereaved parent, too, and she speaks from the perspective of experience and empathy.

August 4

A few days ago, a dear friend went for a final checkup after a medical issue. Tests showed what was thought to be a minor condition requiring a routine procedure as treatment. When the procedure went from routine to unusual, my friend's world was tilted on its axis as she awaited more test results for three days.

Another "three".

In the space of those three days, I prayed off and on for my friend. Over the last few months, I've come to an even better understanding of my prayer relationship with my Father. I don't need to be fancy. I don't need to be wordy. When I'm being held to the flame or am praying while working or sleeping, my prayers often consist of one or two words.

The one word? Father.

Two words? Father, and the name of the person on my heart.

For three days and nights, it was "Father, (my friend's name)..."

On the day she was waiting for the phone call, I emailed her several times. I wanted to be sure she knew that she was on my heart and I was lifting her up.

At lunch, (2:08pm to be exact) I sent her an email prayer asking God for healing or something even better.

At 2:09pm I received an email (and a phone call) with the good news that God had answered our prayers.

Blessing #3.

From that time forward, the words of my prayer were the same, but the emphasis changed.

"Father! (My friend's name)!"

Friends, when your heart is crushed and just breathing is a chore, persevere in prayer. It doesn't have to be fancy or fluent. It doesn't have to be eloquent or expressive. It doesn't have to be verbal or verbose. It just needs to be *genuine*. God wants your heart - not your words, not your works - just your heart. When you reach out to Him in truth as well as love, your relationship with Him will become deeper and more intimate than you can ever imagine.

My friend stopped by and spoke to me at work today. She shared a little of what our Father revealed to her during her three day wait. I believe He's laid a seed of hope in her heart, a heart that has diligently sought His will for her life's calling, and followed Him wherever He has called her to go.

And my friend? She is the first person who recognized in my story the words of hope and encouragement for others. If you're reading this in book form, her desire to follow God's call on her life is the reason it came about.

To God be the glory.

August 5

It wasn't until a few days ago that I realized I am scheduled to work on September 2. We buried William on September 2 last year. My first inclination was to trade Saturdays with someone. However, we're currently understaffed. In addition, I've already requested time off surrounding the anniversary of his death. In light of all this and after praying, I decided to go ahead and work that day and trust God for the outcome.

I was sitting here thinking about it when I remembered a discussion we had at work about that specific weekend and some other schedule changes that needed to be made. I got up just now to check.

That Saturday I'll be working with the only other employee on staff who has experienced child loss.

Blessing #4.

God is good.

All the time.

August 6

Today at church, I caught up with a dear friend so I could tell her something. I did. Then she told me something.

Several weeks ago, she had requested prayer for an unspoken need. It concerned a chronic condition and its effects. The request she made initially had been answered some time ago, but the condition itself remained a constant source of uncertainty and anxiety.

This week, while contemplating the issue, my friend told me she felt frustration about having to live with this condition for the rest of her life. She said she thought to herself, "This is more trouble than it's worth."

The next morning, she woke up, and every single symptom of the condition was gone.

Every single symptom of a condition she's had for almost twenty years.

Gone

Just like that.

Blessing #5.

William died on a Tuesday night. Wednesday morning I went straight to church to a ladies' prayer group. They were my first line of support that day. They cried with me, prayed with me, made me eat breakfast. They were the hands and feet of Jesus on a day that even now is foggy in my mind.

This year August 23 will fall on a Wednesday, so I checked with one of the members of the group to make sure they still meet. She said they do. I asked to join them on the 23rd and explained why. When I told her, she looked shocked. She said she couldn't believe it had been a year. I can't either, but I imagine most people I know think it's been longer. That my friend has even a small sense of the freshness of my son's loss to me every day is a blessing to me.

So, God is slowly filling those days I opted out of work. I don't doubt there'll be a blessing in every one. Looking for them will keep my eyes and mind on God and off myself.

Milestones in this valley can be opportunities - for God to work in you, and for you to work for God. Will that make them easier to navigate? Not really, but it will give you something to focus on besides your grief and it will bring God glory in the process. And, just maybe, your determination to bring God glory will encourage someone else.

August 7

Today my ex-daughter-in-law posted on social media.

My grandson has told her he wants to be baptized.

Blessing #6.

August 8

Today a "sister in loss" (I just read that term online) posted a picture from Niagara Falls, where she and her family are vacationing. It shows a rainbow at the Falls.

R - emember

O - ur

Y - ahweh

G - od's

B - lessings

I - n the

V - alley

Blessing #7.

August 9

I spent a good portion of this morning having to tell people their items were due on August 23. It was dreadful. It nearly choked me the first two times. It pinched my heart *every* time.

I'll be spending a good portion of this afternoon doing the same thing.

I dragged home for lunch and saw a dragonfly on the porch. It was green. It reminded me of William's high school colors.

And, of course, the epic "dragonfly chase" across the hospital parking lot last year. (See July 4.)

Blessing #8.

August 10

I have never been one to join all sorts of groups and organizations. I'm not put together that way. However, I have learned that on this journey, there is safety and encouragement in numbers. I have joined a couple of social media groups specifically geared for bereaved Christian parents. Today I read a child loss post that contained a link [91] to a short devotional about the storms that occur in our lives. The author pointed out that although the storms pass, the rain that falls from them remains behind in all the places where it fell and is absorbed. In essence, the storms we endure are what produce fruit in our lives. It also contained the following quote:

"The rainbow!—see how fair a thing
God hath built up from tears."
—Henry S. Sutton

The rainbow reference reminded me of the working title for this journey...

Joy in the Mourning: Viewing the Rainbow from the Vale of Tears

A reminder...and blessing #9.

I saw another social media post about how so many who sympathize tell us that they can't imagine surviving child loss. Well, we couldn't either, until we had to. The post pointed out that survival is only the beginning of the journey for bereaved parents. Once we can breathe and function, our next question should be "What does God want me to do with this?"

What *does* God want me to do with this?

He wants me to live it in His strength.

He wants me to give it to His keeping.

He wants me to share it for His glory.

August 11

My devotional today was about the if-onlys that often dog our steps in the wake of a tragedy. (https://odb.org/2017/08/11/if-only/). Included in the entry was this prayer:

"Father, You have carried me through hard circumstances before. Thank You for teaching me to trust Your heart of love even when I don't understand what You are doing in my life." [92]

I'm approaching the one year mark, and I'm still sometimes swamped by a wave of grief so strong it takes God's strength for me to reach the surface. I will always remember when I first heard the news. It felt as if someone smacked my head with a 2x4, and I remember being puzzled by the fact that my heart could continue to beat and my lungs continue to expand and contract as if my world had not just exploded into pieces - pieces that I've spent months trying to rearrange and refit, knowing all the while that there's one important piece missing.

It's in heaven.

That prayer is one I'm still learning how to live.

The devotional also included the following quote by Charles Haddon Spurgeon.

"To trust God in the light is nothing, but to trust Him in the dark—that is faith." [93]

As I approach an anniversary no mother ever wants to see, these were just what I needed to remind me to be careful where I step in this valley and to always hide His Word in my heart, so that it may be a lamp for my feet and a light for my path.

And they were blessing #10.

August 12

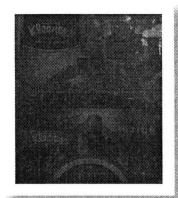

While running an errand this afternoon, I came across a packet of tissues in a checkout aisle that reminded me of my son.

I felt a little silly, but I posted it to William's memorial site with the comment:

"Went out to run an errand. Saw this while in the checkout line. Had to buy it, but doubt I'll ever use them, no matter how badly I need them.

And I need them more often now than I did before last year.

I miss you."

Within one minute I got this response from his childhood friend:

"I just bought that same pack."

Blessing #11.

Someone recently gave me a picture of the "stages of grief". It resembled a large "U" with the "stages" printed down one side and up the other. I thanked her (she meant well), and my first thought on looking at that "U" is that the "experts" may have gotten the "stages" part right, but they missed the boat on the progression. When I saw that "U", I immediately saw child loss as a ping pong ball dropped in that chasm, pinging and ponging off the sides in a chaotic, random fashion. That's what my child loss experience has been like. My second thought when I saw it was actually a question. Which one of the "experts" who drew that figure had lost a child? My guess would be none.

August 13

Time sat heavy on my hands yesterday. As a consequence, today I woke up with a sigh. If you're in this valley, you know the sigh I'm talking about. I forced myself out of bed and began my morning routine, beginning with my quiet time and devotional (https://odb.org/2017/08/13/from-fear-to-faith/). [94] I hunted up the scripture and began reading aloud, as is my habit. I'm ashamed to say I was only half paying attention, until I got to the last verse.

The Lord God is my strength, and He will make my feet like hinds' feet,
and He will make me to walk upon mine high places.
Habakkuk 3:19 KJV

See July 16.

Blessing #12.

August 14

Last night I received the details for my grandson's baptism. It will be August 20.

Two days after the one year milestone of my mother's death.

Three days before the anniversary of his father's (my son's) death.

Joy...in the mourning.

Blessing #13.

My Bible reading today included Jeremiah 29:11.

> "For I know the plans I have for you," says the Lord.
> "They are plans for good and not for disaster,
> to give you a future and a hope." NLT

It's an oft-quoted verse to those facing an intense trial or struggle. However, context is key. God gave this message to a backslidden rebellious people whom He'd sent into exile for their disobedience. I believe this message was to encourage them that once disciplined (for their own good), He would restore them.

If you are tempted to share this scripture with a bereaved parent, I suggest you reconsider. To the ears of someone swamped in shock and grief, it might be misinterpreted by them as their child's death being part of God's plan and for their good. That's not what you meant, and it's not what it says - in context. Before you offer a scripture to a grieving friend, ask the Lord for His leading.

August 15

I saw the wounded bird this morning. She reminded me that my Father will take care of me as long as I turn to Him. (See July 11.)

Blessing #14.

August 16

I'm coming up on the first anniversary in seven days. My husband, bless his heart, asked me if I wanted to do anything special that day. My sinful self would like to fall in the floor, crying and kicking and pummeling the ground until I'm too exhausted to lift a finger or shed one more tear. My spiritual self recognizes that it won't change a thing - just give me a headache and body aches to go with the heartache. I am grateful to God for His presence in the hard places. It's comforting to know He's aware of all that I'm feeling and loves me still.

Today there was a children's event at work. One of the children that came recognized me from some summer events we did and gave me a hug. Another one smiled as she told her mother about one of the stories that was read to them in those summer events. There's nothing sweeter than a freely given hug or smile from a child. They reminded me of my grandson, who I hope to see baptized in four days.

Blessing #15.

August 17

This morning at work, the dear friend who gave me the scarf came in. It was a "God-incident" that I saw her, because I wasn't scheduled to be working with the public when she came in. She asked me how I was doing, and I explained that tomorrow would be one year since my mom died.

That's when it happened. Blessing #16. Because my friend looked up and said, "When is the 17th?" I told her it was today. Surprised, she told me it was the two year milestone since her mother died. In all the times we've spoken, this is the first time we've talked about dates. I had no idea our milestones were only one year and one day apart.

But I know Who did.

I was able to share a small gift and card with my friend, and pass on a blessing to her. After all, blessings are meant to be shared, not hoarded.

Keep your eyes open. God will give you opportunities to be a blessing to others. Be watchful for them.

August 18

A year ago this evening, my mother passed into eternity. By all accounts it was peaceful. For that I am grateful, but it does not mean that I don't miss her.

We didn't always see eye to eye, my mother and I. She thought I made some bad choices here and there. I thought she didn't understand me. I can see now that we were both right.

But that didn't mean we didn't love each other.

Mom sacrificed a lot for us. She worked for 37 years at a job she really didn't seem to like so that she and Daddy could give my sister and me things that they never had as children. She sewed our clothes. She and Daddy scrimped and saved to put us in private school. They gave us the opportunity to go to college.

And she sat back and let me make mistakes she knew would break my heart, because she also knew it was the only way I would discover certain truths for myself...

1. I am broken.

2. I am not in control of my circumstances.

3. I *am* in control of my choices.

4. I cannot use #2 to excuse #3.

I was involved with the Awana program for over fifteen years. While completing one of the handbooks, there was an exercise that required me to write a letter to my parents. Being the t-crossing, i-dotting person I am, I just now went through my Awana stuff and - sure enough - I found the copy I filed with my handbooks. I've attached the pictures, but here's a transcription:

"February 3, 1995

Dear Daddy and Momma,

I am writing this letter as part of an assignment in my Awana JV handbook. My assignment is to write a letter to my mom and dad and thank them for what they do for me, making sure to mention some of the things I found in the scriptures I had to look up.

Deuteronomy 6:7-9 tells us to teach our children God's laws. You made sure we went to church and learned God's laws. Thank you for making sure I learned God's laws.

Proverbs 22:6 tells us to teach our children the way they should go. I believe this means parents should set a good example and be a role model for their children. You both set good examples for me. You are upright, honest, hardworking, and dependable. While you never preached against smoking and drinking, your own lives - free of smoke and drink - were a testimony far more impressive than words. Thank you for teaching me the way to go.

2 Corinthians 12:14 tells us to supply food for our children. I know as a child I never missed a meal, and even as an adult you've fulfilled this command! Thank you for always providing for me.

Ephesians 6:4 admonishes us not to scold or nag our children. I know as a child I did some things - foolish things - that you were tempted to scold and nag me about. (I know this because as a mother this is one area I am sorely tempted in myself!) You never gave me the attitude that failure was final. While I didn't like failure, I learned from each one. Thank you for not nagging *me or scolding me.*

1 Timothy 5:8 tells us to care for our children when they need help. You always helped me. I especially remember all the times you cared for me when I was sick. I'm a lousy patient, but I appreciate your taking care of me. I tried your patience, I'm sure! Thank you for taking care of me when I needed help.

1 Timothy 3:12 tells us to teach our children obedience. You did a great job teaching me this. I knew your word was law. And when I was small I knew when you said, 'one more time' you meant absolutely one more time. Thank you for teaching me obedience by setting boundaries for me and sticking to your guns.

I hope you enjoy this letter. I have enjoyed writing it.

Love,
Leslie"

It's not fancy or inspirational, but I remember my mother commenting on it after she got it, saying how it was good to hear how much I appreciated her. It made me glad I'd been required to write it, and that my parents were alive so that I could mail it.

If your mom is alive and you are old enough to understand the sacrifices she's made for you, do her (and yourself) a favor. Tell her so. Write it. Message it. Text it. Draw a picture. Take a photo. However you communicate the best, tell your mother how much she means to you. Tell her you appreciate the life she gave you. While you still have time...

Tell. Her.

Her children stand and bless her.
Her husband praises her:
"There are many virtuous and capable women in the world,
but you surpass them all!"
Charm is deceptive, and beauty does not last;
but a woman who fears the Lord will be greatly praised.
Proverbs 31:28-30 NLT

I posted the above to my social media today. Finding that letter, considering it's been 22 years since I wrote it, was Blessing #17.

On July 30 I explained I am off from work August 23-27, but didn't want to sit around and mope. I explained God would no doubt help me fill the days with activities that would honor Him. Today He filled in the last day. I had no plans for Friday, August 25. Then I received an email announcing an information booth and donut sale to support Trinity's Angels Bike Rally.

It's being held Friday, August 25.

Blessing #18.

August 19

Yesterday my husband explained to me how to enlarge pictures on my computer device. This morning I was standing in the kitchen with him practicing how to do it, when our wounded cardinal came to the birdfeeder. (She's on the feeder on the left. You can just barely see her wounded left leg dangling below her.)

To make sure I knew Who sent her, I found this in my apple this morning.

Blessing #19...and 20.

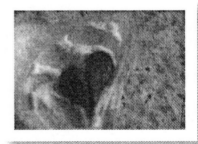

August 20

My family drove up to Oliver's church today and watched my grandson make a public profession of his inward decision to follow Jesus by being baptized. The enemy truly wanted to keep us away. Our GPS sent us down a road that sported the sign "Bridge out." We had to take a detour. From the church to the river, the GPS flat out lied, trying to send us in the opposite direction of the instructions I held in my hand. After that, it refused to recognize the city where my grandson lives. At the baptism itself, the battery on my husband's device he was using to film the event went nearly dead. Oh yes, the enemy was far from happy about how God has taken what he meant for evil and used it for good.

But we made it. We witnessed it. And it was glorious.

Blessing #21.

Before going down to the river, we attended service at the church. The pastor was speaking on Psalm 37. He was reminding people that the struggles of life can be used by God. One statement struck me right between the eyes. I'm sitting in a strange church of another denomination in another state, and the pastor says, "*Your struggle may not be about you. God may be preparing you to help somebody else.*"

Blessing #22.

I know I seem wishy-washy about the point of recording my journey, but God knows that about me. He loves me in spite of it, and even sends me confirmation again and again to encourage me to keep pressing on.

During the church service, we sat behind Oliver's great-uncle and great-aunt, who themselves have lost a son. After the service, Oliver's great-uncle pulled me aside. He had noticed me signing during the singing, and it reminded him that he wanted to ask me something. He quietly explained that last year he filmed my son's funeral with his cell phone, and he asked if I thought I'd like a copy.

Blessing #23.

If you had asked me before William died what I thought of services being filmed, I might have looked at you askance. That's because I was completely ignorant of the absolute shell-shocked state that comes when you suffer the sudden loss of a child. A lot of that day I don't remember, and most of what I do is the stuff I'd rather forget. Just in the last couple of months, I've wondered about bits and pieces of the service. My ex-sister-in-law was kind enough to share pictures she took, and I was thankful for them. I had no idea a film existed, and I am blessed beyond measure that he has offered me a copy. Will I be able to watch it? At some point, I think so. I don't think God would have offered me the opportunity if He didn't believe that at some point I would be ready to receive it. So, my first tears of the day were happy ones.

One of the unusual things that landed at our house after William died was his bath towels. I don't know why, but they ended up in the house and not in storage. I tried to get rid of them, and I couldn't. I couldn't conceive of ever using them, so there they sat. I had no idea what to do with them. Today, after his baptism, Oliver used one to dry off. It seemed a fitting way to draw William into the ceremony.

And it was blessing #24.

Dear William,

Your son made a beautiful profession of his faith in Jesus today by deciding to be baptized. Even though my heart is cracked, it is overflowing with gratefulness to God for bringing this beauty from the ashes of last year's tragedy. I love you and miss you. Even though you weren't here in body, each of us that knew and loved you brought our part of you with us.

Love,
Mom

August 21

This morning's devotional message (https://odb.org/2017/08/21/be-still-4/)[95] included the first two verses of Psalm 46:

> *God is our refuge and strength,*
> *always ready to help in times of trouble.*
> *So we will not fear, even if earthquakes come*
> *and the mountains crumble into the sea. NLT*

I have learned the truth of verse one. God is there *before* you know you need Him. He's ready, because He knows there will be times of trouble. That's why He put this verse in my devotional this morning.

Because I need His refuge. Right now.

And His strength is what will get me through this week.

The solid ground that was my predictable life shook in a violent earthquake almost one year ago, and the mountain of my expectations of what my life would look like, that mountain that I always expected to be there, solid and immovable, crumbled before my very eyes and slid into the vast, churning sea of grief.

Thank You, God, for always being ready to help me in times of trouble.

Because they are here.

Thank You, God, that You are my Rock, the One that will never be moved, never be shaken. Thank You that when my own hands tremble from the strain of clinging to You in the midst of the violent storm of emotions that is my life right now, I can rest knowing that You are holding me and Your grip will never fail.

I'm two days from the one year mark (I won't call it an anniversary - those are for celebrating), and I'm under constant attack by the enemy. After yesterday's baptism, I was feeling decent ("fine" never fits anymore). This morning I woke up feeling like I had swung from the crest of a wave into its deepest trough. I forgot stuff. I cried. I forgot more stuff. I cried more. I got to work and had to go back home because I forgot something. I went *back* to work and warned everyone not to rely on me for anything. I toughed it out, but now I'm not just sad, I'm tired, too. Tired of explaining why I'm not myself. Tired of trying to find a way to answer "How are you?" without being rude or oversharing. Tired of crying. Tired of being tired.

I should have expected the enemy's attack after yesterday's victory.

Part of my job involves children's books. Today I was cataloging and I came across a book entitled "Baabwaa and Wooliam." [96] When William was five, I had a prayer partner with two small children. Her daughter was about two and a half when we started praying together. When she spoke my son's name, it came out sounding like "Wooliam".

Blessing #25.

August 22

So, it's almost here. The anniversary no one celebrates. The one nobody ever wants to see.

My firstborn died a year ago tomorrow.

I am not unaware that there are some on my friend list that don't want to hear about the hard parts of this journey, that think I should be able to keep my focus always on all the time I was blessed to have my son. I also know that as time passes, more people will join your ranks. In contemplating your viewpoint, I have come to the conclusion that there are two questions that I need you to answer so I can understand your perspective.

First, how long has it been since your child died?

I realize you can't get context in a social media post, so I'll just flat out say that I'm asking the question in a curious voice, not a sarcastic one. I really want to know if you have survived this. The reason I'm asking is because I know quite a few people that have, and I have met even more since I joined this club to which no one wants membership. None have taken me aside and said "you need to move on" or "be grateful for the time you had" or however else you would want to pretty-up the phrase "get over it". If you haven't walked in my shoes, your opinion necessarily carries less weight than someone who has. My son was a gymnast in high school. His gymnastics coach, however, had never been a gymnast. When William needed help, he often sought out the advice of the assistant coach - who had been a gymnast - rather than the coach who had not. This is the same principle.

Second, when was the last time you actually spoke to me?

If you're only keeping up with me on social media, then everything you read is out of context, because I am the context. A post is one moment in time, often one that I'm still in the process of working through. If you haven't actually spoken to me or seen me since William died, your view of me is skewed. I am not losing weight. I am not suffering from insomnia. I am not weeping uncontrollably or withdrawing from life in general. I am not sitting at home focusing on all I have lost.

I am working, eating, sleeping. I am engaging with others and staying involved in the work of the Lord. I am reaching out to those around me who've experienced loss. There are many days where my son's name doesn't cross my lips, although it forever rests in my heart. I have even gone for a "spiritual checkup" because I don't want to get bogged down in the grief that I will live with for the rest of my life. Yes, that's what I said. This is never going away.

And I'm sorry if you can't handle that. If it weren't for God's strength and comfort, I couldn't either.

I'm doing the best I can.

Please, pray for me.

I posted the above based on one person's remarks to me and two others that are using more subtle ways of getting their point across. I didn't want to say anything, because I really do understand that they haven't a clue, and I don't hold it against them. However, I finally decided that, in the interest others coming behind me in this journey, perhaps I should address the issue. My hope is to stimulate those on the outside to compassion instead of criticism. It's rough terrain we have to tread, and it doesn't come with a detailed map. We really are doing the best we can.

What I didn't expect was the multiple responses from friends in support of me. My sister offered to do something totally unexpected, which made me chuckle at a time when I didn't think I could. My "new" son offered some "physical enlightenment" to the offenders. Again I laughed. They both lightened a very heavy moment for me.

And that laughter was blessing #26.

As I was posting on social media, I came across a post by a former coworker. She had also lost her son sometime last year. What I didn't realize was that her son died the day before mine. I hate that we share this connection, but I know God allowed us to discover this fact so that we can share the comfort He's given us.

The opportunity to share His comfort with her today on her one-year milestone was blessing #27.

Our church's evening praise and worship service is this Sunday night. I usually volunteer to sign one of the songs that the leader chooses. This month, she has chosen "Ever Be". [97] It's about always praising God, whatever the circumstances. That's the beauty of His holiness. Praising Him, especially in song, is one of the places I feel the most free of my loss, my grief. I guess, in order to raise my hands, I must first lay down what I'm carrying.

August 23

My older son William died a year ago today.

I will *not* allow the enemy to claim one more inch of territory in this tragedy. I *will* allow God to use me as a vessel for His glory. I *will* praise Him for the time I had and trust Him with the time I didn't. I *will* offer Him the sacrifice of praise, even if I have to do it with tears streaming down my face.

While I was trying to think of words for today, God implanted in my thoughts... rose petals. So I did a little research.

We've all smelled roses, right? Some have a stronger scent than others, but they all seem to have some aroma. There are all different kinds and sizes and colors, and even when they grow on the same bush, no two of them are alike.

The petals of a rose can be used to make rose oil which can be used to scent products like soap and massage oil. Rose oil is more potent than rosewater, because the process is more intense. The petals are crushed or shredded or bruised. They're dropped in a jar of oil, which is then submerged in boiling water. The more you repeat the process, the stronger the fragrance that the petals will yield.

The last part of 2 Corinthians 2:14 says that God uses His children *"to spread the knowledge of Christ everywhere, like a sweet perfume."* NLT

We, the children of God...are roses. We're all different. Some of us are weaker, some stronger. We are made for the purpose of spreading the perfume of Christ. When life goes along like it's supposed to, that's what we do. Some of us are more potent that others, but we all emit the essence of our Savior in one form or another.

When life gets hard, when we are crushed, bruised, shredded - that's when we have the opportunity to allow the fragrance of God to intensify in our lives. When the boiling water of trials comes into our lives, we can be used by God in an even more powerful way. If we rest in the oil of His anointing, we will exude more of His presence as the enemy applies the heat of trials and suffering to our lives. The more trials we experience, the more potent our

Christlike fragrance can become.

That's my hope for my journey. I hope it has brought me to a place where I am spreading the knowledge of my Savior to everyone I meet, like a sweet perfume. Like the perfume Mary used on the feet of Jesus in John 12:3, I hope His scent fills the air around me. I hope those who don't recognize it are intrigued, and begin to inquire about the source of the fragrance.

It won't change what has happened, but it will redeem it.

For those of you who never met my son, there is a video that his friends lovingly put together for his funeral last year. You can view it at his memorial site. Forgive my shadow on the first part. William would have done a better job of it, but I'm a little technically challenged.

I posted the above entry to social media just shortly after midnight, because I assumed the rest of the day would not find me too coherent. A few minutes after I did, I received a message from one of William's closest friends. She shared some memories with me, and how much she still misses my son. Then she shared this: *"You would be happy to hear that I have turned to God to seek comfort in coping with Wil's loss, and I have you to thank for that. Sharing your journey has been an inspiration and left me longing to rekindle my relationship with God."*

Blessing #28.

I went to the ladies prayer meeting today as I had planned. One of ladies came in a few minutes after I did. I knew her name, but I can't recall ever being introduced before, though we've both been members for quite some time. And while I remembered her, there was one important fact I had forgotten.

She lost her 25-year-old daughter seven years ago.

When she came in, she shared how the morning had been one little crisis after another. It culminated in misplacing her keys, and she said she was a hair's breadth from just giving up and staying home. But she didn't.

Blessing #29.

Praying with someone who's walked this path is a precious, intimate thing that can't be described. Even talking with her, knowing that I don't have to explain myself with more than a few words...it was truly a gift from God.

After we prayed, we exchanged information on social media and we talked back and forth. In the process she shared that one of her regrets for her first loss year was that she didn't keep a journal. She encouraged me to do so.

Isn't God amazing to keep ensuring I remain on course?

Blessing #30.

Tonight my younger son and his girlfriend cooked dinner for us. They did something similar last year, shortly after the day that changed all our lives. It was a breath of fresh air to have them here. Just their presence in the house makes our lives a little lighter.

Blessing #31.

As this terrible difficult and exhausting day wound to a close, I received the following email from a sister in Christ. She doesn't use social media and had no way of seeing what I posted in the wee hours of this morning. As I read her email, I felt a sense of expectation rising in me, but even I had no idea what was about to happen.

Date: August 23, 2017 at 9:50:59 PM EDT

Dear sister in the Lord,

You have been on my heart today knowing it must be a very tough one....I woke up in the middle of the night last night and thought of you and what I might say to bring some comfort. I immediately thought of Joshua 1 about being strong and courageous, but knew that was not it....When I was thinking of you going through this and generously sharing with us all through your writings, I realized what you are giving to us, a story unfolding of your awesome intimacy with our Holy God....What a story and gift you are giving! AND, in all of that, God is strong and courageous through you as you take one step or word at a time....even when it must be sometimes overwhelming. I think that is why God brought strong and courageous to mind about you. His strength and courage is lived out in your intimacy with Him. THEN, my verse this morning seemed so right to share with you...2 Cor 2:14 " But thanks be to God, who always leads us in triumphal procession in Christ and through us spreads everywhere the fragrance of the knowledge of him." That is what you are doing, Leslie! Glory to God! May the peace that passes understanding continue to sustain you....

When I wrote this morning, I kept wondering, *why are You giving me roses?* Then, just before bedtime, to get my friend's note with THAT SAME VERSE! I ended up not going to sleep until almost 2:00am, but it wasn't grief that kept me up, it was glory!

GLORY, GLORY, GLORY!

Blessing #32!

August 24

I was so awed by God's last blessing to me last night, I didn't even try to go to bed until 1:00 this morning. When I did, the song "Count Them All" [98] was playing when I turned on the radio. It struck a chord with me, because that's what I felt led to do for most of this month. However, I had been looking for one blessing in each day. Now God told me to go back and look more closely.

Count them all.

So that's what I did. I got up today and set about recounting. I went back and counted them all. Just before I finished, I remembered my son and his girlfriend making dinner and had to go back and add it in.

Imagine my surprise when, as of yesterday, they came up to 32. William was 32 when he died.

Our God is an awesome God.

I could continue to count my blessings, but I think I've learned what God wanted me to see. Blessings are all around you. Even in the darkest of days, you can find a reason to praise God. You can.

Believe me, if I can, you can.

August 25

In speaking to my sister-in-loss at the prayer meeting Wednesday, she answered a puzzle for me. I have often stumbled over the question about how many children I have and where they live? My friend told me that when others ask about her daughters, she says, "I have two daughters. One lives in heaven and the other lives in New York." I like that answer because it's positive and it opens a door to share your faith, if the party cares to walk through it. I'd never heard that before. I appreciate the fact that it focuses on the future, not the past.

August 26

Today I volunteered at a back-to-school church event for kids. There I was approached by a friend. She told me how much she appreciated the Bible verses I post on social media each morning. She said she looks for them each morning, and even when she doesn't click on them, she always reads them.

I may have stopped numbering the blessings, but I'm still counting them.

August 27

It's 2:25 - in the morning and I am wide awake.

I don't know if everyone finds this true, but I sleep better if I wear myself out during the day. I was at an all-day event yesterday that really did the trick. I was nodding by eight and in bed by nine. I slept hard...until my husband starting getting ready for bed. By the time he settled in at about 11:30 last night, I was wide awake.

I haven't read extensively about grief and child loss because I didn't want to be influenced by what I discovered, but I have read a little here and there from other grieving parents in online sites devoted to sharing their walk through this tragedy called child loss. Some of the material I read mentioned insomnia, but I have always imagined that condition as being tired and wanting to fall asleep, but unable to do so. I am simply not sleepy, but I know that three hours from now, when I have to get up, I'm going to be wishing I had been asleep at 2:25 instead of typing.

In an effort to promote relaxation, we disconnect our wifi at night. I was tempted to resurrect it to research the true definition of insomnia. Instead, I went old school and looked it up in our encyclopedia. (Yes, we actually have one.) Among all the horrid causes they listed (such as mental illness, drugs and alcohol), it was defined as wakefulness, so I suppose I have insomnia.

I tried getting a drink of water. (That just led to the inevitable trip to get rid of said water.)

I tried music.

I tried reading.

I tried television.

I even tried a video game, which, surprisingly, usually does the trick.

It didn't.

In the past when I've been awakened around 3:00 or 4:00 in the morning, I've usually found they were calls to prayer, and would search my heart as I lay in bed, looking for the person God had laid on it. Then I would pray until I fell back to sleep.

I started there and prayed for a couple of people, but the wakefulness has persisted, and it has persisted to the point that my mind is now nearly fully engaged and running all those to-do lists that you wake up with when you're ready to start the day.

I do not want to start my day at - now - 2:50 in the morning.

This entry was a last ditch effort to unload some of my "wakefulness" and turn what the enemy wants to use to make me miserable into something good. I decided to use this opportunity to speak to those who find insomnia as a new bedfellow after child loss.

I want you to know you're not alone. And I get not wanting to be awake, because awake in a dark, quiet house with nowhere to focus your attention naturally causes your mind to turn inward. And when it turns inward, the first thing it comes across is a great big flashing sign: "Grief Zone - Enter at Your Own Risk". The minute you try not to think about it, it's stuck in your head and... there you go, right down the rabbit hole you've been working so hard to avoid.

I don't have any advice for you right now, just empathy.

But I will tell you what God just whispered to me.

Remember my calls to prayer usually come between 3:00 and 4:00?

Well, it's 3:15 now, and God is nudging me to head back to bed.

And to pray for all of you who are, or will one day find yourself, wide awake in the wee hours in the midst of a storm of grief and shock and loss, eyes wide open and streaming, heart cracking almost audibly from the waves of pain that are swamping you.

I hope you find some comfort in knowing that there's one broken-hearted momma out there praying for you tonight...I mean, this morning.

Heavenly Father,

I'm coming to you this morning on behalf of my brothers and sisters in Christ who have lost or will lose a child. I pray for those who, one night, find themselves tossing and turning, weary but unable to rest. I pray for those laying in bed, begging You for the oblivion of sleep, but unable to hear Your still small voice over the churning of their broken heart and the anguished screaming of their mind as they try to comprehend the incomprehensible.

Lord, they need to feel You near right now. In the absence of light and sound and activity, let Your presence be made known to them. Let all those scriptures they have hidden in their hearts begin to surface, one by one. With each breath of Your Word they exhale, let them inhale Your peace. Help them Lord, to count their blessings, even in the midst of their overwhelming grief. Help them start with the blessing that is their child's life, however brief it may have been. Show them things they can be thankful for: true things, just things, pure things. Help them to turn away from their grief toward You. Let their tears be healing ones that wash away the sharp edges of their grief. If they seek solace in music, let it be songs of worship that draw them closer to you. Take each wakeful moment and use it for Your glory and their good.

Father, I ask Your mercy upon those that walk this valley without You, whose hope died with their child. Of us all, they, Lord, are the most wounded because their pain is not tempered with eternity. Draw them to Yourself, Lord. Put one of Your children in their path - perhaps one of us that understands a portion of their pain - that can lead them to You. I pray they will seek their answers from the only One who has them, and may they find peace with You to be the only answer they need.

I pray all these things - or something better - in the name of Jesus. Amen.

I have no way to confirm this, though I will try a screen shot. It is exactly 4:00am, which would be about the time I would go back to sleep after being called to pray in the still of the night.

iPad · 4:00 AM · 44%

< Notes

Lord, they need to feel You near right now. In the absence of light and sound and activity, let Your presence be made known to them. Let all those scriptures they have hidden in their hearts begin to surface, one by one. With each breath of Your Word they exhale, let them inhale Your peace. Help them

God is good. All the time. If I start this day sleepy, it will be worth every yawn.

There's an old saying my dad used to use. "The 'tired' tree fell on me."

Folks, I got lost in the "tired" forest.

When my alarm went off at 5:00am, I shut it off and rolled over. When it went off at 6:00am, I hit snooze twice. When I finally put my feet to the ground, I seriously wondered if I should pick them right back up.

Then I remembered whose daughter I am. And that today is Sunday.

I'm up and moving, but occasionally still wondering.

Then I cored my apple. There sat two of the seeds in the shape of a heart.

Even when I pulled the seeds out of the core, they stayed together.

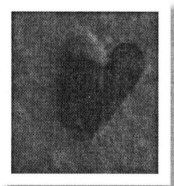

If seeds wrenched from their casing can still hold together, then once I wrenched myself out of that bed, God can hold me together.

Today's message at church was based on Psalm 51. Part of that Psalm (verses 10-12, to be exact) was some of the first scriptures I felt led to memorize when I became a child of God - not for a class or a contest or a Bible study, but for my own spirit. They were a reminder to continually be on the lookout for areas in my life I had not released to God. They're a good reminder on this journey. If I'm not vigilant to keep my mind and heart on God, it will wander. A wandering heart is a potential for disaster on every side. So, on your journey, keep a watch out for chinks in your armor, because the enemy is determined to distract you. He's wily. He'll go for your weak spots. Make sure he doesn't find any, or, if he does, make sure you shore them up before he settles into them.

Create in me a clean heart, O God; and renew a right spirit within me. Cast me not away from Thy presence; and take not Thy Holy Spirit from me. Restore unto me the joy of Thy salvation; and uphold me with Thy free Spirit.
Psalm 51:10-12 AKJV

I mentioned earlier about counting your blessings. Part of the message today spoke directly to that point.

"Some days your best thought is 'Well, God, I don't understand what all is happening in my life right now, but at least when my life is over, I'm going to heaven.'"

If that's the only blessing you can claim on any given day, it is enough.

Because He is enough.

After the second service I was approached by a woman and her daughter. The woman thanked me for signing during the services and shared how it had touched her. I told her it's the Holy Spirit's doing, not mine. We talked for a few minutes, and she shared that someone had told her I had been through a great deal this last year. When she asked, I told her about William. She shared she'd lost her first husband suddenly as well. I was able to share a hug and some words of sympathy with her.

If I had succumbed to the desire to sleep in today, just think of all that I would have missed.

It's 2:45 in the afternoon now. On a normal Sunday, I would be napping about now, but guess what.

I'm not a bit tired. I'm reminded of William's elementary/middle school's theme verse:

> But those who trust in the Lord will find new strength.
> They will soar high on wings like eagles.
> They will run and not grow weary.
> They will walk and not faint.
> Isaiah 40:31 NLT

August 30

I know now why I was up in the wee hours of the morning August 27, and I know who I was praying for.

I just got word that an old high school classmate lost his eleven-year-old son on August 26.

Have you ever felt that tug on your spirit? The one that has you wide awake when you shouldn't be? Don't ignore it. Answer the call, and follow the Lord's leading. You just might be the answer to someone's prayer.

We weren't more than acquaintances in high school, so my old classmate might never know I was praying for him and his family that night.

But *I* know.

And God knows.

And that is enough.

September 2

Dear William,

We buried you a year ago today. No wonder I'm having trouble concentrating on that bandanna. Celebrating your life is difficult when I'm also mourning your death.

A whole year...

Only one little year...

Time has never seemed longer...or shorter.

Lord,

This is a tough road you've called us to. Thank You for walking it with us. Thank You for all that You've taught us on it. Thank You for all the miracles - large and small - that You have performed and allowed us to witness. Thank You for lending me William for 32 years. I understand now that he's not my Wil, he's Yours. Thank You for his laugh. Thank You for his incessant talk and his enthusiasm for life. Thank You for his love. Thank You for that twinkle in his eye that meant he was up to something. Thank You for his love for his friends, because watching their dedication

to his memory over this last year has shown me their love for him, which I know is a reflection of his. Thank You for allowing him to experience the gift of fatherhood and the joy of raising his son. Thank You for allowing me to text him that I love him on his last night here, because I know that where he is now, there is no more night.

No Night There [99]

In the land of fadeless day
Lies the city foursquare;
It shall never pass away,
And there is no night there.

Refrain:

God shall wipe away all tears,
There's no death, no pain, nor fears,
And they count not time by years,
For there is no night there.

All the gates of pearl are made,
In the city foursquare;
All the streets with gold are laid,
And there is no night there.

All the gates shall never close
To the city foursquare;
There life's crystal river flows,
And there is no night there.

There they need no sunshine bright,
In that city foursquare;
For the Lamb is all the light,
And there is no night there.

We buried my firstborn a year ago today.

A. Whole. Year.

There are days when it feels as fresh as yesterday, when it's still inconceivable that I have survived my own child. When the grief ambushes me, God is there, waiting for me to reach out, knowing that I will need Him more than ever on those days.

I've made it through the year of "firsts", and tried to describe them the best I could. If I had to sum it up, being a parent-in-loss sucks, but that's okay. The less I find this world attractive, the more my heart longs for its true home. That's not a bad thing, especially if it gives you perspective and motivates you to help others through the valley.

Because we're all in this valley. We entered it the moment we took our first breath. Some are traveling in the upper elevations; they may not even recognize the fact that they're here. Others have been pushed a little deeper, made a little more aware of the darkness the shadow casts, and how far reaching it is.

Valleys are on my mind a lot these days, so I looked up some scripture references to them.

Psalm 84:6-7 reads:

> When they walk through the Valley of Weeping, it will become a place of refreshing springs. The autumn rains will clothe it with blessings. They will continue to grow stronger, and each of them will appear before God in Jerusalem. NLT

Two things stand out to me here. First, you can't have a rainbow without rain. Storms in life are a certainty. God promises to be there with us in every one of them. He also promises that the rains will bring blessings to the valley. I am a witness to that. Many of you are, too.

Second, we are walking "through" this valley. While we won't leave it on this side of heaven, it is a blessing to know that it is not our final destination.

I also found 2 Chronicles 20:26, and it spoke to me in a profound way:

> On the fourth day they gathered in the Valley of Blessing,
> which got its name that day because the people praised and thanked
> the Lord there. It is still called the Valley of Blessing today. NLT

Did you catch that? We walk "through" the Valley of Weeping, but we "gather" in the Valley of Blessing.

That, my friends, is my destination: the Valley of Blessing where I will praise and thank the Lord. That's where William went. That's where my parents went. When it's my time, by the grace of God, that's where I'll go.

Will you?

This morning's devotional asked a painful question of me on this, the anniversary of my son's burial (https://odb.org/2017/09/02/dont-run-alone/).

"Who can I encourage to persevere through difficulty today?" [100]

I don't feel like helping anyone. I just want to crawl up and wait this day out.

But I had to work. At first, I was okay with that, because I was on duty with my coworker who is also a bereaved mother. But she wasn't able to make it in, so one of my other coworkers is filling in. The good news is that all my coworkers are wonderful people, so it was still a good place to be. It's just the cranky side of me doesn't deal well with sudden change sometimes.

"Who can I encourage to persevere through difficulty today?" [101]

I know who. God already laid him on my heart. And I can totally relate to the awful day he's going to have today.

My friend who lost his son on August 26 is having the memorial service today.

I messaged him, but I know he won't reply. He can't hear anything right now over the cracking of his heart.

Lord, my friend is experiencing something beyond difficult. Keep him close, Father. Hide him in the shadow of Your wings.

At work today, there were so many administrative tasks that I was kept busy all day. That helped me to keep my footing on the Rock of my salvation. I worked with one of our youngest employees, who is always cheerful and helpful. He was a breath of fresh air, really.

I found out after I got to work today that one of my cousins passed away in the early hours of the morning.

And later, after work, I developed a walloping headache.

The enemy is working overtime to make me miserable today, but I'm not going down without a fight.

I did drop the ball, though. I was so gobsmacked by the news that my cousin died that I haven't contacted her surviving sisters and brother to express my sympathies. My own grief is no excuse. If anything, it should make me more compassionate, not less.

"Who can I encourage to persevere through difficulty today?" [102]

Father, forgive me, and let me speak Your comfort to my cousins' hearts.

September 3

Today after church I worked some more on the bandanna for the bike rally. One of the things I put on it was William's favorite saying in high school, "carpe diem".

After I finished, I turned on PBS to watch a British dramedy. Within a few minutes of having it on, one of the actors actually said "carpe diem".

It feels good to be hugged by my Dad.

September 8

A few days ago, I wrote a letter to the bikers that have volunteered to come to town and ride for our children to thank them for their sacrifice. I contacted the Trinity's Angels ministry leader and asked if I posted the letter on the ministry's social media page, would all the riders have access to it.

I had no idea what she would suggest when I asked that question.

I prayed, and prayed, and this morning I surrendered.

I am now on the agenda to read the letter at the bike rally.

The last time I spoke in public was at my son's funeral.

That was the memory God gave me when I prayed. It was as if He was reminding me that if He got me through that, He will get me through this.

But it's not going to be easy.

September 9 -Trinity's Angels Never Forgotton Bike Rally

The weather was great for riding today - not too hot, but not cold enough to need a jacket. Since my husband and I had no idea what to expect, we headed up to the venue early. It gave us an opportunity to explore the vendors and visit the displays. There were four large displays holding pictures of over 100 children whose families have been left to grieve their loss.

In the decorations across the stage there were cartoon dragonflies. I even saw a woman with a dragonfly barrette in her hair. I suppose they'll forever conjure up a picture in my mind of William chasing one down in the hospital parking lot when my mom had her last stay there.

There were all sorts of booths, some games, food, face-painting...

And bikers. There were bikers everywhere. I've never seen so many tattoos or so much leather in one place in my whole life. In the past, such a sight might have caused me no small amount of apprehension. Today, I felt only appreciation.

At about noon, after a heartfelt prayer, the riders began to mount up. Our little Yamaha among all those Harleys looked like a Volkswagen in a sea of Cadillacs. Just as everyone began starting their engines, I heard a radio on a nearby bike playing "Born to be Wild" [103] sung by Steppenwolf.

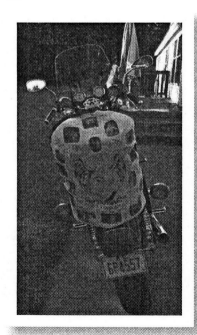

It felt good to laugh. It also felt good to think what a kick William would have gotten out of the moment, too.

Due to our inexperience in riding in a pack, my husband asked to be one of the last riders. Because we were, we were witnesses to an impressive sight as 100 bikers roared past in a solemn assembly. It was incredible. It was moving.

And a little painful. Each of those riders - us included - represented a family fractured by loss and living with a grief so profound that there are no words that can adequately describe it. Each rider was given a bandanna to wear or sport on their bike. The names of the children and their likenesses were on the bandannas, and families had decorated them for the riders. Since we were riding, our bandanna was displayed on the back of our bike. We had decorated it with pictures of William at various points in his life. Interspersed among the pictures, I wrote sentiments that friends and family have posted to William's memorial site and quotes that they had requested.

The riders had scheduled two stops for breaks. We made our first stop after about 40 minutes. One hundred motorcycles wrapping around the back of a large gas station in two rows is quite a sight. I can't imagine what the cashier thought when she saw all those riders filing in for drinks, snacks, or smokes. What, to my eyes, was an impressive sight, may have been quite intimidating to someone who didn't know their purpose. If there's such a thing as a panic button at gas stations, I don't imagine the employees strayed too far from it.

While we were at the first stop, I was walking around, trying to take pictures that would do justice to the magnitude of generosity of the riders who volunteered for this rally. In the process, I came across a woman trying to do the same thing (full sun and cell phone cameras are not a good match). After a while, we began to talk, and I learned that she, too, was a bereaved mother. Her daughter was 20, a nursing student, when she died in a single car accident. That was nineteen years ago. She shared how her daughter had told her dad, who was a motorcyclist before he married, that when she graduated, she was going to buy a Harley. She didn't have that opportunity, but her father did. This bereaved mother and her husband were riding in memory of their daughter.

Our second stop was similar to the first. I fully expected to be so stiff that I'd have to be pried loose from the back of the bike, but God invigorated both me and my husband. When we mounted up for the last leg of the journey, I was almost disappointed that it

would soon be over.

There was an unexpected moment when we passed a wedding ceremony in progress. It sounded as if the riders did what they could to quiet their engines, but a hundred Harleys are going to make a distinctive sound, no matter what you do. I suspect no one at that wedding will ever forget that ceremony.

And isn't that an amazing illustration of our lives as grieving parents? Life was going along just as we expected, when something unexpected, over which we had no control, roared through our lives and left them forever changed.

You have a lot of time to think and pray when you spend two and a half hours on the back of a motorcycle. In that time God showed me a great metaphor for life.

From what little I've learned about motorcycle riding so far, the passenger's role is to follow the lead of the Rider. If He leans right, you lean right. If He leans left, you lean left. If you do the opposite, you're pulling against the Rider and making the journey more difficult than it should be.

As a passenger, you go where the Rider takes you. You have no control over the conditions you face, only your attitude towards them. Do you experience pouring rain or liquid sunshine? Are you thankful for the smooth parts of the journey, or do you spend most of your time fretting over the hard places? Do you enjoy the fresh air and sunshine, or worry about bugs in your teeth and sunburn?

I also learned that as the passenger, you can't see everything the Rider can. He has a much better perspective. Oh, you can try to peer around Him, but you still can only see a fraction of what He does. And at some points in the journey, you should probably be grateful that you can't see what's coming.

Oh. Don't I know the truth of that.

In fact, when the wind begins to blow and you feel buffeted by its force, you can "hide" yourself behind the Rider. His Presence will shelter you from the worst of the storm.

I also learned - the hard way - that it's not a good idea for a passenger to lose focus. If you let yourself "wander", then the bumps in the road are liable to unseat you. If you keep your attention on the Rider, attuned to His leading, then even the bumpiest parts of the journey become bearable. Maybe not enjoyable - possibly even painful - but still bearable. And when you trust the Rider completely, then you can rest in the knowledge that the destination is worth the trip.

Yes, indeed. God can teach you a lot of things in a couple of hours on the back of a motorcycle.

After the ride, there were speeches, music, and presentations. One part of the ceremony involved the reading of each of the names of the children that have died. I had volunteered to be one of the readers of the names some time ago. I had explained that I didn't mind reading my son's name, but that I was fine reading whatever part of the list they needed. I tracked down the leader and received my portion of the list.

It did not have William's name on it.

What it did have, right near the middle, was the name of the young girl whose mother I spoke with at the first stop.

Isn't God amazing?

I tracked her down and showed her what God had done - for me and for her - and after the reading, I gave her the sheet. You can't begin to imagine what it felt like to share God's comfort with another sister-in-loss. And, knowing a little of her daughter's story made reading her name more meaningful, because it was more than just a word on the paper. She had a face and a family, and I will enjoy meeting her when we all are called Home.

Near the end, the ministry leader asked me to read my letter to the bikers.

Thank You Letter to Riders

The last time I stood before a microphone was 53 weeks and 1 day ago, in a veterans' cemetery in Suffolk, Virginia, when we buried my baby. I share that so you can under-

stand the depth of my gratitude for what you did for our children here today.

Speaking as a bereaved mother, I want to try to explain what your gift means to me. My son left this earth suddenly, without warning. A part of my heart went with him, and it cracks a little more as I watch his friends pick up the pieces and go on with their lives - which is as it should be. Still, with each passing day his name crosses their lips a little less and my heart breaks a little more. They can't help it. I wouldn't want them to be stranded in the past, but it still hurts that my son won't be in their future. It's like losing him a little more each day.

My son accepted Jesus as His Savior when he was young, so I will see him again when I join him in heaven, in God's time. But it's the time between now and then that hurts so much, because each day I hear his name less.

Events like this help me know that there are people who, though they may not feel my grief, do understand my need to memorialize my son. Yes, he's dead, but he lived. He left behind memories. He left behind loved ones. Even after a year, I feel his absence keenly, and even more so with each family gathering or family milestone he misses.

Your memorial ride has been an unspeakable gift to me. To know that you were willing to spend an afternoon riding in memory of a child you never met is a blessing beyond measure. Your gift encouraged me that our children's lives matter - present tense. You felt so strongly about these children and us, their grieving families that you volunteered to wear their names and ride in their honor. If I could, I would hug each one of you.

It's the hugs I miss the most, being wrapped in the arms of my son.

This first year, God made it possible for my husband and me to ride with you (albeit at the back of the pack). I can't begin to explain what an honor it was for us to join you in celebrating the lives of Trinity's Angels. Thank you for being willing to ride to remember them.

God bless you all.

It was quite a day, and I know a lot of people around town must have wondered what was happening.

The sound of over a hundred motorcycles roaring through the countryside was probably quite a surprise for some people. It might have shocked others, because they weren't expecting it. Some may have even been dismayed at the disruption of their day.

What they experienced for one moment, we as bereaved parents experience every single day. Surprise. Shock. Dismay. And it doesn't stop after the funeral is over and life resumes its routines.

It happens all over again at the milestones: birthdays, holidays, family events.

It happens when we least expect it and are unprepared: the scent of their cologne, the sound of their favorite song, the sight of someone who could be their twin.

And it happens with each passing day as our child's name crosses other's lips less and our hearts break a little more.

This is the existence of a parent who survives their child. It's not for the faint of heart. It is hard. It is messy. And it is not what we signed up for.

We do the best we can to carry on, picking up the pieces, and going on step by step. Some days are less hard than others, but none are easy. We left easy at the side of a grave we never expected to see.

Trinity's Angels Never Forgotten Bike Rally helped ease our pain. For one day, our children's names were spoken freely, their memories were shared lovingly, and our tears flowed without self-consciousness. For one day we were able to set aside the sorrow of living with their deaths and concentrate on celebrating their lives.

And that was all possible because of the sacrifice of several motorcycle clubs and riders. Each rider rode in memory of one of our children. They did so willingly. They did so feely. And it is my fervent prayer that God blesses each one of them for their sacrifice. It meant the world to us.

So, the next time you hear a motorcycle roar down your street, perhaps you'll think about the bike rally for grieving parents.

And perhaps you'll say a prayer for us.

Epilogue

So, that's it. That's God's story of how He pulled me through the first year of my new reality. I've learned a lot, made a lot of mistakes, and hopefully have come out on this side a little wiser and a lot more compassionate. I've learned that our grief is as individual as our loss; it doesn't look or feel the same for any two people, though it shares some common traits. No one travels this grief journey at the same speed or in the same steps. It's hard. It's messy. It's painful. And the scars it leaves are permanent.

But this valley I now walk - we all walk - is not my final destination. I'm just passing through. I didn't expect William to run ahead of me, but then, he did always seem to do everything at a full run. As much as missing him hurts, God has been faithful to His Word. He has taken what the enemy meant for evil and used it for good. He's used it to teach me many things I probably wouldn't have learned in any other way. I can rejoice in the blessings while still mourning William's absence. Some of the most encouraging blessings have come in the form of how God has used the walk I have with Him to move in the hearts of William's friends and family.

"You have always reminded me how important faith in God is."

"Watching you this past few days shows me the true faith that Christians should have."

"Many of the verses you have been posting have been a balm for my own heart in

broken areas God has been trying to heal for years now. Thank you."

"Whether you know it or not, you have helped me many times reminding me of His power, forgiveness and love."

"Thank you for your encouragement to us."

"You continue to inspire me on my journey with the Lord. Your faith is, and has been, a guide for me."

"You have inspired me to explore returning to church and to look to God for comfort as I try to make sense of all this."

"Leslie, I've used your testimony twice today as I mentor women who have not the faith you have, yet face much less tragedy and are crumbling from it all. I am using your story as a means to show how much we truly have to be thankful for."

"Tears are rolling down my cheeks and once again I am reminded by you to treasure the gifts of God each and every day."

"FATHER is using you as a example of walking humbly before the God of all creation knowing HE will carry you through all the dark places."

"You have made me sad, happy, joyful, and thankful all at the same time with your comforting words! Your courage as a mother is inspiring to me, your love for God through this tough time is amazing."

"My son and I are going to church this morning with my aunt and uncle. He's been asking a lot of questions lately and he's old enough now to find the answers and understand them for himself."

"I have found myself distant from God the past few years and was questioning things. I have had many situations the past few months that have reopened my eyes. You have no idea how much your faith has showed me that He is real, I am missing out, and now is the time for me to grow stronger in my faith as well. I look forward to your morning posts and I know God has a plan for all."

I've mentioned previously my fondness for crossword puzzles. In the same newspapers my mother saved for me (and yes, I'm still working through that stack, even a year after she went home), there is another puzzle called a "Cryptoquip". This puzzle is a message that has been encrypted. It starts with a one-letter clue, like "O equals S". As each letter is replaced, you begin to recognize words that lead to more letters and more words. The true meaning is hidden until the very last letter is revealed.

My story is the same way. Right now, I can see some of what God has revealed through this tragedy, but the final letter won't be revealed until I see Jesus face to face.

And that's okay. I trust the One who has all the answers.

Endnotes

[1] Anna B. Warner/William B. Bradbury, "Jesus Loves Me," 1860.

[2] Cindy Hess Kasper, "Making Preparations," taken from *Our Daily Bread®*, © 2017 by Our Daily Bread Ministries, Grand Rapids, MI. Reprinted by permission. All rights reserved.

[3] Albert Lee, "Hold On," taken from *Our Daily Bread®*, © 2017 by Our Daily Bread Ministries, Grand Rapids, MI. Reprinted by permission. All rights reserved.

[4] Randy Phillips/Bernie Herms/Matthew Joseph West, "Tell Your Heart to Beat Again," *Hope in Front of Me*, 2014.

[5] Victoria Bylin, *Until I Found You* (Minneapolis: Bethany House Publishers, 2014), pp. 298, 300-301.

[6] Bill Crowder, "Your Journey," taken from *Our Daily Bread®*, © 2017 by Our Daily Bread Ministries, Grand Rapids, MI. Reprinted by permission. All rights reserved.

[7] Randy Phillips/Bernie Herms/Matthew Joseph West, "Tell Your Heart to Beat Again," *Hope in Front of Me*, 2014.

[8] Zach Williams/Mia Fieldes/Jonathan Smith, "Chain Breaker," *Chain Breaker*, 2016.

[9] Chris Stevens/Bryan Fowler/Toby McKeehan, "Move (Keep Walkin')", *This Is Not a Test*, 2015.

[10] Bryan Fowler/Ryan Stevenson, "Eye of the Storm," *Fresh Start*, 2015.

[11] Lisa Harris, *Hidden Agenda* (Grand Rapids: Revell, 2015), p. 226.

[12] Jennifer Benson Schuldt, "Seeing Well," taken from *Our Daily Bread®*, © 2017 by Our Daily Bread Ministries, Grand Rapids, MI. Reprinted by permission. All rights reserved.

[13] Susan May Warren, *Take a Chance on Me* (Carol Stream: Tyndale House Publishers, 2013), p. xiii.

[14] Priscilla Shirer, *The Armor of God* (Nashville: LifeWay Press, 2015).

[15] Becky Wade, *My Stubborn Heart* (Bloomington: Bethany House Publishers,

2012), pp. 182-183.

[16] Becky Wade, *My Stubborn Heart* (Bloomington: Bethany House Publishers, 2012), p. 252.

[17] Becky Wade, *My Stubborn Heart* (Bloomington: Bethany House Publishers, 2012), pp. 254-255.

[18] Becky Wade, *Meant to Be Mine* (Bloomington: Bethany House Publishers, 2014), p. 354.

[19] Colleen Coble, *Twilight at Blueberry Commons* (Nashville: Thomas Nelson, 2016). p. 35.

[20] Laura Story, "Blessings," *Blessings*, 2011.

[21] Mark Schultz/Cindy Morgan, "Different Kind of Christmas," *Different Kind of Christmas*, 2014.

[22] Becky Wade, *Undeniably Yours* (Bloomington: Bethany House Publishers, 2013), pp. 34-35.

[23] Becky Wade, *Undeniably Yours* (Bloomington: Bethany House Publishers, 2013), p. 182.

[24] Becky Wade, *Undeniably Yours* (Bloomington: Bethany House Publishers, 2013), p. 338.

[25] Susan May Warren, *It Had to Be You* (Carol Stream: Tyndale House Publishers, 2014), p. 156.

[26] James Banks, "Serving God With Our Prayers," taken from *Our Daily Bread*®, © 2017 by Our Daily Bread Ministries, Grand Rapids, MI. Reprinted by permission. All rights reserved.

[27] Colleen Coble, *Mermaid Moon* (Nashville: Thomas Nelson, 2016), p. 259.

[28] Amy Boucher Pye, "Losing to Find," taken from *Our Daily Bread*®, © 2017 by Our Daily Bread Ministries, Grand Rapids, MI. Reprinted by permission. All rights reserved.

[29] Marie Monville with Cindy Lambert, *One Light Still Shines: My Life Beyond the Shadow of the Amish Schoolhouse Shooting* (Grand Rapids: Zondervan, 2013).

[30] David Wilkerson, *Have You Felt Like Giving Up Lately?* (Grand Rapids: Revell, 1980), p. 152.

[31] C.S. Lewis, *A Grief Observed* (New York: HarperCollins Publishers, 1961), p.

xxvi. A GRIEF OBSERVED by CS Lewis © copyright CS Lewis Pte Ltd 1961. Used by permission.

[32] Amy Boucher Pye, "The Lighthouse," taken from *Our Daily Bread®* , © 2017 by Our Daily Bread Ministries, Grand Rapids, MI. Reprinted by permission. All rights reserved.

[33] Amy Boucher Pye, "The Lighthouse," taken from *Our Daily Bread®* , © 2017 by Our Daily Bread Ministries, Grand Rapids, MI. Reprinted by permission. All rights reserved.

[34] Matt Crocker, "I Surrender," *Cornerstone*, 2012.

[35] Matt Crocker, "I Surrender," *Cornerstone*, 2012.

[36] Matt Crocker, "I Surrender," *Cornerstone*, 2012.

[37] Lori Wick, *The Visitor* (Eugene: Harvest House Publishers, 2003), p. 113. Taken from *The Visitor*. Copyright © 2003 by Lori Wick. Published by Harvest House Publishers, Eugene, OR 97404. www.harvesthousepublishers.com. Used by permission.

[38] Taken from *THE TOUCHPOINT BIBLE, NLT*, p. 116, by V. Gilbert Beers and Ronald A. Beers. Copyright © 1996. Used by permission of Tyndale House Publishers, Inc., Carol Stream, Illinois 60188. All rights reserved.

[39] C.S. Lewis, *A Grief Observed* (New York: HarperCollins Publishers, 1961), p. 11. A GRIEF OBSERVED by CS Lewis © copyright CS Lewis Pte Ltd 1961. Used by permission.

[40] Dave Branon, "The Land of 'What Is,'" taken from *Our Daily Bread®* , © 2017 by Our Daily Bread Ministries, Grand Rapids, MI. Reprinted by permission. All rights reserved.

[41] C.S. Lewis, *A Grief Observed* (New York: HarperCollins Publishers, 1961), pp. 56-57. A GRIEF OBSERVED by CS Lewis © copyright CS Lewis Pte Ltd 1961. Used by permission.

[42] Priscilla Shirer, *The Armor of God* (Nashville: LifeWay Press, 2015).

[43] Taken from *THE TOUCHPOINT BIBLE, NLT*, p. 154, by V. Gilbert Beers and Ronald A. Beers. Copyright © 1996. Used by permission of Tyndale House Publishers, Inc., Carol Stream, Illinois 60188. All rights reserved.

[44] Kirsten Holmberg, "Spilling Through My Fingers," taken from *Our Daily Bread®*, © 2017 by Our Daily Bread Ministries, Grand Rapids, MI. Reprinted

[45] David McCasland, "Running and Rest," taken from *Our Daily Bread*®, © 2017 by our Daily Bread Ministries, Grand Rapids, MI. Reprinted by permission. All rights reserved.

[46] Kirsten Holmberg, "Cradled in Comfort," taken from *Our Daily Bread*® , © 2017 by Our Daily Bread Ministries, Grand Rapids, MI. Reprinted by permission. All rights reserved.

[47] Jonathan Nelson/Kenneth Shelton/Darien Dennis, "Expect the Great," *Better Days*, 2010.

[48] Jonathan Nelson/Kenneth Shelton/Darien Dennis, "Expect the Great," *Better Days*, 2010.

[49] Taken from *THE TOUCHPOINT BIBLE, NLT*, p. 231, by V. Gilbert Beers and Ronald A. Beers. Copyright © 1996. Used by permission of Tyndale House Publishers, Inc., Carol Stream, Illinois 60188. All rights reserved.

[50] Taken from *THE TOUCHPOINT BIBLE, NLT*, p. 231, by V. Gilbert Beers and Ronald A. Beers. Copyright © 1996. Used by permission of Tyndale House Publishers, Inc., Carol Stream, Illinois 60188. All rights reserved.

[51] Taken from *THE TOUCHPOINT BIBLE, NLT*, p. 232, by V. Gilbert Beers and Ronald A. Beers. Copyright © 1996. Used by permission of Tyndale House Publishers, Inc., Carol Stream, Illinois 60188. All rights reserved.

[52] Helen Lemmel, "Turn Your Eyes Upon Jesus," 1922.

[53] Max Lucado, *Every Day Deserves a Chance* (Nashville: Thomas Nelson, 2007), p. 69.

[54] Joth Hunt/Andy Harrison, "I'm Free," *Overflow*, 2016.

[55] Tim Gustafson, "The Gift of Giving," taken from *Our Daily Bread*®, © 2017 by Our Daily Bread Ministries, Grand Rapids, MI. Reprinted by permission. All rights reserved.

[56] *Back to the Future*, directed by Robert Zemeckis (1985; Universal City CA, Universal Pictures Home Entertainment, 2016), DVD.

[57] Taken from *THE TOUCHPOINT BIBLE, NLT*, p. 345, by V. Gilbert Beers and Ronald A. Beers. Copyright © 1996. Used by permission of Tyndale House Publishers, Inc., Carol Stream, Illinois 60188. All rights reserved.

[58] Taken from *THE TOUCHPOINT BIBLE, NLT*, p. 345, by V. Gilbert Beers and

Ronald A. Beers. Copyright © 1996. Used by permission of Tyndale House Publishers, Inc., Carol Stream, Illinois 60188. All rights reserved.

[59] Taken from *THE TOUCHPOINT BIBLE, NLT*, p. 346, by V. Gilbert Beers and Ronald A. Beers. Copyright © 1996. Used by permission of Tyndale House Publishers, Inc., Carol Stream, Illinois 60188. All rights reserved.

[60] Taken from *THE TOUCHPOINT BIBLE, NLT*, p. 346, by V. Gilbert Beers and Ronald A. Beers. Copyright © 1996. Used by permission of Tyndale House Publishers, Inc., Carol Stream, Illinois 60188. All rights reserved.

[61] Taken from *THE TOUCHPOINT BIBLE, NLT*, p. 346, by V. Gilbert Beers and Ronald A. Beers. Copyright © 1996. Used by permission of Tyndale House Publishers, Inc., Carol Stream, Illinois 60188. All rights reserved.

[62] Molly Reed/Jeff Pardo/Francesca Battistelli, "Giants Fall," *If We're Honest*, 2014.

[63] Molly Reed/Jeff Pardo/Francesca Battistelli, "Giants Fall," *If We're Honest*, 2014.

[64] Joel Houston/Matt Crocker/Salomon Ligthelm, "Oceans (Where Feet May Fail)," *Zion*, 2013.

[65] Jari Villanueva, "Taps Bugler," tapsbugler.com, 2010, http://tapsbugler.com/lyrics-or-words-to-taps/. Used by permission.

[66] Jari Villanueva, "Taps Bugler," tapsbugler.com, 2010, http://tapsbugler.com/lyrics-or-words-to-taps/. Used by permission.

[67] Jari Villanueva, "Taps Bugler," tapsbugler.com, 2010, http://tapsbugler.com/lyrics-or-words-to-taps/. Used by permission.

[68] Jari Villanueva, "Taps Bugler," tapsbugler.com, 2010, http://tapsbugler.com/lyrics-or-words-to-taps/. Used by permission.

[69] Jari Villanueva, "Taps Bugler," tapsbugler.com, 2010, http://tapsbugler.com/lyrics-or-words-to-taps/. Used by permission.

[70] Jari Villanueva, "Taps Bugler," tapsbugler.com, 2010, http://tapsbugler.com/lyrics-or-words-to-taps/. Used by permission.

[71] Chris Quilala/Josh Silverberg/Mia Fieldes, "Fierce," *Let It Echo*, 2016.

[72] Shauna Niequist, *Present Over Perfect: Leaving Behind Frantic For a Simpler More Soulful Way of Living* (Grand Rapids: Zondervan, 2016).

[73] Louie Giglio/Chris Tomlin, "Amazing Grace (My Chains Are Gone)," *See the Morning*, 2006.

[74] Kirsten Holmberg, "Table Rock," taken from *Our Daily Bread®*, © 2017 by Our Daily Bread Ministries, Grand Rapids, MI. Reprinted by permission. All rights reserved.

[75] Pat Barrett/Anthony Brown, "Good Good Father," *Never Lose Sight*, 2016.

[76] Pat Barrett/Anthony Brown, "Good Good Father," *Never Lose Sight*, 2016.

[77] Tim Gustafson, "Taking Shortcuts," taken from *Our Daily Bread®*, © 2017 by Our Daily Bread Ministries, Grand Rapids, MI. Reprinted by permission. All rights reserved.

[78] Taken from *THE TOUCHPOINT BIBLE, NLT*, p. 317, by V. Gilbert Beers and Ronald A. Beers. Copyright © 1996. Used by permission of Tyndale House Publishers, Inc., Carol Stream, Illinois 60188. All rights reserved.

[79] Shauna Niequist, *Present Over Perfect: Leaving Behind Frantic For a Simpler More Soulful Way of Living* (Grand Rapids: Zondervan, 2016).

[80] Shauna Niequist, *Present Over Perfect Study Guide* (Grand Rapids: Zondervan, 2016).

[81] Shauna Niequist, *Present Over Perfect: Leaving Behind Frantic For a Simpler More Soulful Way of Living* (Grand Rapids: Zondervan, 2016).

[82] Xochitl Dixon, "Destroying the Divides," taken from *Our Daily Bread®*, © 2017 by Our Daily Bread Ministries, Grand Rapids, MI. Reprinted by permission. All rights reserved.

[83] Lawrence Darmani, "Approaching God," taken from *Our Daily Bread®*, © 2017 by Our Daily Bread Ministries, Grand Rapids, MI. Reprinted by permission. All rights reserved.

[84] Julie Schwab, "Are You Being Prepared," taken from *Our Daily Bread®*, © 2017 by Our Daily Bread Ministries, Grand Rapids, MI. Reprinted by permission. All rights reserved.

[85] Hannah Hurnard, *Hind's Feet on High Places* (Wheaton: Living Books/Tyndale House Publishers, 1977).

[86] Scott Davis/Scott Krippayne, "What Faith Can Do," *It Is Well*, 2009.

[87] Lauren Daigle/Michael Farren/Paul Mabury, "I Will Trust in You," *How Can It Be*, 2015.

[88] Chris Greely/Bobby Strand/Kalley Hailigenthal/Gabriel Wilson, "Ever Be," *Without Words: Synesthesia*, 2015.

358

[89] Liz Johnson, *The Red Door Inn* (Grand Rapids: Revell, 2016), p. 92. Used by permission.

[90] Michael Blalock/Michael Farren, "Count Them All," *As Long As We Can Breathe*, 2016.

[91] http://womenofchristianity.com/the-fruit-comes-afterward-streams-in-the-desert-0728/

[92] Cindy Hess Kasper, "If Only...," taken from *Our Daily Bread®*, © 2017 by Our Daily Bread Ministries, Grand Rapids, MI. Reprinted by permission. All rights reserved.

[93] Cindy Hess Kasper, "If Only...," taken from *Our Daily Bread®*, © 2017 by Our Daily Bread Ministries, Grand Rapids, MI. Reprinted by permission. All rights reserved.

[94] Karen Wolfe, "From Fear to Faith," taken from *Our Daily Bread®*, © 2017 by Our Daily Bread Ministries, Grand Rapids, MI. Reprinted by permission. All rights reserved.

[95] David McCasland, "Be Still," taken from *Our Daily Bread®*, © 2017 by Our Daily Bread Ministries, Grand Rapids, MI. Reprinted by permission. All rights reserved.

[96] David Elliott, *Baabwaa and Wooliam* (Somerville: Candlewick Press), 2017.

[97] Chris Greely/Bobby Strand/Kalley Hailigenthal/Gabriel Wilson, "Ever Be," *Without Words: Synesthesia*, 2015.

[98] Michael Blalock/Michael Farren, "Count Them All," *As Long As We Can Breathe*, 2016.

[99] John Clements/Hart Danks, "No Night There," 1899.

[100] Amy Peterson, "Don't Run Alone," taken from *Our Daily Bread®*, © 2017 by Our Daily Bread Ministries, Grand Rapids, MI. Reprinted by permission. All rights reserved.

[101] Amy Peterson, "Don't Run Alone," taken from *Our Daily Bread®*, © 2017 by Our Daily Bread Ministries, Grand Rapids, MI. Reprinted by permission. All rights reserved.

[102] Amy Peterson, "Don't Run Alone," taken from *Our Daily Bread®*, © 2017 by Our Daily Bread Ministries, Grand Rapids, MI. Reprinted by permission. All rights reserved.

[103] Mars Bonfire, "Born to Be Wild," *Steppenwolf*, 1968.